Causeway to a
Bigger World

Causeway to a Bigger World

by Dan C. West

MOUNTAIN ARBOR
PRESS

Mountain Arbor
Press

Alpharetta, GA

ISBN: 978-1-63183-391-5

Printed in the United States of America   0 8 2 0 1 8

⊗This paper meets the requirements of ANSI/NISO Z39.48-1992 (Permanence of Paper)

to Sidney

Contents

Acknowledgements

I wish to thank first, Sidney Claire Childs West, my wife of 55 years, whose companionship and partnership in this adventure largely made it possible. Not only did she participate in most of the projects and activities I have described, she helped shape them. And, she generously read this manuscript twice, for accuracy and style.

I also wish to thank my children who continue to amaze and inspire me with their accomplishments. Andrew also read the manuscript and made important corrections and additions.

To my parents and my siblings and their families, I owe much and I treasure their love.

Sara Caroline Moseley, daughter of my mentor, John D. Moseley, is a gifted editor who added much, in quality and style, to this.

Finally, I wish to thank all those who guided, led, inspired, taught and influenced me, many of whom are named, but there are many more. I think especially of those with whom I have worked, including my critics and opponents. I have learned much from them all.

Causeway to a Bigger World

A word of introduction. When I left Galveston, Texas, in 1949, with my family at the age of nine, we crossed over what is called the Causeway that connects the island with the mainland, on our way to Houston. In so many ways that was the route to a wider, bigger world that, over the years, for me extended from China in the east to Hawaii in the west, and from Alaska in the north to Peru in the south. It was also the crossing into an intellectual and personal expansion, from the narrow confines of what I later saw as a parochial Texas into a greatly expanded vision of what I came to see as a better life for me and a wider view of reality.

154~ New Causeway showing Four Lane Highway, Galveston, Texas

My ancestors were German and English immigrants to Galveston on my mother's side and Scotch-Irish migrants from the North Carolina Piedmont on my father's. I have yet to do the genealogical research that would tell me more. This much I know. My mother's mother was the daughter of an English couple named William Pilfold and Ann Taylor. It was her mother's second marriage as she had been widowed by the death of Mr. Taylor. Mr. Pilfold had been transferred from Cork, Ireland, by the Mexican American Cable Co., and after leaving Ireland my grandmother, Nan Taylor Pilfold, was born on the ship as they crossed. I often think, as I grow older, about the immigrant status of my great grandparents. They arrived in Galveston in January, 1890. Her parents were Anne Jane Howard Taylor Pilfold. Her first husband died. The homeland of the first immigrant processed at Elis Island, New York, was Ireland. Her name was Annie Moore, and she was from County Cork. She passed through Ellis Island on January 1, 1892 – two years AFTER my grandmother and her family arrived in Galveston.

My mother's father, John Frederick Junker, was the son of German immigrants who met and married in Galveston after their arrival

there. He, my grandfather, was a laborer, an hourly wage earner, who got piecemeal jobs anyway he could. My grandmother inherited a small amount of money from her mother and with it bought the house in Galveston, at 1610 Ave. O, in which they lived and begat 7 children. One died in infancy, another died as a young unmarried man, and I knew the remaining five who survived into adulthood. They were Marguerite (Meyer), John F. Junker, Jr., Hazel (Spatz), Mildred (West), my mother, and Lois Jane (Bonawitz). My mother was a graduate of Ball High School in Galveston.

My father, Embry Carlos West, was the son of Embry Gustavus West and Gladys Gertrude Wood. Each of these, my paternal

Embry G. West, 1901

grandparents, had (unusually for that time) some college education and each had been school teachers. They divorced in 1933 while my father was in high school. It was during the Great Depression. My father's sister, Hester Gray (Ollis) stayed with her mother. They lived eventually in Springfield, Missouri. Gladys Wood West later married U. S. Tegarten. Hester Gray West later married Lawrence Ollis. The Ollises had two children, Ronald and Betty. I have lost touch with both.

My father was sent to live with his mother's sister in Oklahoma until he had been graduated from high school. Then for a while he lived and moved about with his father, who bounced from job to job, trying to survive. Finally, out of desperation, my father volunteered for the U. S. Army in Galveston where there used to be a base called Fort Crockett. He served from January until September of 1936.

As the story is told, my mother was skating along the seawall Boulevard one day and was spotted by my father who asked her out.

After they married they lived on 16th St. and then P St. and then N ½ Street, almost directly behind my grandmother. I was born May 29, 1939. By this time, Dad was working as a debit salesman for Moody Insurance Co.

Mildred and Carlos West, 1938

Chapter 1

Galveston

The hospital where I was born, St. Mary's Infirmary (run by a Catholic order of sisters), still stands though it is no longer a hospital. It is a structure now owned by the University of Texas Medical School, Galveston, and is overshadowed by a campus of high rise and other modern buildings that occupy much of the east end of the island.

I was named Dan, not Daniel as many people assumed during my life. My mother chose the name from the Old Testament. It was one of the twelve tribes of Israel and, in Hebrew, it means judge. Carlos is also my father's name. He was Embry (after his father) Carlos West. I was always told that my grandmother chose the Spanish Carlos (Charles) because she thought the Spanish people to be romantic.

I have little recollection of my father prior to his leaving to go to war in 1944. He had been drafted into the Army, even though he was married and had two children. At the time, he had a management job, I think it was in personnel, at Todd Shipyard, on an island separate from Galveston. I do recall his leaving, with my mother in tears, and my sister and me equally upset. He told me that in his absence I was "the man of the family" and that I should look after my mother and my sister. This was meaningless, of course, given that I was only five, but I tried to take it seriously. He entered the Army Transport Service, a branch of the military which had been created during the war. He became the senior transportation clerk and was later promoted to ship's administrative officer on a large transport ship, an air corps repair ship. The second rank he was

1

given was the equivalent of Purser on a civilian ship or Supply Officer on a Navy ship.

My mother got a job with the U.S. Army Corps of Engineers in Galveston. They had offices in the Santa Fe building above the railway station. I don't know her job; but because she worked, my sister and I were under the care of our maternal grandmother. Nan Taylor Pilfold Junker, Granny, lived almost directly across the street from us on Ave. O, close to 16th Street.

My grandfather, John F. Junker, had died the day before I was born in 1939. He suffered a fatal heart attack at work, on the Galveston wharf. My mother literally got up from her hospital bed, two days later, to attend his funeral.

My maternal grandfather was bald, as was his son, my uncle, John F. Junker, Jr. Male pattern baldness is inherited from the mother's side. I went bald in my thirties, as did our son, Andrew. In "The Comedy of Errors," Shakespeare has one of the characters say, "There's many a man has more hair than wit." II.ii.85

Granny was a huge influence in my early formation. She wasn't a beautiful woman but she was always immaculately groomed and dressed. Because of her English and Irish heritage she always drank afternoon tea. She did crochet work and was a fine housekeeper. When we lived across the street she still had two of her children living with her, my aunts Hazel and Lois. The house was tiny. She loved Nan and me, and later Janet and Bill too, as much as her own children. I adored her. I was heartbroken in 1960 when she died. I asked for leave to come home, in uniform, from the Naval Academy, for her funeral.

My sister, Nan Gay (named for two grandmothers, Nan and Gladys) was born in 1943. Of course, we must have played together but the only memory I have of that is pedalling my tricycle on the sidewalk while she stood on the back and held on to me. She was blond and precious.

I started public school at age five. At that time, Texas had half day kindergarten. I went to Alamo School, within walking distance of where we lived. I don't remember my teacher's name but I recall enjoying the time at school and resting, at mid-morning after a snack of cookies and milk, on a rug spread on the floor.

I was promoted to the first grade, also at Alamo. On the first day of school, no one had told me I was now expected to stay beyond midday, so I left the school at noon and began walking home to my grandmother's. She was called by someone at the school and told I was missing. She grabbed her hat and purse and started walking toward the school. She met me, turned me around, and told me to return and stay till the end of the school day.

Later, I attended two other elementary schools in Galveston, San Jacinto and Stephen F. Austin. I am unclear about their locations and which grades were in which school. The reason I attended three schools before the end of the 4th grade is that after my father returned from the war, we moved four times before leaving Galveston. We lived in two different houses on Menard St. and another place on Ave. R. At one point, we moved for a few months, to a house in LaMarque, TX, on the mainland, then, back to Galveston.

I have a very vague recollection of being in Mobile, Alabama, close to the end of the war when my father's ship put in there, and then of living in a mobile home in a trailer camp in New Orleans where my father was stationed before his discharge after the end of the war. In 1945 I was six years old.

Back in Galveston, my most memorable experience was being taken to my Grandfather West's farm one summer. I must have been eight. Granddad, as we called him, remarried, a woman named Olive whom I called Aunt Ollie. I do not know her last name. They had two children. Nadine Joy was a year older than I, and Ronald West was a year younger. The farm was a throwback to another age, though I am certain there were still many people in the country living in such condition that year. It was what we now call subsistence farming. The farm comprised 100 acres and was close to Alma, Arkansas. The road in front was dirt. They grew most of what they ate and tried to grow enough extra to sell for badly needed cash with which to buy staples such as salt, flour, sugar, coffee, etc. They kept chickens, hogs, rabbits and at least one cow. There was one horse, Jim, who pulled a farm wagon, their only means of transport. There was no running water or electricity or indoor plumbing. The well, with bucket and a pulley, was behind the back porch. There was an outhouse half-way to the barn. Lighting was with kerosene lamps. Aunt Ollie cooked on a wood burning stove. The farm's main crop was corn, some of which was used to feed chickens and hogs; but much of it was hauled into town for sale. Granddad also grew rows of Gladiolas which he sold to florists in Alma. In the summer, the whole family hired out to a nearby farmer with an orchard to pick peaches to earn cash. The fields were plowed with Jim pulling a turning plow blade or a harrow. We were expected to use a hoe to chop weeds.

There are two amusing stories which my son requested me to include. At breakfast one day, Grandad mentioned that a neighbor's horse had died. Ronald and I were fascinated and asked where the dead horse had been taken. Granddad said it had been dragged to the creek bottom for the buzzards to deal with. Quickly finishing our meal, we raced to the creek, eager to see the corpse. There it was with a buzzard circling overhead. As soon as we got a glimpse of the dead animal we ran away as fast as possible, terrified!

On another day, Ronald and I were in the hay loft of the barn, with a box of Aunt Ollie's matches, taken from her kitchen without permission. We piled some loose hay in a little mound and lit it. The plan was that I would quickly stamp out the fire with my cowboy boots. But, the fire quickly spread. We ran, panicked, to the house. All five of us rushed back to the barn with brooms and quilts and shovels, and, with great difficulty, extinguished the spreading fire. Granddad, a normally gentle, quiet man, said sternly, "I'll see you boys at the back porch." We knew what was coming. Bent over, we received a whipping. He used his belt, and we never considered playing with matches again.

Aunt Ollie cooked enormous breakfasts, lunches and suppers. There was lots of pork, some of which had been cured in a smokehouse, and chicken or fried rabbit for meat. There were biscuits, cornbread, cakes and pies. There were fresh vegetables and also fruit and vegetables that had been canned and kept on long shelves in the pantry. We drank fresh, unpasteurized milk not long after it came out of the cow. We ate well and a lot and then worked it all off. Neither Granddad nor Ollie were the least bit overweight. We went to bed early and got up before dawn. There were no fans, only open doors and windows to allow any breeze. We attended a Primitive Baptist Church on Sundays, dressed up as well as possible and all riding in the flatbed wagon behind the adults on the seat.

It was a hard life in many ways; but I don't remember anybody complaining much; and the family was close knit but also welcoming of me. It was a three-month experience that must have influenced my thinking for the rest of my life. I have never taken comfort or convenience, income or job, for granted. I have never disparaged or discredited poor people. Most of them work hard, just to get by. And I have never forgotten the relatively modest circumstances from which I came.

Later Granddad sold the farm and moved his second family to Lubbock, Texas, where his aged mother, one sister and two bothers lived. His father, Gus West, had been a grocery store owner there. His two brothers, Jack and Lamar, owned lumber yards in Lubbock and nearby Levelland, respectively. His sister, Aileen, worked as a secretary for many years and then, late in life, married a wealthy widowed businessman. At the time of his death, Granddad earned a modest salary writing a column on gardening for the Lubbock Avalanche Journal. I did not keep in touch with Aunt Ollie or with Ronald and Nadine after he died. All three are now deceased.

Once, while we lived in Galveston, Granddad, Ollie, Nadine and Ronnie came for a visit. I believe it was while we lived on Menard St. We had a fairly large back yard. Granddad dug and planted a vegetable garden for us while he was there. I have no idea how they got there - perhaps by bus, which my father must have sent them the money to pay for.

Beginning very early, perhaps even before Dad went to war, we were regular attendees at First Presbyterian Church. All of the Junkers were raised Presbyterian because my grandmother's family had been Anglican in England and Ireland and my grandfather's family were German Evangelical (Lutheran) and thus Protestant as well. The First Presbyterian Church was one of the most prominent in Galveston. Its pastor was the Rev. Dr. Wil R. Johnson, an

Australian immigrant who had been a journalist before his call to the ministry. I don't know about college but his seminary had been the Moody Bible Institute of Chicago. He was fundamentalist. He was bald, wore pince nez glasses, and until the forties wore formal morning dress (frock coat, wing collar, striped trousers) in which to preach. I idolized him. Once, when I was seven or eight, about the time I was "taken in to the church" (confirmed) he told me I should consider the ministry for my career. I resolved to do just that and continued in that choice until late in high school.

Memories of that church include Sunday School classes taught by my Aunt Hazel, vacation Bible school, ice cream socials in the park-like lawn behind the church, floor fans, lots of stained glass windows, and Dr. Johnson's preaching, always forceful but literate and well delivered. Both of my aunts were married there. My sisters and I were baptized there, and Dr. Johnson conducted my grandmother's funeral. He was quite proud that I became a minister. Sidney and I had lunch with him during our honeymoon in Galveston in 1963. The Session of First Presbyterian invited me to be the summer intern minister in 1963; but I had already accepted a similar job at First Presbyterian Church, Sherman, TX.

My younger sister, Janet Sue, was born in 1947, the third child to be delivered at St. Mary's Infirmary. It was unusual in those days for a Protestant to use a Catholic Hospital. My mother believed, however, that because sisters (nuns) owned and ran such places they took better care of women patients. Janet was as brunette as Nan was blond, and just as adorable. Pictures of the three of us in Galveston show happy faces and bright eyes. Some of our happiest times occurred when we had picnics and went swimming on the beach.

Dad returned to Todd Shipyard after the war but at some point, changed careers and began work with the Beneficial Life Insurance Co. He had his own insurance agency for a brief time. Then he was hired by Blue Cross-Blue Shield of Texas and was told he had to move to Houston. That was in 1949.

Chapter 2

Houston and Tyler

At first, we lived on O St. or maybe it was Ave. O, close to Wayside. We rented one half of a duplex. Dad talked my mother's sister, Hazel Junker Spatz, and her husband, Bernie, into moving to Houston and living in the duplex next to us and Bernie went to work for Ideal Baking Co. I remember we had next-door neighbors named Stover; and their son Lyn and I became fast friends. Mr. Stover was a plumber, and so he made some money and they acquired a television set, first in the neighborhood, and would let us come over and watch some.

I believe I attended two different schools in Houston, as a fifth grader, because we moved before the year was up. It was a new suburb and I don't remember the name of the school. While we lived on Ave. O I had a teacher named Miss Smith who taught me cursive handwriting. I liked her very much, the first teacher I can remember, and I was sad when I had to leave that school. The other thing that happened while I was there was I acquired a violin (a very inexpensive instrument made available through the school) and started learning to play it.

My mother became pregnant while we were in Houston, for the fourth time. And Blue Cross promoted Dad to regional director of its East Texas region that comprised such places as Tyler, Longview, Gladewater, Lufkin, Commerce, Athens, etc. So, we moved again and the result is that I attended the fifth grade in two cities and three different schools.

I finished the fifth grade at Gary Elementary in Tyler. It was a block from the First Presbyterian Church; but we were not church goers at that time. I remember that part of the time we were in Houston we attended a Methodist Church (my father was raised Methodist).

Between Gary Elementary and the church was a Mobil Gas station and the man who owned it was named Casey. For some reason my Aunt Hazel and Uncle Bernie Spatz moved from Houston to Tyler; and, unable to get a job at a bakery, Uncle Bernie worked for a while at that gas station.

We lived first on Donnybrook St. and later on W. First St. Bill West was born in August after we moved to Donnybrook; and I was very happy, after having two sisters, now to have a brother. The house was in a relatively new development (we were the second occupants) and across from undeveloped land which provided great play space. I remember building a fort over there. There was a long, climbing hill, from our house to the road at the top, maybe it was New Copeland Road; and Mom often sent me on my bike for single items she needed, e.g. milk, bread, etc. Pumping up that long hill built up my legs and improved my stamina but I did not have an opportunity to gain upper body strength to correspond.

I was a poor athlete. And because I wasn't good at anything like that I lost interest in sports. I recall that at Gary School, I was such a lousy batter in softball that they usually asked me to be the umpire.

Next door to us lived a railroad conductor named Hewett whom I idolized. He liked me too; and we often spent time together as he was a great gardener and yardwork man.

Behind our house the previous owners had built a chicken yard and when we arrived it was grown up in grass and weeds. It had a fence around it and couldn't be mowed easily and Dad said I could turn it into a garden. He got somebody to bring a tiller and turn it up and I planted as much stuff as I could find seed for. It was a luxuriant garden, because of the chickens who had occupied it. I remember old fashioned white squash which were the size of dinner plates!

I attended the 6th, 7th and 8th grades at Hogg Jr. High School on S. Broadway in Tyler. I played in the school orchestra. No sports. I ran for student council and lost. I had good teachers but I don't remember a single name. In those days, the school allowed us to leave for lunch if we wished. I remember riding my bike to downtown Tyler where there was an old-fashioned boarding house, and for 50 cents you could have all you wanted. The food was in the middle of the table, family style, and my friends and I would absolutely consume helpings of this stuff, and then pedal like crazy to get back to school before the hour was up. Even though I wasn't an athlete, I had an enormous appetite.

Dad sold our house and bought another on W. First, off Noonday Road. We had chickens in back. I think there were three bedrooms. The girls shared one and Bill and I the other. Once again there was a wooded area, undeveloped land, behind us and I played there a lot. I had a friend named Bernie Kemp who lived a block or two away.

One Sunday I attended Sunday School or church at First Presbyterian. It must have been with a friend. I remember coming home and telling Dad that I missed going to church and thought it was not good that the family had stopped doing that. We became active at First Presbyterian. Mom and Dad were co-presidents of the Young Marrieds Sunday School class. I was in something called Christian Endeavor (Sunday evening). I also joined a Boy Scout troop sponsored by the church. I remember my Scoutmaster's name was Don Hill. The minister of the church was Sherrard Rice. I worked with him to earn the God and Country Award in Scouts. I remember enjoying two summers at a Boy Scout camp. I think it was called Camp Mohawk. Somehow, even though I was born on the Gulf Coast, I'd never learned to

West family, 1950

swim and did not do so, when I should have and maybe could have, at camp those summers. Otherwise I loved Scouting. I achieved the Order of the Arrow and earned a number of merit badges.

I was a newspaper courier in Tyler too. It was an afternoon (except on Sunday) route for the Tyler Courier Times. My papers were left for me on the traffic island on Glenwood Blvd. I would go there each day, fold the papers into a compact bundle, load them in my paper sack stretched across the front of my bike on the handlebars, and throw them from the bike to land on customers' porches. In those days' people expected their papers to be at the door; and I'd get a complaint if it wasn't. Collecting was a chore. Often people put me off or even stiffed me. But it was how I made spending money.

Next door neighbors were a couple named Stedman. He was a barber. We kids called both of them "Steadie." They were kind to us and we loved them. Across the street was a lawyer, who had lost an arm, named Bill Wood. He'd managed to get elected to the state legislature. Once he took me to Austin with him and I met some of his colleagues and saw the House chamber, etc. Very exciting.

Chapter 3

Dallas

Sure enough, after three years in Tyler, we moved again, this time to Dallas. Dad had been promoted to Sales Coordinator by Blue Cross. Blue Cross was founded in Texas as a non-profit company. Each state now has its own plan. Later, I figured out that his job in Dallas, was the equivalent of sales manager or VP for Sales. His immediate supervisor was Gen. Harley B. West (no relation but he liked Dad, maybe partly because of the name). The CEO was a man named Walter McBee. I met them both more than once when Dad would take me to the office and introduce me to people. Another man there with whom I became friendly was Melvin Munn, responsible for advertising and public relations.

We lived on Morningside Drive, between Greenville and Skillman, in northeast Dallas. It was 4-5 blocks south of Mockingbird Lane. Our next-door neighbor was Mrs. Harris (either divorced or widowed), a teacher at a technical (vo-tech) high school in downtown Dallas. I think it was Crozier Tech. She talked Mom and Dad into sending me there. I didn't like it. I sensed I was out of place. There were classes in auto repair, cosmetology, home construction, cooking, etc. I transferred to the closest public high school where we lived. It was Woodrow Wilson, in the Lakewood area. Years later it became clear to me that it was one of the best in Dallas. It had a classical college prep curriculum. I took two years of Latin, got a strong background in math, had excellent English teachers, enjoyed history classes a lot. There was an algebra teacher,

Ruth Abernathy, an unforgettable character, and an outstanding teacher. I learned to "recite" in math. What that meant was that, almost every day, you went to the blackboard where everybody could see, including Miss Abernathy. You were given a problem and told to solve it. Homework every night. Tests almost every day. Single piece of paper folded once, lengthwise, name clearly written on outside top. If you did any of that wrong – 0 for the day! No one was late. No wisecracks. No misbehavior of any kind. This woman was tough and we lived in shock and awe of her. I never had another moment's trouble with math.

Leona Sealy taught Latin. She was a career teacher and a dedicated professional. Students today do not understand the value of Latin. After two years of it I never had a minute's difficulty with English grammar, spelling, or syntax. Miss Harris and later Miss Hill were the English teachers. Miss Harris drilled us in diagramming sentences and made us memorize Chaucer. There were others; a chemistry teacher whose name has left me, was very good. Two other math teachers (I took trig, both kinds of geometry and even some calculus). There was a good speech teacher and at least two good history teachers. The Principal was a man named Ashmore. We called him Pop Ashmore, and we loved him. He ran the school like an extended family.

Almost immediately I decided to join Junior Army ROTC. I loved it and did well. After 10th grade, I went to ROTC summer camp at Camp Walters near Mineral Wells, TX. It was one of the hottest places I ever survived. We lived in tents atop wooden platforms. I remember sweating a lot. Once there was a particularly memorable parade. I was on the Regimental staff., standing behind the regimental commander. Flying in on a helicopter to inspect us was none other than Gen. Harley B. West of the Texas National Guard, my father's boss. I was quaking in my shoes. As he inspected the Regimental staff, he stepped in front of me, called me by name, asked a question or two, then told me he'd seen my father that morning and had been asked to convey a greeting. Of course, I was surrounded by friends when we fell out, asking me what that was all about.

During my senior year, I was Regimental Adjutant and was promoted to Major. Woodrow, as we called it, was a large high school (there were over 600 in my class alone), and I'm guessing that half to two-thirds of the boys were in ROTC. I'm guessing there were maybe 600 or 700 in the regiment. We paraded before school every Wednesday morning. As the Adjutant I "formed the parade." That meant I walked the field after each company had formed up, checking alignment. Then, on the dot, maybe it was 8 o'clock, I saluted the regimental commander and reported the parade was formed. He then ordered me to "post." At that point I did a rapid strut from the end of the formation to the middle of the field and assumed my place behind the Colonel. Because of this weekly visibility, a lot of people knew who I was, even though I may not have known them. That played in my favor insofar as popularity was concerned.

It was then that I became aware of my unusual walk. Friends teased me by calling me "dancin' Dan." The adjutant-walk, during parade, demonstrated this for all to see. Who knows where or why I walk the way I do. I can say I've never been sensitive about it. After all, I can't see it.

In high school, I learned to be friendly. It was the thing then to speak to everybody whether you knew them or not. I wanted to be accepted and popular, if possible, but two things were against me. I was a newcomer. I had moved in from Tyler at the beginning of the 10th grade. Many of my classmates had known each other since kindergarten. Most people, I began to learn, did not move as often as we did. Second, I was not an athlete. Football players were at the top of the heap. If you were a football player AND in ROTC, you were assured of great prestige. I wasn't any good at ANY of the sports Woodrow offered. I tried basketball and I tried track, but it was hopeless.

I concentrated on ROTC and academics and tried to be friendly. I almost got elected an "all-school favorite" (a meaningless accolade) my senior year. I think there were 12 boys and 12 girls. But I narrowly lost out. I was elected to the Student Council, and I had a number of friends who were among the most popular kids in the schools. One was Dean Hozier. He seemed to like me a lot. Still, I can't complain; as a relative newcomer, an outsider, and a non-jock, and, oh, there was another thing. I looked very young for my age. I was not only scrawny, as a high school student, I looked like I was still in junior high.

I had several very close friends. Marvin Brown and I rode to school each day. Bill Wilson lived in the next block and got me interested in politics, Democratic Party-style politics. Robert Fulkerson and John Gorman, who had been inseparable friends from infanthood, somehow allowed me to become part of their friendship. Nick Lund, a year behind, was a friend from church.

Back to Bill Wilson. He and I decided that in 1956, as Adlai Stevenson and Dwight Eisenhower once again squared off for the presidency, we were the only two kids in the whole school who supported Stevenson. The whole state of Texas went wild for Ike both times he ran. My parents, previously life-long Democrats, were among them. My sister Janet remembers that my mother and I argued fiercely over this.

I remained active in Scouts in Dallas. I became an Explorer and earned more merit badges. I was a member of a post sponsored by the East Dallas Christian Church. I would have and should have earned the Eagle, but I still didn't know how to swim. There are at least three, maybe, four required merit badges for Eagle: swimming, rowing, lifesaving, canoeing, perhaps. You have to know how to swim for each of these. I got to be Life Scout but not an Eagle. A great regret.

During two of the summers we lived in Dallas I worked at a YMCA Boys Camp called Camp Grady Spruce on Possum Kingdom Lake. I was a cabin counselor; and during the day I taught classes in fishing. I loved it.

I had a paper route in Dallas, for the Dallas Times Herald, an afternoon paper, except on Sunday. At first, I delivered with my bike. Later I earned enough and saved enough to buy a used 1949 Chevrolet, with four doors. I named it Agatha and it was robin's egg blue. That was the last year Chevy made the so-called torpedo body. The car was very useful for delivering papers and very useful for dating, which I learned to do at some point. I remember when I went to take the test for a driver's license I scored perfect on the written test and failed parallel parking on the driving portion of the test. I had to go back for a second try. I have hated parallel parking until this very day.

I don't remember actually being in love; but I do remember how much fun it was to go out with girls, especially after I got a car. Sadly, with one exception, I have forgotten the name of all I liked. There must have been a half-dozen girls, all pretty, all very nice and fun to be with. The usual drill was a movie and then a snack or a coke somewhere. Also, there were quite a few dances. ROTC had a ball each year and there were a couple of other school-sponsored dances. And then there were private dances, at places like the Lakewood Country Club or the White Rock Lake Pavilion. I guess these were given by wealthy parents for their kids and I must have been invited to some of them because I remember going to quite a few. That was expensive. Everyone dressed formally. You were expected to buy and take a corsage for your date. And, afterward, it was expected you would take her someplace for a late-night snack or meal.

What else? I was in some plays. One was "The Old Lady Shows Her Medals." Another was a circus performance and I was the ringmaster. My aunt Lois Jane and Uncle Barney Bonawitz came up from La Marque to see me in that. And I played violin in the school orchestra.

The one girl I dated and am now in touch with is Maidee Longaker (now known as Mary Hope). Maidee was, of course, a nickname. Her dad was a lawyer. She was, and is, beautiful. And she was smart, and funny. We had lots of good times. After graduation, she went to Randolph Macon Women's College in Virginia. Then she transferred to the University of Texas, Austin. She became a school teacher and remained single for years. She met a widower, several years her senior, and they married. He already had five children, and they had one of their own. We reconnected after years of no contact through a mutual friend, Carolyn Holloway, with whom she had become close in Dallas.

The church was very important to us in Dallas. We were active members in Northridge Presbyterian Church on Bob-O-Links Drive. I was active in the Senior High Fellowship.

The minister was a man named John Knox Bowling. He managed

to get his wife and his daughter employed as well. One was organist and the other was choir director. Sadly, he was discovered to have pilfered funds from the church's treasury. He was tried and found guilty and dis-ordained by the presbytery. The congregation split. Some remained loyal to him and refused to vacate the church property. Others, including my family, remained loyal to the presbytery, hired a lawyer, sued the Bowling group and after meeting for months in a school auditorium, won the lawsuit and reoccupied the building. I became disenchanted with church, ministry, and religion. I had planned to enter the ministry since age eight, but no more. My newest hero was the Jewish lawyer who took our case and won. I decided to be a lawyer.

The minister who followed Bowling, after we won back the property, was Walter Johnson, who became very influential in my life and gave me good counsel. He was followed by a man named Robert Watkin who performed our marriage in Anson in 1963.

I applied to five colleges in my senior year: Rice Institute, UT Austin, Austin College, Harvard, and one other which I have forgotten. I was accepted at all except Rice. I wasn't upset about that. I had applied to Rice only because it had Naval ROTC (one of only two schools that did so in Texas). And I knew it was mostly an engineering school, which did not attract me at all.

I was excited about Harvard which also had Naval ROTC. But I knew there was little chance I could go. There was no money. Harvard had a two-step process, after admission you applied for financial aid if you needed it. I applied, but my grades, while good, were not perfect and my test scores were also not good enough. Even then Harvard was very competitive. Besides that, how could I afford to travel to Massachusetts?

I went to the University of Texas because of finances. It was the least expensive place and I got into ROTC so I got a small stipend and help with the cost of my books.

Just as I prepared to leave for college the family moved to Ft. Worth. Dad had been transferred once again. I think he was head of that region. My sisters, poor things, and brother Bill, were going through the same experience I had, changing houses and schools far too often.

My father was something of a dreamer who always thought he could improve himself and his family's circumstances. Wherever we lived was not good enough for him and so he traded houses and cars frequently, usually, I suspect, losing money in each deal. He stayed way over his head in debt most of his adult life. He was not a good money manager. My mother put up with this until, in their retirement, she balked and made it clear she would move no more.

I think Dad was driven, in part, by his mother's attitude. She had left his father because, he said, she thought she had married beneath herself; her husband, my grandfather, was not ambitious enough or successful enough or wealthy enough. Later, Dad felt her disapproval of him for the same reasons. And, my mother always felt her mother-in-law's disapproval. Dad was haunted by the way his mother sided with his sister, Hester Gray, and he felt less than successful compared to Hester's husband. These feelings were apparently confirmed when my grandmother died and left a much smaller inheritance to Dad than to Aunt Hester. It is terrible what parents do to children with such attitudes.

For all that, Dad was a decent man, a gentleman in the way we used to use that appellation. He was kind, seldom raised his voice, worked hard, earned a living to support his family sufficiently to enable my mother to stay at home, at least until the 60's, and was universally liked by everyone he met. He was a born salesman who, without any college, rose to a high rank in a major corporation in Texas. He was a handsome man, the son of a handsome man (my grandfather, as a young man had movie star looks). He was fastidious about his grooming and appearance. He spoke to everybody, was accepting of everyone, was honest and treated us, his children, with love and affection. He left most of the parenting to my mother, at least while I was home; but he could administer discipline (almost never corporal punishment) when necessary.

My mother was attractive if not pretty as a young woman. She too was a high school graduate. She was intelligent, could be funny, took her housekeeping and cooking duties seriously, often put herself last when money was short, set a nourishing meal on the table each evening when we sat down together, and made money go farther than the best manager. She was long-suffering in listening to many of my father's schemes for getting ahead. She loved to read; and I can remember her reading to Nan and me as a young child. I feel that my love of history came from her. I felt her love and support for as long as she lived. John Corbin wrote, "Surely there is no influence more potent than a mother's and no voice so long remembered as a mother's voice." Her death at 67 from lung cancer (she smoked heavily from teenage years) was devastating to me. She was insecure, somewhat self-denigrating, often at odds with relatives and neighbors, and drank too much. But I forgive her all of that. I believe she was a good person; and she did the best she could in sometimes less than good circumstances.

Chapter

The University of Texas

I chose the University for two important reasons. It had NROTC and it was the least expensive. I had very little money. Dad had driven me to Austin and found a relatively inexpensive boarding house, on 23rd St., about four blocks from the campus. Such places were common then, as many students could not afford the more desirable dormitories on campus or the fraternity and sorority houses just off campus. The place was clean but basic. Someone had added a two-story wing to the back of an old two-story house. My room was on the second floor. My roommate was named Asa but I have forgotten his last name. We got along well. He taught me to smoke.

Meals were served in the main house's dining room. I'm sure there was a housemother but I cannot recall her. There was another resident with whom I became friends and his name too is lost to me. He loved Broadway musicals, had a record collection and would invite me to his room. I recall hearing "My Fair Lady" for the first time, in this way.

The university was overwhelming, in spite of the fact I had come from a large city and a large city high school. I believe there were 16,000 students at the time. Walks across campus often ended when I had not only seen no one I knew, but no one I recognized as ever having seen before. People typically did not speak. I enrolled in September of 1957. Registration was in the gym. It was one of the most frantic, confusing, crowded scenes I had ever witnessed. I was intimidated, and wondered if I really belonged there.

I was accepted or assigned (I don't remember asking for it) to something called Plan II. This was a kind of honors program in the sense that good students were placed in more advanced classes and given extra challenge. I do not remember any of my professors. I vaguely recall enjoying an English composition class and a history course.

I listed myself as a pre-law student but I don't think that made any difference in my choice of courses, as a freshman.

My most vivid classroom memory was finding myself in an introductory biology class with over 600 students. Seating was assigned alphabetically so I was in the last row. We were in a large amphitheater. I was so far back I never really knew what the professor looked like. Had I seen him on the street I would not have known him. He entered the pit by a side door, gave his lecture, entertained no questions, and left as soon as the bell rang. If we needed help or had questions, we were expected to make an appointment with a teaching assistant, a graduate student who probably also graded our tests. We were assigned to labs where, among other things, we dissected dead animals (which I hated); and the graduate students there were called lab assistants. They could be somewhat helpful, but nobody was much concerned about us. We were freshmen! This was my introduction to big, state-owned universities and I did not like it. The memory of it dissuaded me, later, from ever even entertaining the idea of working for a state-supported university; and it also influenced me to insist that my children attend an independent college or university.

Money was a chronic issue for me. I was never sure I would be able to return for a sophomore year. My father prevailed on relatives, my Aunt Lois and Uncle Barney Bonawitz,, to send me $600, which saved the day as I was really broke. I had virtually no spending money. A fraternity (required for being accepted socially at that time) was out of the question. I walked past several fraternity houses on the way to my boarding house and remember looking at the young men lounging on their porches drinking beer. I joined a group called APO (Alpha Phi Omega), a service fraternity that accepted any and all. It was affiliated with the Boy Scouts. I also joined the Westminster Fellowship at University Presbyterian Church (where I worshipped). It was an active group that provided a free supper on Sunday nights (when dorms and my boarding house did not offer any meal). And also, there were a number of beautiful girls who came. Dating, however, was out of the question. What would I invite a girl to do, walk across campus?

As I look back, my estrangement from the church must not have been that serious. Though I had given up any ambition for the ministry, I still attended church school class and worshipped each Sunday. I must have been very active in the Westminster Fellowship, because close to the end of my freshman year I was invited to join something called the Faith and Life Center. This was a group of Protestant students who formed an experimental communal living arrangement in a house not far from campus. They engaged in service and daily acts of devotion. I might have joined had I stayed at the university.

I got a part-time job at a drugstore on Guadalupe St. (known as "the drag" to us students).

It was called Falkner's Pharmacy. The owner was a sour old man who trusted no one, paid stingily and seemed not to like me, or anyone else. You had to be busy or appear busy at all times. At first, I was responsible for whatever needed to be done: stocking shelves, sweeping the floor, helping customers find things, dusting the shelves, taking out trash. Later, he let me check folks out, sometimes. Maybe he'd been stolen from in the past; but I always felt he was trying to catch me taking something or doing something I shouldn't. I got off late and walked to the boarding house, where the cook would have put my plate in the oven. It was so late it would have long since cooled to cold and I sat in the dark kitchen, grateful to get what I had.

My enrollment in NROTC provided a bit of financial help. I got a small monthly stipend, my uniforms, and some help in buying textbooks.

In spite of my penury, I enjoyed many aspects of university life. Classes were often interesting. I loved the library, in the tall tower in the campus center. Football games in the enormous stadium were amazing. I got to go to New Orleans to march in a Mardi Gras parade with my NROTC unit. I got off campus a few times to visit the state capitol and other such interesting local sites. Even though I was only there a year, I value the experience. It gave me good insight into large, state-owned universities, big campus life, football frenzy; it taught me careful money management as well as time management and frugality which served me well later in my life.

I think it was in November of that year that a telephone call from Dallas changed my life.

My friend from high school, Robert Fulkerson, called to say that the Congressman from Dallas, Bruce Alger, Republican, was offering a competitive exam on a Saturday, for anyone interested in an appointment to the U. S. Naval Academy. I'd never given a thought to such a thing but Robert said he felt I should go with him to take the exam. It wouldn't cost anything. I saw it as an excuse to go home to see my family for the first time since leaving. By now they had moved to Ft. Worth.

I took the exam and must have done well. But I thought little of it and expected to hear no more of the matter when I left to return to Austin. Unknown to me at the time the student who sat next to me in NROTC class at UT took the same test. I don't recall his name. We were friendly but not close. Later I got a telegram telling me I was offered a First Alternate Appointment to Annapolis. My classmate and seatmate received the Principal Appointment. There were four other alternates, ranked according to their scores on the test. Apparently, my friend Robert did not score highly enough. I learned, somehow, that the man in my class had the appointment. I was pleased I'd done well on the test, but not especially excited. I assumed the matter was settled. Then, I got instructions to take the Naval Academy entrance exam and a physical exam at the Dallas Naval Air Station.

I don't remember where I took the entrance exam. The Navy paid for me to go, by bus, to Dallas, for the physical. In the dentist's office, upon checking my teeth, the Navy dentist got very excited and called his colleagues in to look at my mouth. At the age of 18 I had no cavities and my teeth were straight. I never wore braces. I'd never chewed gum or eaten candy and had even stopped using sugar in iced tea.

Incredibly, the man next to me in class failed the English part of the Academy entrance exam and I was offered the appointment! I was astonished. Such good fortune, that so many dreamed of and never obtained, had fallen into my lap and I had done little to deserve it. I didn't even like the Congressman because he was Republican!

Now I faced a decision. In retrospect, it was a "no brainer." The Academy offered to pay for everything: tuition, books, uniforms, transportation to Annapolis, and even a small monthly salary for spending money. I faced the very real prospect of having to drop out of college to work and find more money to pay for it. I accepted the appointment.

My fascination with the Navy stemmed from an interest that began with the reading of a series of books by C. S. Forester called the "Hornblower" series. Horatio Hornblower was a fictional character whom Forester modeled after Admiral Horatio Nelson, hero of the Battle of Trafalgar. The series began with Hornblower as a midshipman and continued with his career ending as he became a knighted Admiral. This happens during the 19th century. I found the detailed descriptions of life at sea, battles fought by the British Navy and Hornblower's exploits fascinating. My experience in Junior Army ROTC had taught me a lot, so I resolved that in college I wanted to continue military training, but in the Navy version of that.

Chapter 5

The U. S. Naval Academy: A New World

Looking back, I understand that Texas was very parochial, very limiting. The state is so big, so self-contained, so proud (the only state to be a sovereign nation before statehood) that many who grow up and live there believe there is no place better. There is. I met many from other parts of the country. I was exposed to the east coast, an area with even more history than Texas, I had instructors who had traveled widely and came from many different places and experiences. Annapolis was the capital of Maryland, one of the original 13 colonies. I became interested in colonial American history.

During my years at the Academy, I had roommates from Michigan, Pennsylvania, Wyoming, Missouri, and friends from a variety of other states. There were no African American or Hispanic midshipmen and few Jews, but there were many Roman Catholics and one of my closest friends was a Morman.

Chapel was required. You had to attend either Catholic mass or Protestant chapel. We formed up and marched, as a company, to one or the other. A band, positioned in a band shell in front of the chapel, played such things as "Onward Christian Soldiers" with drums and cymbals as we marched in. At the end of the service, as the organ played, "Eternal Father, Strong to Save," first the Navy flag and then the U. S. Flag were dipped in front of the altar and then paraded out with an honor guard. It was an impressive service, full of pageantry and a mixture of church and state. For a while I elected to attend Sunday services in the town (which one could do with the permission of the Chaplain) and I visited Methodist, Episcopal, Presbyterian and Christian Science congregations. I was fascinated with St. John's College, also in Annapolis, with its Great Books curriculum. I sometimes went to lectures there.

The coursework in those days was a prescribed curriculum, no electives. Even though many, as I did, had previous college work, you took the same courses in the same sequence. I had one classmate who was a graduate of Yale and he did just as the rest of us. I loved the English and the history classes. My English prof, Plebe (first) Year, was Richard West. He liked me because of the name. He awarded me a 4.0 in the course, a perfect score. I stood No. 1 in my class (of about 600) in English. This brought an unintended consequence. Several First Classmen (seniors) in my company (the 11th) made me edit and correct their senior theses.

I had a math professor in calculus who was an unforgettable character and who made a lasting impression. His name was Samuel S. Saslaw and he signed his name S^3 (S cubed). He was a Russian Jew who had fled the Soviet Union. He dressed impeccably in three-piece Harvard Square suits from Brooks Brothers. He always wore bow ties. EVERY class he taught included his thoughts or illustrations or opinions in other areas than math (politics, history, art, religion, science). He taught us that math and music were closely related, that religion and economics were intertwined, that history could not be understood apart from biology. One day, in a statement that still reverberates in my head, he got the point through to me that ALL knowledge is interrelated; that its division into separate disciplines (philosophy, language, math, chemistry) are artificial constructs invented by us for our own purposes. That was like a revelation and a blinding one at that. For years, it has helped me deal with the popular notion that religion and science are separate and qualitatively different realms. Not so.

We often had lectures by visiting scholars, exhibits in the museum, talks by important government officials or high ranking military leaders, concerts by visiting musicians or even symphony orchestras. I loved all that and attended at every chance. We marched in parade every Wednesday. Once the visiting dignitary was Britain's First Lord of the Admiralty. I was intrigued.

There were dances and balls in the Arsenal. We wore full-dress uniforms. Your date was in a formal dress with corsage. You lined up at the receiving line, presented your card to an aide and were introduced to the Commandant (a Captain) or the Superintendent (an Admiral) and his wife. Only then could you enter the dance hall. There were classes in ballroom dancing, in table etiquette, in diplomatic language. Classes in the politics of other countries. It was a wide new world to me, and I reveled in it. I subscribed to the Christian Science Monitor, discovered the Atlantic Monthly and the New York Times in the library, went to Washington, D. C. on weekend liberty three or four times to visit important sites; and explored every inch of Annapolis.

Once I talked a classmate into accompanying me to D.C. and we toured the Capitol on our own. I'd read enough about it that I knew where to go. It was late afternoon and I wanted to see the Speaker's Chambers after we came out of the House Chamber. In those days, you could wander around freely. As we headed to the Speaker's side I spotted the man himself, Sam Rayburn of Texas. Accompanied by just one assistant and with no security detail he came toward us in his customary three-piece black suit and with a beat-up Stetson on his bald head. Summoning all the courage I could muster, I said, "Mr. Speaker, may I speak with you? I'm from Texas." He stopped and said, "Certainly son, where you from?" "Dallas sir." Then I said, "It's a great honor to meet you." Then he said, "Who's your friend?" I introduced my classmate, who was awestruck. Then this from

Rayburn, to his aide, "Remember these boys. They're gonna be admirals someday." And, "Good luck young men." I remember every word and syllable. He'd been a hero since I watched him chair the Democratic National Convention in 1952. My mother and I had watched as we stood on the sidewalk outside a car dealer's place in Tyler where a TV set had been positioned inside the showroom window.

In January 1961 I volunteered to march in John Kennedy's inauguration. It was one of the coldest days I've experienced. We stood for hours, freezing, before the parade began.

I got to see both Kennedys as we passed the reviewing stand in front of the White House.

Kennedy was very handsome and very tanned; he'd been in Florida on vacation. Jackie was extremely beautiful. The freezing temperature and the hours of waiting were suddenly of no consequence.

That evening our duties were to act as escorts and ushers at one of five inaugural balls. The one I was assigned to was in some enormous armory, I think. My job was to stand at the cloakroom, take coats and hats and retrieve them when people exited. In the door, to my amazement, came Sam Rayburn and Adlai Stevenson together. Both were divorced and so they had agreed to be each other's date, I suppose. I took their coats and hats and they disappeared inside. Hours later, they reappeared and Rayburn was drunk and Stevenson was obviously trying to get him to leave. But he didn't want to do that.

Stevenson ordered me to get the hats and coats and I helped them both with their coats. Then, Stevenson put the Stetson on Rayburn's head, who immediately snatched it off saying he wasn't going anywhere. Somehow Stevenson edged him out the door and into a waiting limo. Amazing!

Being a student at Annapolis was unlike being one at other colleges. We marched to class, in uniform, of course. We "recited." That meant if you were called on you stood up, either at your seat or at the blackboard, and answered the question or solved the problem. Half our profs were Naval officers, assigned to the Academy for a year or two, to teach. Most of the courses were Navy related: steam engineering, celestial navigation, ordinance and gunnery, seamanship (including knot tying), U. S. diplomacy, Naval history. There was also math, chemistry, physics, engineering.

Some of the Naval officers were barely competent, knowing not much more than we did. Many of the civilian profs were real characters. One man was egregiously profane, sometimes obscene, and flew into a rage if anyone went to sleep. This was a calculus class that met right after lunch. We had a somewhat overweight classmate who invariably dozed off. The prof pelted him with erasers and chalk. Another man, in history, had such an incredible memory that he would stand for the entire hour without notes and reel off facts, names, dates, details far beyond what you could find in any book.

He loved to give tests with throwaway questions: "what color was Napoleon's white horse?" or "when was the War of 1812?"

Everyone was required to do a sport. I was in a quandary about which sport. For a week or two of my first year I was on the "Submarine Squad." I had never learned to swim. You could not be in the Navy and not know how to swim. Solution: you joined the Submarine Squad until you learned. The Submarine Squad was Academyese for non-swimmers who would sink beneath the surface of the sea. Great motivation. I learned in about two weeks.

I knew it was hopeless to try out for football or basketball or anything like that. Similarly, no chance with baseball, tennis, lacrosse or soccer.

Being from Texas I'd never heard of the last two. I tried cross country, sailing, handball and squash (another game unknown in Texas), and gymnastics. It was discouraging. Finally, someone suggested I go out for crew (rowing in shells). I liked it and I seemed to be O.K. in that. It turned out to be the perfect sport for me. It takes stamina and discipline and careful teamwork, but not a lot of skill or coordination. It's a repetitive action. I made the lightweight (under 165 pounds; I was a stick) freshman varsity crew. Our most memorable victory was against the Harvard freshmen in spring 1959. I was the stroke (number 8) who sits just forward of the coxswain (a guy as small as possible, who steers with lines attached to a rudder and calls out the cadence and gets thrown in the drink if you win). I am very proud of my success in crew, my only athletic achievement in a sport, once again, never at that time heard of in Texas.

Football was a big deal at Annapolis. We could lose to every team we played including the new Air Force Academy; but if we beat Army it was a successful season. The hazing of plebes (freshmen) was severe but if you beat Army at Thanksgiving time we got to "stand down." That meant your life was much more bearable from then until Christmas vacation. Consequently, plebes were highly motivated to attend pep rallies, encourage football players in the corridors, and yell at the top of their lungs at the game with Army. There were two outstanding, and famous, football players then. One was Joe Bellino, a halfback who won the Heisman Trophy and was in the Class of '61. The other was Roger Staubach, in my Class of '62, who was the quarterback, at least in his final year, and later gained wider fame with the Dallas Cowboys. I knew Roger to speak to; I'm not sure I ever met Bellino off the field.

The Navy mascot is a goat. One year some West Pointers managed to goat-nap it. The Army mascot is a mule, often two mules. At the game, we would scream in unison, "Get your asses off the field." I remember a game with the Air Force Academy. Their mascot was a high-flying hawk. A tender would stand in the middle of the field, remove its hood, and it would soar high into the sky and later land back on the outstretched arm.

Except this year, a prankster, among the Brigade of Midshipmen, rigged a supersonic radio that managed to confuse and disorient the hawk who tumbled head over tail and landed in a heap in the wrong place on the field, a heap of feathers. The Air Force tried to make Navy forfeit the game. They were enraged.

I did well my first year at the USNA. Having had Army Junior ROTC in high school and then a year of NROTC in college helped me a lot. The first year was full of hazing but if you did not screw up too much it was much better for you. I received a very good conduct rating from my company officer, one of the best. My grades were all good and I was happy to be out of plebe status. Youngster cruise was at hand.

The second year is known as Youngster year and during the summer between midshipmen typically go on a cruise. I was assigned to the USS Henly, a Destroyer Escort of WWII vintage. That meant the ship was at least 20 years old. We headed for the North Atlantic, one of the roughest seas in the world. Many of my shipmates were seasick for days. I never was. We steamed into the St. Lawrence Seaway, the newly enlarged entrance to the Great Lakes. Our mission was to provide an honor guard for the official opening by President Eisenhower and Queen Elizabeth II, and then to accompany the Queen on her Royal Yacht all the way to Chicago. Along the way, we put in at a number of smaller cities (I remember Ogdensburg, New York and Manitowoc, Wisconsin as two of them), and were entertained grandly by cities excited to see the first U. S. Naval flotilla of any size on the Great Lakes since the War of 1812. At each port, there were balls, banquets, parades. There were lots of girls eager to be taken on dates. We were sometimes invited to private homes for meals or to beach parties. On board ship, someone would call out the invitation and we would raise our hand if it sounded good. I remember country clubs, beach houses, lovely residences, all much grander than anything I'd known growing up.

At Chicago I stood along her parade route, at attention, as the Queen and the Duke of Edinburgh passed by me in an open convertible. I remember she seemed very small but pretty and gracious, waving to all.

Third Class year went well, as I recall. I do not remember any serious problems or challenges. I made a number of close friends, most in my company. I had roommates, at various times, whom I liked a lot. My favorite was Don King of Wyoming. It was that year, 1960-61, that I went to Washington in January for Kennedy's inaugural.

I remember the food at Annapolis was wonderful. They fed us well, and we had a lot to eat at all three meals. Each table, typically, had 12 midshipmen seated: four plebes on one side, four youngsters on the other, two 2nd classmen and two seniors at each end respectively. Food was served family style and passed first to the 1st classmen, then on down in rank. Most of the conversation involved "running" (hazing) the plebes who had to sit at attention (back straight, chin in, eyes straight forward, squaring their hand with a fork in it to get food to their mouths). All the while they were being asked to recite things required to be memorized, report on assignments they'd been given at the last meal, etc.

Every plebe was required to memorize in its entirety a small handbook called "Reef Points." I still have my copy, dated 1958-59. For example, if a plebe was asked by an upperclassman, "How long have you been in the Navy, Mister?" he was required to recite, flawlessly,

> "All me bloomin' life, sir! Me mother was a mermaid, me father was King Neptune. I was born on the crest of a wave and rocked in the cradle of the deep.
> Seaweed and barnacles are me clothes. Every tooth in me head is a marlinspike; the hair on me head is hemp. Every bone in me body is a spar, and when I spits, I spits tar. I'se hard, I is, I am, I are!"

If a plebe made an error or did anything at all to displease a senior, he was punished. The most frequent penalty was, "Shove out, Mister." Whereupon you sat as though in a chair, but without a chair! Another favorite penalty, if you were in your room when it was prescribed, was the asymptote. That's a word for a curve on a mathematical graph that gets closer and closer to the vertical without ever touching it. We had steel, double decked beds. The top bunk had a head rail and a foot rail. The plebe stretched with his hands on the top head rail and his feet on the foot trail and his back arched. It takes little time to tire and collapse, but we would try our best.

A favorite assignment to a plebe, often given during a meal along with an order to report at the next meal, would be to find the "flush factor" for the third toilet from the end in the north "head" (bathroom). The plebe would hold a roll of toilet paper at waist height with a pencil in the inside after unrolling enough sections for just the first one to float on top of the water. Upon flushing the toilet, he would then count the number of sections of paper which disappeared "down the tube." That was the flush factor for that particular fixture. Etc.

It was forbidden to say, "I don't know," when asked a question about anything. If you did not know the answer, the only acceptable reply was, "I'll find out, Sir." Then, you had better do just that and report back.

There were no women in the Brigade at that time. It is hard for me to imagine what it must be like for those who are there now. And, it was hard to meet girls in town unless you brazenly walked up to one on the street. Sometimes there were "tea dances." Girls from nearby colleges were invited to come for an afternoon informal. You could go up to one, ask her to dance and thereby meet her.

I had two girlfriends while I was there. I can't remember the name of either or exactly when we dated. One was a resident of Annapolis or one of the communities close by.

The other was a Philadelphian who was training to be a nurse. Dates were called "drags." If there was a dance or a party and your drag came from out of town you had to find a drag house in town for them to stay. In this way, I met a woman named Lavinia Fowler with whom I became friendly and often visited on weekends, whether I was dragging or not. On one occasion, I invited a girl I had dated in Dallas to come up for a weekend. She was accompanied by her parents and they stayed at Mrs. Fowler's. During the weekend, I received a telephone call from a neighbor or friend of theirs in Dallas telling me their house had burned. I waited till they were ready to leave on Sunday to tell them, so as not to ruin their visit.

Mrs. Fowler was a Christian Scientist and invited me to her church. I went there on several occasions. I thus became familiar with an American religion I'd only heard of before. Readings during worship each Sunday came from the Bible and also from "Science and Health with Key to the Scriptures," by Mary Baker Eddy, founder of the church. There is a First Reader and a Second Reader. One must be male and the other female and they swap places every few months. It was my first exposure to gender equity in church.

One weekend another midshipman, who also used Mrs. Fowler's house, invited Linda Bird Johnson, daughter of the Vice President, to come over from Washington. She arrived in a chauffeured limo with Secret Service escort. After the dance, she was driven back to

Washington. I suppose it was not safe for her to stay overnight. I thought she was nice, and attractive, and she had an outgoing personality.

None of the girls I dated, either in high school or while at Annapolis had captured my heart. I thought I was in love a time or two but nothing lasted and in some cases, including the three just mentioned, they decided they should continue the search.

Second class summer was a series of training events at a number of different places. The first was Pensacola, Florida for Naval Air Training. Dad owned a station wagon at the time so the whole family drove to Florida with me, as a vacation trip, to deliver me to the first training site.

We flew in trainers, sitting behind a pilot; one day we flew off and then landed back on an aircraft carrier. It was a terrifying experience for me. But not as scary as the Dilbert Dunker, a plane fuselage into which you were strapped, that flew down a rail into water and turned upside down. You were then expected to unbuckle yourself, open the canopy and exit underwater, swimming then to the surface. Later, we did Frogman training and a turn with the Seabees in Quantico, Virginia. There was a submarine cruise, though I can't remember where we embarked. I remember damage control (putting out a fire set in a listing ship's hull), gas mask training, and a lot more. Once, in Philadelphia, we ate our meals in the mess hall of a brig (Naval prison) and it was disturbing to see prisoners come in each day, under guard, for their meals.

Chapter 6

A Change in Direction

Second class (junior year) began in September 1961 uneventfully. Sometime that fall, I learned of a Quadrennial Youth Conference of the Presbyterian Church in the U.S. It was to be held in Dallas during the Christmas holiday time. I was very interested and thought I should go since it was so close to my family who lived at that time in Ft. Worth. I registered and attended. I do not remember the names of the speakers but I remember sitting, in one session, in the sanctuary of the First Presbyterian Church in downtown Dallas when I had a strange feeling, a kind of epiphany. I remember shuddering a bit at the moment it occurred. It was, in retrospect, a religious conversion. I felt God had touched me, that I was on the wrong course, and that I needed to get back on track with my original plan to enter the ministry.

Two other things happened at that conference. My childhood minister, Dr. Wil R. Johnson, was there. He'd brought some young people from Galveston. I saw him again for the first time since my grandmother's funeral and we talked. I also met a girl, Jane Langston of Beaumont, and I fell for her. We talked for hours. She was a Presbyterian and a student at Austin College. I left Dallas with my head and heart full of all sorts of conflicting ideas and questions.

Eventually it became clear to me, I had to become a minister. The question was how and when.

After returning to Annapolis I took the first opportunity to buy a bus ticket to Richmond, Virginia, the location of the nearest Presbyterian Church, U.S. seminary, then called Union Theological

Seminary in Virginia. I took a taxi from the bus station and as I got out of the taxi, in front of Watts Hall, down the steps from the front door came Professor Balmer Kelly who would later become one of my favorite seminary teachers. I was in uniform. He greeted me warmly and asked if he could help me. I told him I was visiting as a prospective student. He stood there, on the steps, and we talked a long time. Later, a man named Priestly Conyers, Assistant to the President and Dean of Admission, was also very friendly and told me I would need to have a college degree but then I could apply.

There would be financial aid available, and he strongly implied they'd be glad to have me when I was qualified to enter.

Back at Annapolis we had final exams after Christmas. I did well on each except Electrical Engineering, a course which I hated because I had no interest in it at all. I failed the exam. The required grade for every course was 2.50. I think I got a 2.46 on the exam and 2.49 for the semester. I would be required to repeat the course and might have been required to repeat the entire semester, after dropping out till the next fall. That was called a "turnback." In those days, you had to pass every course and all were required. I would have to go before the Academic Board and they would decide my fate.

The low grade in that exam seemed an important signal to me, a kind of confirmation that I was on the wrong career path; further, it provided a way out. The events I have described seemed more than coincidental. I felt strongly guided, strangely propelled, to go in a different direction for my career. And, I felt increasingly as though I was coming home, coming back to an original path and plan that I never should have left in the first place.

I remembered how I had felt almost forced to take the Annapolis appointment, for financial reasons. I thought about a certain disillusionment I had experienced insofar as a career in the Navy, and in military life in general were concerned. I had already decided I would not stay in beyond the four years I would be obligated for after graduation. When I had entered Annapolis, I was sure I would be an admiral, but I figured out that promotion was too arbitrary, too fluky, too happenstance. It was all a question of where you were and when and whom you knew and who liked you. There did not seem to be enough attention to merit and too much accidental occurrence at the base of it all. Certain aspects of military life discouraged me as well; way too much inefficiency - lots of rushing to wait. My enthusiasm had waned.

Meanwhile I figured out that staying and finishing at the Academy would take a year and a half. Then, I would be obligated for four years of active duty. Thus, it would be 5 ½ years before I could enter seminary. On the other hand, if I left at that point in mid-year, returned to Texas, took a course or two at TCU, earned some money, and then went to college for a bachelor's degree, I could be in seminary a year and a half from then.

There were two other circumstances that contributed to the direction I was moving. First, at the end of second class year (junior year) no one was allowed to resign from the Academy and the Navy. After that amount of time the government had so much money invested they could not allow such to occur. In another 3-4 months, I would not have been allowed to leave. And, we were at peace in the world. The Viet Nam war was not yet in sight. Kennedy had just been elected. There was no thought that I was exiting when the country was threatened. A number of my classmates later lost their lives in Viet Nam, but in January, 1961, that was not yet a clear possibility.

I went before the Academic Board, comprising the heads of all the academic divisions. The Captain who was chair of the English, History and Philosophy Division (we called it the Bull Division) was my strong advocate, because I had stood first in my class in English at the end of Plebe year. He knew I was a good student. They told me I could repeat the course I'd failed. I thanked them, respectfully, but said I'd decided to resign my commission, finish college elsewhere, and then enter seminary as I'd had a change of heart and now wanted to be a minister. They tried to dissuade me; but I'd thought about it and prayed about it too much, and my mind was resolved. As I did an about face and walked out of the room I felt a strange peace descend and a huge burden lift.

My parents said, of course, I could come to Ft. Worth and stay with them and my siblings. I was sad about leaving my friends at the Academy. I worried that there had been wasted time and missed opportunity because of my decision to go there. But later, I decided that the experience there was invaluable; and that, if I had it to do over again, even if I knew I wouldn't finish there, I'd do it again. It had been so broadening, so interesting, so helpful to me in many ways. I'd learned discipline, time management, decision making, organization, planning ahead and much more. These were all skills most college students do not learn, and I would find them all very helpful later. Much of my course work had been on a different level and from teachers of far more varied experience than I would have had at most other colleges. I had seen a part of the country and met people from other parts of it that opened to me a much broader perspective. I had taken heavy doses of science, engineering and math. All of that helped me later, but I would have done little of that had I stayed at UT Austin or gone to another college, as a humanities major.

Thus it was that, in the summer of 1961, I got a job at a shoe store in downtown Ft. Worth. It was called Baker's and it sold women's shoes, less expensive ones. I worked there a couple of months, and learned a lot about human psychology and observed a lot about the behavior of women, at least while they are shopping. One day a woman came in and, maybe because we had a sale on or perhaps because she liked me, she bought 15 pairs of shoes! The manager thought I was a hero. I had no idea what I'd done, if anything, to prompt such extravagance.

Later, I don't remember why, I quit that job and took another at the main branch of the Ft. Worth Public Library. I probably saw an ad in the paper and thought it sounded interesting. Because of that experience and a later job in the library at seminary, I learned my way around libraries, always afterward felt comfortable in them, even enjoyed them. Books have been important to me for years. I own far too many, and I'm always surrounded by them. Someone said that he or she always imagined that heaven would be something like a library.

While I was working and trying to save enough money for college, I enrolled as a part-time, summer student at Texas Christian University. I took either two or three courses. One was a course in Bible, another was in early American history. I liked being on the campus and enjoyed the courses.

Though I hadn't planned it that way when I was in high school, it took five years and four colleges to earn a bachelor's degree. What a checkered career as an undergraduate! I told dozens of students, in later years, there was no disgrace in being a college drop-out or a transfer student. More importantly for me, I actually attended, as a student, four distinctly different institutions in the U. S. higher education system: a large state-owned university, a government-operated military academy, a large independent university, and then, finally, a small, church-related, liberal arts college. Each experience proved invaluable in what became my career in colleges.

In addition to changing colleges I changed career paths, four times! I began as an aspirant for the ministry. Then I wanted to be a lawyer. Next, a naval officer. Then, back to the ministry. In the end, I became a college administrator. Some might have thought this a tortured path. Nowadays it seems more typical, as many students have several choices, are qualified to go in alternative directions and often have difficulty deciding. I learned to be open to change, expectant of surprises, and amazed at the fascinating turns my life has taken.

I applied to Austin College (where I had been accepted in '57) and was accepted for entrance in fall, 1961. My close friend Nick Lund, from Dallas days (we often fished together) told me I could be his roommate in Luckett Hall. I was happy about that. A meeting with the Registrar, Forrest Bryant, concluded with three important discoveries.

Many of the courses I'd had at Annapolis would not transfer. Austin College did not teach such things as steam engineering or celestial navigation or ordinance and gunnery.

On the other hand, I had taken enough math that they would admit me as a math minor.

Finally, we figured out that, if I took every history course Austin College offered in 1961-62, and the college accepted my academy history courses, including Naval History, I could be graduated as a history major in the spring.

There remained only the question of how to pay for this. I had a little money saved from working, and the college gave me a scholarship, a loan, and a job (as resident assistant in Luckett Hall).

Chapter 7

Austin College

The year I spent at Austin College was momentous in several ways. My happiness was great as I plunged into life on a small campus, full of confidence, having attended three other institutions, all much larger. Maybe because I was already a senior, perhaps because of the prestige connected with an appointment to one of the service academies, possibly because I had matured more than the average college student, I was well received by faculty and students alike.

I made several close friends, in addition to Nick. Don Renfroe, a football player, lived across the hall. I took up with David Hornbeck and Tom Finley Brown and a number of others with whom I have remained friends until now. Nick and Don urged me to pledge their fraternity, Phi Sigma Alpha, a local there. In retrospect, it was a silly thing to do. But I wanted to be accepted. There was no cost beyond minimal dues as there were no frat houses, and so I pledged as a senior! I couldn't believe I was being hazed again, but after Annapolis' plebe year it was child's play and it was over in a week or two.

I had tried to pursue into a romantic relationship the acquaintance I had with Jane Langston of Beaumont. We dated some but she eventually said, no thanks.

I liked the courses I was taking, except for one: Greek. The prof was a man named Jefferson Davis Sadler. He was teaching classical Greek in a very dull way, by rote. We were all pre-theology students; and we were all male except for one woman who was the star of the class. Judy Singleton was the daughter of a minister and was brilliant; Sadler loved her and barely tolerated the rest of us. He wanted us to read aloud in class so he could criticize our pronunciation. We felt sorry for Tom Brown, from a small town in Arkansas, with a distinct twang. He would get two or three words out and Sadler would cut him off, "Thank you, Mr. Brown, that will do." I barely passed the course both semesters. I disliked it a lot and I'm sorry for the experience. Though I had a much happier time with Greek in seminary, my first encounter more or less dampened my enthusiasm for it.

Other courses were wonderful. Ed Phillips, a Harvard grad and an Easterner, admired my knowledge of Naval history and often called on me with questions in class about that. He wanted me to read everything by Samuel Eliot Morrison, the great historian, and I did read a lot of that. Elmer Flaccus taught me much in his classes in Russian history and Latin American history. I took a psychology course for the first time. I already had enough credits in Spanish; so I did not take a language that year.

Perhaps the most important course (for my development) was by Charles Ramsey, a Presbyterian minister with a Ph.D. in ethics. He was famous for rolling his tie up to his neck while he lectured. It was he who introduced me to the important field of Christian ethics, and inspired in me what has become a lifelong concern for those who suffer from deprivation, injustice and discrimination. I believe it was he, more than anyone else at Austin College, who prepared me best for seminary and made of me a true "bleeding heart liberal" who has never wavered from that political and theological persuasion. Even though that label is no longer fashionable either in U. S. politics or in theology, I claim it proudly. Of course, I am liberal if that means progressive politics, compassion for the poor and the victimized, and determination to hold faith and reason in tandem.

Ramsey was huge in my thinking for another reason. I'd been a political liberal since high school. I would never think of voting for a Republican for any position. Now I had opened to me the theological equivalent to that, progressive Christianity, socially conscious religion, New Testament based compassion. As someone raised, at first, in a very conservative church, I eagerly adopted my new identity. As someone headed for seminary and the ministry after that I moved forward, committed to left field!

I ran for the student senate and was elected. I teamed up with another senator, a woman, to revise the constitution of the student government, and that was done.

At one point, I contracted encephalitis which is a very serious condition that can lead to brain damage. I have no idea how or why that occurred. I was a patient in Sherman Community Hospital; my parents came when they were called and told about this. I recovered and returned to my coursework.

I was happy to be there; and I remember being very busy, engaged, fulfilled. Looking back, I am sure this was one of my happiest years.

The fall term ended, I went home for Christmas in Ft. Worth, and then, back at campus, final exams and the end of the term. My grades were fine.

The spring term was just as good. I took Glen Maxwell's course in introductory philosophy. He was an interesting character, ascetic looking, austere, very formal. And he expected literal memorization out of the text for answers to test questions. I would not do that and usually got a B, but he liked me anyway and we had several fascinating conversations in his office. I sat on the front row, next to Sidney Childs, one of the most popular girls on campus and one of the prettiest. I do not know how we came to sit together. I probably chose that seat next to her. Anyway, that's how and when we met, at the beginning of the spring term. Eventually I asked her out. I took her to my fraternity dance. She says I sat most of the time. She danced with my fraternity brothers. Anyway, I was smitten. I must have told my friends. Don Renfroe teased me every time he saw me. "Hey West," he would say, "is it moonglow or the real thing?" For me it was the latter, but Sidney wasn't so certain.

There was an election for president of the student body. My close friend David Hornbeck ran and asked me to be his campaign manager. He lost. Richard Hull was elected and neither of us has ever forgiven him.

There was another election: for "student body favorite." One man and one woman were elected. It was a meaningless accolade except that you got a larger photo in the yearbook. A woman named Sue Farr was elected female favorite and I was elected male favorite. It was only a popularity contest.

It was at Austin College that I met John D. Moseley, president of the college, and his wife, Sara Bernice. I learned that Sidney was at the college, in part, because of them. Her parents had known the Moseleys for years. Sara Bernice's parents, the Honeas, lived across the street from Sidney's grandmother in Anson, TX. Indeed, Mrs. Honea, Sara Bernice's mother, had been Sidney's first grade teacher. The Moseleys were liked and highly respected by everyone. He dominated the campus and was the driving force behind many new programs and policies. Years later it was clear to everyone that he had saved the college from probable extinction in the 50's, and became its defining president. I admired him and his work. He became a model and later would become, even more, the standard by which I measured my own performance.

I was active in what was called the pre-ministerial association. Once I was asked to preach in chapel. I wasn't very good. I didn't save my notes, for good reason. I became friendly with a student named Steve Schlosstein of Dallas. He was a philosophy major, an agnostic and a great Nietzsche fan. He liked Nietzsche's famous declaration, "God is dead." I thought Steve was one of the most intelligent people I'd ever met. We argued endlessly. He knew much more philosophy than I and I was not happy about that. Once he invited me to go home with him to Dallas to meet his family. They were a gracious, cultured, well-educated group and I liked them as well as him. That may have been the first Jewish family whom I visited in their home; I am sure he was my first Jewish friend. (I do not remember meeting a single Jewish midshipman at Annapolis.)

Toward the end of the year I applied for admission to Union Theological Seminary in Virginia and was told that I was accepted pending receipt of my final grades and transcript. At another point that spring I was examined by the Candidates Committee of Northeast Texas Presbytery and accepted as a candidate for the ministry "under the care of" Northridge Presbyterian Church in

Dallas where my membership had remained. Before I met with the committee I was required to take a series of tests administered by a clinical psychologist, retained by Presbytery for this purpose. Her name was Gladys Guy Brown. The idea was to determine whether candidates were suited, psychologically, for the ministry - a good idea. I clearly remember taking the famous Rorschach ink blot test and a number of others. Dr. Brown had reservations about me. She felt I was "too decisive." This came up in my meeting (and oral exam) with the committee. I explained that I had spent 2 1/2 years at the Naval Academy where you are taught to make decisions quickly and well, and also taught that hesitation could have dire consequences. That seemed to satisfy the committee.

There were two women, devout members of Northridge Presbyterian Church, each of whom had been mentors of mine since high school days. Their names were Naomi Blaize and Margaret Pettey. Mrs. Pettey had taught me Bible in a program then recognized by the public schools in which you could take a course in Bible, off campus, and receive high school credit for it. Beginning in the year I enrolled at Austin College and continuing through my graduation from Union Seminary they each sent me money, always enclosed in a nice card with a handwritten note. They were small amounts but always welcome to a student usually in need. I have never forgotten their kindness to me. They were both thrilled that their church had produced a candidate for the ministry, and tried to do whatever they could to encourage and support me.

There are some fools who proudly call themselves "self-made man." Horse feathers!

There is no such thing. (I remember that a writer named John Bright once said of someone, "He is a self-made man and worships his creator.") We are all helped in ways great and small and often in ways we do not ever realize. I have been helped along the way by so many people, far more than I deserved, and sometimes without my knowing.

There is no way my life could possibly have been so interesting and rewarding without their help: parents and grandparents, teachers, ministers, friends, neighbors, and others. I owe them all.

In a development I cannot explain because I do not remember

why or how it happened, I was hired to be the summer student minister of the Presbyterian Church in Nocona, Texas. I had had no seminary training at that point. Someone must have called the college and asked for a student's name to contact. For three months, I lived in an apartment above a motel on the highway that ran through the town; and every Sunday I would try to say something, in a sermon, that was as intelligent and meaningful as I could manage. My mentor was W. L. Scott, owner of a local hardware store and also the town undertaker and owner of the only funeral home. There were two other elders in the tiny church. One was manager of the local A. & P. grocery store. Session meetings often occurred in his stockroom as the four of us stood in a circle.

The spring term ended; my parents and siblings came for commencement. They were proud and I was proud - five years, four colleges, and three career plan changes later I was finally ready for graduate work. I was very happy in every way, except that Sidney Childs had made it clear, sometime in that spring semester, that she wasn't interested in pursuing our relationship. She told me years later that at least two of her closest friends urged her not to stay with me. That was a disappointment; but I went home to Ft. Worth for a short while before driving to Nocona, thinking that the year had been a great one for me in so many ways.

On my birthday, May 29, 1962, I received a telegram from Sidney with birthday greetings. I was surprised and excited. Maybe she wasn't over me yet. I called her and she said I could come to see her in Wichita Falls where her family had moved from Anson as her father changed jobs. The relationship blossomed and I was overjoyed.

Nocona is about halfway between Sherman and Wichita Falls. It was easy to drive back and forth to see her. She came, at least once, to see me and my set-up and to listen to me try to preach, in Nocona. During one of her visits I asked her to marry me and she accepted. At the time of this writing that was over 53 years ago, but I remember the moment vividly. What a marvelous development! What joy! How amazing was that?

I drove to Wichita Falls and formally asked her father for her hand. He agreed. Her family was very accepting, very welcoming. Later, she told me that her mother's comment was, "There will be fireworks ahead." I invited her to Ft. Worth. She had been to our home in Ft. Worth for Easter in 1962 so she already knew my family. At any rate, I had borrowed money from Nick Lund's mother, Doris, and bought her a diamond ring for $200, a small fortune to me at that time. I took her to dinner at a restaurant and put it on her finger. We were so happy.

Chapter 8

Summer and Seminary

The summer in Nocona flew by. My biggest accomplishment was organizing a preaching event, getting all the churches in town to participate, and asking Melvin Munn, a colleague of my father's, at Blue Cross in Dallas, to come and speak. He was not a minister; but he did a presentation in which he recited from memory the entire Sermon on the Mount, Matthew 5, 6 and 7, from the King James Version of the Bible. It was an inspiring performance, even moving at times. It was the only possible way to get those various congregations and their pastors, from six or seven different denominations, to sit together. How could any Christian of any brand possibly object to hearing the Sermon on the Mount, from the 1611 translation?

There were two other developments that summer. I met a man who was a minister in the Church of the Brethren. The church he pastored was tiny and out in the countryside. He was very intelligent and well-read and I liked him a lot. He died suddenly, perhaps from a heart attack. All of the ministers, including me as a would-be minister, attended his funeral, sitting together in the front pew. I was pained over his disappearance.

Another clergyman I met was a Pentecostal minister, from a nearby town. He taught me to fast, explaining that when one goes without food, blood that is needed for digestion can more readily be available to the brain and one thinks more clearly, concentrates more keenly than when one's stomach is full. That is true. Once he invited me to a service in his church. It was a full-blown event with speaking in tongues, lots of shouting, moaning, crying, dancing in the aisle, falling down. I'd never seen such behavior in a church. But I respected the minister. He obviously loved his people, they adored him, and the whole lot of them were sincere in their faith and their unusual (to me) form of worship.

I remember being back in Ft. Worth, in the brief time between the end of my work in Nocona and my departure for Richmond. I had a call from Priestly Conyers, Director of Admission at the Seminary. He said there would be an African American student (the only one) at the seminary and asked if I would be his roommate. I answered immediately, that I would, of course. I never knew why I was chosen for the privilege, but I'm glad I was.

At some point I had gotten rid of a worthless used car, a French Renault, and bought a used Oldsmobile. I loaded it with all my worldly possessions and set out alone for Richmond. In Forrest City, Arkansas the car threw a rod. I had obviously failed to check the oil. I called the seminary and Mr. Conyers put me in touch with two Presbyterian ministers in the city, one southern Presbyterian and a Union Seminary grad, the other a Cumberland Presbyterian. Someone found a mechanic who tried to help me.

We drove to West Memphis and found a motor in a wrecked car in a junk yard that would fit in my car, drove back and installed it; but it would not work. I gave up and sold the car for junk. I stored my belongings in a closet at the Presbyterian Church and caught a bus to Richmond, arriving a day or two late. The Rev. Tony Dick later packed my things and shipped them to me at the seminary. He had been out of town when all this happened and I never met him, but I shall always remember his kindness. I also remember the other minister, whose name I have lost. He invited me to his church where they were having a pot luck supper and I got a good meal, free.

My roommate at Union Theological Seminary in Virginia was John Linton of Tuscaloosa, Alabama. He had attended Tuskegee College and then finished at Stillman College. We became good friends. He heard me refer to a group one day as "those troops." From this he derived a nickname for me, "Trooper." One day, completely frustrated, he came in from Hebrew class and said, "Trooper, I couldn't pass Hebrew if Moses was the professor." And he didn't. He later transferred to a seminary in Memphis that did not require Hebrew.

John was very bright, very talented and very funny. But he suffered from being the only black man at the seminary. One professor, trying to be funny and friendly, called him 'Black sheep." John told me amazing stories about growing up in segregated Alabama. He had struggles in college because of a poor self-image and an inadequate high school education. I realized how fortunate I had been in having three years in a very good, all- white school in Dallas. He had almost dropped out of college on several occasions. One person who had saved him, when he was at a very low point, was a white Presbyterian minister, the chaplain at Stillman College. John wasn't the first Black man to attend Union. There had been at least two previously, but he was one of the first.

Richmond was still segregated, still very racist. He attended a Black Presbyterian Church in Richmond and somehow learned of places he and I together could eat out, without being harassed. One day, however, we wanted to see a movie and were not allowed into the theatre. I was outraged. He wasn't surprised.

We cooked up a scheme to get even. He had a black Ford sedan, four-door. We washed and waxed it. He put on his best suit, white shirt, formal tie. I too donned a suit with a white shirt and black bow tie and borrowed his flat black leather cap. He sat in back. I drove the car. We headed for a department store called Thalhimers, the largest in the city, occupying an entire block between Broad St. and Main St. I drove to the door, hopped out, ran around the car, and opened the door for him, then scurried to the door of the store to open it for him as he entered. Pedestrians stopped in their tracks. Jaws dropped. I ran back to the car, drove it around the block, and was standing by the car, holding the door open for him as he exited the store and took his seat. Again, passersby were wide-eyed. As I drove down Main St. we both started laughing so hard I nearly ran over the curb. It was a delicious moment.

I had three-part time jobs in my junior (first) year at seminary. I had the laundry and dry- cleaning concession, and the paper route

(The Richmond Times-Dispatch), and, I worked in the library, shelving and dusting books, etc. I was trying to make and save enough money to pay off the engagement ring and then to get married in the coming summer. The papers were delivered early, at daybreak. People expected them at their door. John and I lived on the top (third) floor of Westminster Hall. It was the oldest and creakiest dorm on campus. Because he had a hard time waking up, John depended on me to wake him each morning. He told me once that each morning as I came up the wooden stairs which creaked and groaned from my weight, he thought it sounded like death approaching. I usually had to call him more than once to get him up and out. One morning, after repeated calls had no effect, I grabbed the end of his steel, cot-like bed, and upended it, spilling him out on the floor. He was astonished and then, fortunately, we both started laughing and could not stop.

There were a number of African American people on the service staff of the seminary. One was the main cook in the refectory. He and other Black people took a special interest in John, of course, trying to support and encourage him as they could. One morning, as the two of us ate breakfast we decided to have a contest to see which of us could eat the most eggs. The cook heard about it and started frying eggs one after the other as we asked for more. Finally, we stopped. I don't remember who won, but we'd each swallowed about 3 dozen eggs. As we staggered out of the refectory back to the dorm, John said to me, "Trooper, if we could get a breakfast like that every morning, we could take the world!"

I loved him and one of the great disappointments in my life is that we've lost touch. I wrote him once, but got no reply. Last I heard he was a pastor in Houston, but he may have left the ministry by now.

My courses at seminary were almost all interesting and engaging. I had arrived in late summer to take "Baby Greek" from Balmer Kelly, the man who'd greeted me when I'd visited from Annapolis. He was a brilliant New Testament scholar, though largely unpublished. Later I learned he was also an accomplished concert pianist. I took at least two courses from him. One was a study of Galatians. He taught using a pure Socratic method. You had to be prepared. He simply asked questions, drawing you out, helping you teach yourself. He was a fabulous teacher. He had an inflexible rule, announced on the first day of class. He did not care whether you came to class or not; he did not take attendance. But he required you to be on time. To make this clear he would close and lock the door as the bell rang. If you were late, you were out.

I took four semesters of Hebrew from Howard McRae who was also the Registrar. He was a saintly man, careful, kind, patient. It was difficult but amazing to learn to read the Bible in both original languages, Hebrew and Koinonia Greek.

Other memorable teachers were John Bright, a well-known Old Testament scholar, James Mays, also in Old Testament, John Newton Thomas, systematic theology, John Leith, doctrinal theology, E. T. Thompson, church history, and James Smylie, also in church history. There were others; the faculty was very good and very dedicated.

Chapel was held each morning and I always attended, sitting in the same pew in Watts Chapel. The preacher was a faculty member, graduate student or visiting clergyman.

One semester we had, as a visiting professor, the famous David Buttrick, minister of Madison Avenue Presbyterian Church in New York City. He was awe-inspiring. There were sometimes speakers, lecturers, preachers from other countries or other cities. I lapped it all up.

The first year I was there I often visited a different church in Richmond, just to learn about other denominations and hear good preaching. The Second Presbyterian Church had a minister from Scotland, John Clarke, who was quite good. I remember worshipping there the Sunday after Kennedy was assassinated. It was a memorable service. Clarke was very literate, often quoting from Shakespeare or other writers, very impressive.

Another place I visited more than once was the First Baptist Church on Monument Ave.

The man there was Theodore Adams, well known in Baptist circles. In the 60's he still wore a cutaway coat when he preached. One Sunday (not a day when I was there) two well-dressed young Black men presented themselves at the altar when Adams issued the call, in Baptist fashion. They wished to join the church. Adams somehow delayed, saying the Board of Deacons would have to meet. The newspaper got hold of it. They did some digging and discovered the two young men were from Africa, Ghana I think, and were the sons of Baptist ministers who'd been converted by missionaries from that very same congregation. The story flew around town. Adams was in a spot. His church was still segregated, the Southern Baptist Convention was still all white. Many in the city, whether Baptist or not, opposed allowing the African students to join, because of their color. To his everlasting credit, Theodore Adams, in 1962, in Richmond, told the Deacons and the congregation that if the two students were not taken in he would leave at once. They joined the church.

The President of the Seminary was James Archibald Jones, former minister of a prestigious church in Charlotte. He was wealthy. He'd either married money or inherited it. The seminary owned a large mansion in Ginter Park, just steps from the edge of campus. The story was that Jones and his wife had spent a good deal of their own money fixing the place up. It was gorgeous. They entertained occasionally, and both were very gracious. He was a good preacher; and though we didn't see him much, he knew most of us and, was always friendly; we liked him and respected his leadership. Later I understood that he was gone a lot because he was busy raising money. I got a lot of scholarship money because I had so little of my own with which to pay. He had to find the funds to support people like me.

At some point, I knew I needed to buy another used car. I'd saved just a little, but hardly enough for a decent down payment. I went to see the Treasurer, the Rev. W.W. "Duke" Norfleet, Jr. He told me which car dealer to go see and which bank to go to for a loan and gave me names of men at both places to ask for. I was accorded a friendly reception and sold a car, first, and made a loan, second. Norfleet had called ahead to each. So respected was Norfleet by the local business community that his request for help for one of his students was granted without question. It was one of a number of occasions when I learned that, in business, trust is basic; and one's word and honor are precious. When a promise is broken or respect is lost, doing business becomes very much more difficult.

Sidney and I carried on our long-distance romance. She had to finish her senior year and get her degree. There was never any thought otherwise by either of us. It was hard. We missed each other a lot. I wrote every day and she did too. Phone calls were expensive. We talked a few times but mostly wrote. I remember making one trip to Austin College, for Sidney's commencement. She came to Richmond once, to interview for a teaching job. Neither of us could wait for the summer to come. The wedding was set for June 29th.

Largely because of Sidney who was active in the First Presbyterian Church of Sherman, Texas, I was offered a job as summer student assistant there by J. Allen Smith, the pastor.

At almost the same time Dr. Johnson, now retired as pastor of First Presbyterian Church, Galveston, suggested me to the Session there for the same job. Someone called. I had to say, with heavy heart, that I had already committed myself to Sherman. I often wonder what that might have been like to go home again, to Galveston. I was lucky to get the job in Sherman. It was a great church; and Allen Smith was a wonderful minister from whom I learned much.

Chapter 9

Marriage and Richmond

Sidney worked in Anson for the first month of the summer, June, 1963. I started my work with Allen Smith at First Presbyterian Church, Sherman. I can't remember where I stayed. I knew a number of the members of the church from my year in Sherman at the college as a student. And, of course, Sherman was already familiar to me.

Our wedding was on June 29, 1963, in Anson. I was surprised at how many of our friends and family managed to get there. The officiant was the Rev. Robert Watkin, pastor of Northridge Presbyterian in Dallas. Sidney did not have a home pastor as the little Presbyterian church in Anson where she grew up could not afford one and later closed. We were therefore married in the First Methodist Church, where her grandmother had been a fixture and where her mother was raised. Louise Childs, my soon-to-be mother-in-law, had changed to the Presbyterian Church when she married Sidney's father Claire Carmon Childs, originally of Minneapolis, Kansas.

I remember riding to Anson with Sara Caroline Moseley and staying overnight in her grandmother's house across the street from Sidney's grandmother, where Sidney spent the night.

Those who stood with me included my friends Robert Fulkerson and John Gorman of Dallas, and Don Renfroe, Nick Lund, and Howard Bethel from Austin College. Sidney's attendants included her cousins Ann Lee and Andrea Bess Castles, her college roommate Lynn Hartman, my youngest sister Janet (my older sister Nan was pregnant), and her good friend from Anson, Sue Ann Cross. Her close friends Honey Altman and Lynn Galbraith were candle lighters and another friend, Florence Spragins, was the soloist.

The weather was unbearably hot, even at 8 o'clock at night. We sweltered inside the church. There was no air conditioning, and the large floor fans that circulated the air were so forceful that they had to be turned off for fear they would blow out the many candles. The reception was at the nearby home of a friend of Sidney's and her family. My car had been well decorated and we were pelted with rice. We were escorted to the city limits by the Sheriff, Woodrow Simmons, another close friend who adored Sidney, as did just about everyone else in the small town.

Our honeymoon was in Galveston (we could afford nothing grander) where Dad had driven and booked a hotel room on the beach. He made sure it had a kitchen but Sidney had no intention whatever of cooking anything while we were there. I showed her about the city, driving past places I could find where we'd lived and also schools and the church. We had lunch with Dr. Johnson in Luby's Cafeteria. We walked the beach and rode bikes.

Back to Sherman. The church housed us in three different places. We lived a few days in the old Grayson Hotel downtown, long since closed. Then we lived for about a month each in the homes of two different Austin College professors who were active members of the church. One was Graham Landrum who taught English. I can't remember the name of the other. We were well received; Sidney knew many more people than I did. I preached a few times. I learned a lot from Allen, an impressive preacher, a fine pastor, and a lovely man in every way. We loved his family too: Lois, his wife, and his three kids, Martha, Jim and Philip. We saw a good deal of the Moseleys, who were members of the church and who were very supportive.

It was a wonderful summer, filled with work among people and in a place we both enjoyed, and filled with the joy of newly-married life. It was a great prelude for the trip to Richmond where I would resume seminary and Sidney would embark on her teaching career, using her elementary education degree from Austin College.

In 1963-64, my Middler Year, we lived in Smith House, a three-story Victorian heap on the edge of the campus that had been converted to a married student's dorm. We were in one room, which had been the kitchen; but we had our own bath and an outside entrance, formerly the back porch, on the campus side and on the first floor. Our closest friends in Smith were Hannah and Parker Williamson. They later divorced, and he became well known in Presbyterian circles for his ultra-conservative advocacies. Next door, in Melrose House, another former residence turned into a dorm, were close friends Jim and Dian McCall. Jim was a year ahead of me. They too are since divorced. She was a classmate of mine at Austin College and well known by Sidney. Other married couples with whom we socialized included Don and Frances Swope and Dick and Mary Allee Baldwin.

We took all three meals in the Refectory which was good. Sidney had no cooking to do and we met many more people that way.

She began her teaching at the Highland Springs Elementary School in Henrico County. She loved the kids, enjoyed the teaching and was well received by her colleagues and the principal. She taught the fifth grade. We owned one car, a Chevrolet two-door, in which she commuted each day. Her school in Highland Springs, Henrico County, burned the second year; she spent most of that year in temporary space in another school.

Parker and I shared a study on the second floor. I applied myself to course work, free of part-time jobs because, with Sidney's salary, I did not have to do that. So, she put me through the last two years of seminary, for which I shall always be grateful. One of her friends at school was another teacher named Diane Wake. We became friendly with her and her husband, Gary, a medical student, and that gave us friends outside the seminary.

The second year we moved to the Rice Apartments, across the street from Memorial Hospital, and two blocks from campus. We had a two-room apartment with a tiny kitchen. I fashioned a study out of a storage room in the basement. We were very happy. We ate lots of casseroles. Sidney would buy a pound or two of hamburger meat and make it last through two or three meals. In the years since, she has often remarked that although we had very little money or anything else, those were some of our happiest times. Gore Vidal said, in his book, "Creation" that "no man knows when he is happy, he can only know when he was happy." (p. 253)

We ushered at the Symphony concerts because that gave us free seats. We took trips into the Virginia countryside or to places like Williamsburg and Yorktown, with friends. We went to movies, ate out a few times, and explored Richmond.

Between Middler and Senior years I was hired to be the student intern minister at Starmount Presbyterian Church in Greensboro, North Carolina. I have no recollection how that came about; but the minister must have called the seminary and someone must have suggested me. As Sidney was on summer break from teaching she went too. Once again, we lived in the homes of church members who were out of town on vacation.

The senior minister of the church was Allen McSween, and I liked him a lot. It was a new, suburban church; and he was a good (not great) preacher, a fine administrator, and a good man. He had a wonderful sense of humor. On my first day, he told me that if I would go to a nearby shopping center and stand on the corner outside the ABC (state owned Alcohol Beverage Control) liquor store I could easily meet half the congregation! Sidney and I loved him and his wife, Queenie, who was pretty and elegant. The members of the church were warmly accepting and helped us both gain in confidence and maturity. At the end of the summer I guess I had visions of being the pastor of just such a church, but that was not to be.

One of the people in the church with whom we became close was a dentist. It could be that his house was one of those in which we lived temporarily (there were at least two). He gave us money (maybe it was $200 which was a big deal then) and told us that after we finished my last year at seminary he wanted us to travel, and we did.

Back in Richmond we became friendly with a professor named James Bear, who taught world missions, and his wife. They lived in a huge house, on campus. He gave me his old rolled top desk which I used in our room in Smith House at first, and then upstairs in the study room there, and later in the basement of Rice. They also introduced us to Florence Robertson, daughter of a seminary professor of the past and then a concert pianist who lived in the Westwood Tract two or three blocks away. She asked us to babysit her teenage daughter and her young son, on several occasions. This was good because she and her husband were wealthy (he was an executive with Reynolds Tobacco Corporation there in town) and their refrigerator was always stocked with many kinds of food, none of which we could afford. It was pleasant duty. She later gave us an old breakfront secretary which Sidney "antiqued" and, now refinished, we still have in one of our guestrooms. Florence loved Sidney. We stayed in touch with her for years. She is now deceased. I don't think I ever met her husband. He traveled a lot and wanted her to go with him. Thus, our babysitting jobs also supplemented our income.

One year while I was there my "fieldwork" (required of all students) included serving as a weekend chaplain both in a charity hospital (every patient was Black) and in a juvenile detention home. I preached in the latter. What could I have possibly said that might have helped? But I recall that the inmates in both places seemed, in most cases at least, pleased I was there. In another semester, I preached on weekends in a number of small country churches, all without regular pastors as they were dying out. Sidney would sometimes accompany me. These were churches that had existed, in some cases, since Colonial days. One had a slave balcony in the rear of the sanctuary. They were in farming areas in the Shenandoah Valley and members had owned their land for generations. Traditions, customs and attitudes were entrenched. Still another semester I taught an adult church school class at the Ginter Park Methodist Church, several blocks from campus. I remember the minister was a good preacher. He memorized every word of his sermons and delivered them in a smoothly polished but slightly stilted manner. Nonetheless I was impressed with his memory. I think he had what is called "total recall" or "photographic memory." Every time I've come to know someone with that I've been envious. My memory is very selective.

I remember preaching in chapel at the Cathedral School for Girls, an Episcopal institution. Such invitations were welcome. They not only stretched me to prepare, but supplemented our income, from Sidney's salary.

We made trips home to Texas by car, a long drive each way. On our first trip over from Texas in late August, 1963, we pulled a rented trailer with all our clothes and the little bit of other things we owned (fortunately the seminary apartments we occupied were furnished). It was before an interstate highway was completed in the Chattanooga area. As we approached that city we descended a winding, two lane highway with many hair-pin turns. I think it was raining. The trailer felt as though it might "jack-knife." We were both worried. As we came out of yet another sharp turn, there appeared in front of us a large sign - "Prepare to meet Thy God." Someone's idea of a "teaching moment."

I was elected president of the student body in my senior year. I don't know how that happened. I don't remember asking for it or campaigning. There was no student council. I do remember meeting with the seminary president, whom we called "Jas A." but not to his face; then it was "Dr. Jones." It reminds me of when, years later, I was a college president and students called me "Dan C.," when they didn't call me worse things.

We had one African American in our class and two women. It was brave of Pansy Cameron and Ruth Currie to go to seminary then. That was before women could be ordained to the ministry. We also had a South Korean Presbyterian, C. Yoo. There were about 55 in our class. Most of us dressed formally, suit and tie, every day, especially for class or chapel. Professors often addressed me as "Mr. West."

Sidney and I were caught up in the civil rights struggle. As we drove back to Richmond from Texas in August, 1964, we listened, transfixed, to Martin Luther King, Jr.'s "I Have a Dream" speech, delivered on the steps of the Lincoln Memorial in Washington. I had a call one day from my friend David Hornbeck (of Austin College days) who by this time was a Middler at Union Theological Seminary in New York. He said he was trying to recruit seminary students from the east coast, to come to Washington and demonstrate for the Voting Rights Act which Lyndon Johnson was trying to get through Congress in spite of fervent opposition, from Republicans and southern Democrats. We drove over and I remember standing across the street from the Lincoln Memorial, holding signs and handing out leaflets, for hours. Some motorists would honk in agreement, others would make obscene gestures or shout various epithets. We stayed in a convent where Catholic nuns supported what we were doing and fed and housed us. It was a thrilling experience.

Our parents, back in Texas, were dumbfounded, but did not criticize.

Later, a Unitarian minister from New England, the Rev. James Reeb, was killed in Mississippi as he tried to help register voters. This struck us as heartless. I came up with a plan to organize a march in Richmond. I contacted C. J. Malloy who was a senior and president of the student body at Virginia Union University's School of Religion, a half mile or so from my seminary. It is a Black Baptist seminary. We would lead the march, in support of voting rights and also in solidarity with those brave volunteers who were registering voters in places like Alabama and Mississippi. It was a daring, even foolhardy thing to do. There was much racism still abroad in Richmond. There were thugs and ruffians who must have been sorely tempted to shoot or at least throw something at us. We could have been killed or arrested or roughed up.

I got a permit from the Richmond police who promised to protect us the best they could, if we remained peaceful. James A. Jones, seminary president, called me to his house and asked me to call it off. I respectfully told him I would not. Such cheek! A few faculty members marched with us (I am almost certain Jim Smylie was one of them), as did a handful of progressive souls from the city. We marched down Brook Road to Virginia Union, where we were joined by hundreds of black Baptists, and continued to the steps of the capitol of Virginia. We marched in silence and there was not a single ugly incident.

I have no idea how many participated. As I stood on the ground and looked up at the steps it seemed to me the steps were full, and there are a lot of steps there. Next day a large photo of C. J. and me was on the front page of the Times-Dispatch, with the marchers behind us. That same photo was republished on the fortieth anniversary in 2005. At the Capitol, there were speeches, calling on Congress to pass the Act and offering support for people who had gone south to register voters. Then we sang the "Battle Hymn of the

Republic" at the capitol of Virginia, spiritual heart of the Confederacy, in Richmond, capital of the CSA! It was an amazing moment.

I have wondered why the seminary has never acknowledged or recalled in any way that event. It was a dramatic moment in the life of both seminaries and in the life of that city. In the years since I have come to believe that the faculty of Union at that time were very conservative, politically as well as theologically. I am convinced most of them did not approve.

A call came from Dr. Martin Lither King, Jr. following the ugly incidents in Birmingham and Selma when police used dogs and tear gas and truncheons to prevent demonstrators from exercising their right to peaceful protest. He would lead a march from Selma to the steps of the capitol in Montgomery, and he wanted religious leaders from across the country to participate. Four of us, students at Union, decided to go. We would have to ride the train, flying was too expensive. And we did not have the funds on our own.

Other students donated money to help pay our way. The others included my classmates Donnie Cross, whom everybody loved, and John Turner, a top student who became a philosophy professor. The fourth was Louis Weeks, a year behind me, who would later become president of the seminary after he had been Dean of Louisville Seminary in Kentucky. Later I learned that Professor James Mays, on our faculty, also went.

We rode all night. In Atlanta, the train stood for hours in the station and we did not know why. Then we were told that upon reaching Atlanta the train had to change crews. The railroad had difficulty finding a crew, as it was known the whole train was filled with demonstrators on the way to Selma. Finally, after hours of delay, we left the station and arrived in Montgomery. From there we were to be taken by bus to join the parade route. As we walked along the sidewalk from train station to bus station, a car full of rowdies feinted running over us, shouting vulgarities. We had to dodge and run out of their reach. When we reached the line of march it had already been underway for some while.

The delay in Atlanta had cost us that. But there were still miles to go and we fell in with many others. We walked silently.

One of my vivid memories is of passing two different African American elementary schools. The children were lined up along the curb at both. They were in their Sunday best and almost every one held a tiny American flag.

We reached the capitol grounds and we stood before it, a magnificent Greek revival building. M. L. King and other speakers stood at a rostrum on the pavement beneath the steps, not under the portico. National leaders had come. I remember seeing Archbishop Iakovos, head of the Greek Orthodox Church in the U.S. in his robe and headdress and a crozier in his hand. Also, Walter Reuther, head of the AFL-CIO.

As King began to speak the crowd was rapt, mesmerized. Later, I decided that when he spoke, in a beautiful cadence and style that is distinctive to the Black Church, it was almost like singing, certainly like calling forth to evoke response. His words were poetic and beautifully so. We applauded a long time when he finished.

My education and my spiritual development progressed apace at Union, of course. In the classroom, every session began with prayer, offered by the professor. Chapel was held daily.

Many of the guest speakers and preachers were outstanding. I remember, for example, a man from England, a Blake scholar. I don't remember his name. His talk on William Blake was amazing for its erudition and breadth of understanding. He had made himself one of the world's leading Blake scholars. One of my professors remarked afterward that this man was an example of how, when focusing narrowing on one subject, one learns a lot about many other things in the process of understanding one's narrow objective. An important lesson. My interests have always been very varied and widespread, maybe too much so.

I've thought about my attitude toward the seminary, in the years since. In 2015 it was 50 years since I was graduated there. My view now, with the benefit of the other colleges and universities I have worked or studied in, is that Union was an outstanding opportunity to engage in biblical studies. The heavy lifters on that faculty were the Hebrew and Greek scholars who spent lifetimes understanding and teaching either the Old or New Testaments: Bright, Mays,

Martin, Kelly, Rissi. I learned much from each of them; I remember being thrilled to learn how to do serious biblical exegesis. The two church historians I had were also quite good. They were the great W. T. Thompson and James Smylie. Smylie took an interest in me and guided me through some papers of which I remain proud, especially one I did on Woodrow Wilson, one of my heroes.

Instruction elsewhere in the curriculum was relatively weak. Homiletics, pastoral counseling, ethics, historical theology, church administration, and worship, were all areas where we needed much more help than we got. Most disappointing to me was the lack of much strength or emphasis in systematic theology (the effort to develop an order, a rational account of the faith, using a particular viewpoint or "system"). That has always been my special interest in theology. The place was heavily tilted toward Bible study.

That was good and it was a lot but it wasn't enough.

I have come to believe that even though Union was the oldest and the strongest of the four seminaries in the southern part of Presbyterianism at that time, it was too parochial, too isolated, and too denominational for me. I'm glad I went there rather than any of the other three, but I now believe that the best seminaries are those which are part of a university: Harvard, Yale, Chicago, Duke, Vanderbilt, Emory. Good theological education costs money and seminary alumni/ae don't have much of that. The "divinity school" within a great university stands a much better chance of adequate financial support. It also benefits from the proximity to and interaction with scholars and students in other fields.

I have never felt especially close to Union in the years that have passed since then. A lot of that has to do with my locations. First, in the southwest and then the Midwest and then the northeast. Union is a regional school, primarily focused on Virginia and North Carolina. I was never asked to speak at Union, through more than 20 years of tenure as a college president. In contrast I was a chapel speaker once at Austin Seminary and was asked to be the president of Louisville Seminary. I attended only one reunion of my class at Union, maybe it was the 25th. I have contributed small amounts of money to Union every year since I left, but it isn't my first love.

In my files, I found a copy I'd saved of a student newsletter, printed on cheap paper and with a mimeograph machine, entitled "Expression." I don't know how many issues were produced. I sent the original to the archives at what is now called Union Presbyterian Seminary, but I did not keep the date. I imagine it was in 1964 or 1965. The lead story was written by my classmate John Ames. It soundly condemned our denomination, the Presbyterian Church in the U.S., or "southern Presbyterian" for being hopelessly conservative and fixated on consensus building. Another article which I wrote, accused the police in Alabama and Mississippi of causing much of the violence, and some brutality, against Blacks and their white supporters. I also offered a strong defense of Martin Luther King, Jr. and observed that only four white PCUS ministers had participated in the Selma to Montgomery march. My views were clear to all at the seminary and I am sure they were not welcome to many.

On the other hand, after attending or working for so many colleges and universities, how could I possibly feel equally enthusiastic about every one? I am intensely grateful for the instruction I got at Union; and especially am I thankful for the financial support.

I do not remember getting any inquiry from any direction from a church or other organization, except the one I shall describe. That is another thing that puzzles me. I was a good student and a leader at the time. I was very proud of the honorary Bachelor of Theology degree I received from the Faculty of Theology of the Reformed Church of France, located at Montpellier. Union had an exchange arrangement with them. I was presented that at commencement because I was president of the student body and it was customary to do that each year for the one occupying that post. It wasn't surprising that I received no call from anyone in Texas because I had strayed too far east to be considered interesting to Texas Presbyterians. Perhaps my political and theological views were regarded as too much outside the mainstream by some. Oh well, what happened is that the Executive Presbyter of Nashville Presbytery, Mac W. Freeman, called his friend John Leith (not my favorite professor) and asked him to recommend someone for the Smyrna Presbyterian Church in Smyrna,

Tennessee, which Mac was trying to fill. They extended a call and I took it. It was the only one I received.

In a fascinating (to me) sidelight, the leading elder of Smyrna Presbyterian Church at the time was Franklin Weakley. He told me, in 1968, as I was preparing to leave, that after they had called me he received in the mail, from a business acquaintance in Richmond, a clipping from the paper there with my picture, leading the march! His friend urged him to rescind the call. Instead he chose to "take a chance." I am not clear whether he told anyone else or if anyone, other than his wife, Lenora, knew. It never occurred to me to mention this to him or anyone else in the church. Besides, they knew, soon enough, what my views about such things were.

My parents drove up from Texas for my graduation, their only visit while I was there. I was thrilled to have them. One day, before graduation, I drove Mom and Dad to Washington. Sidney could not go as she was teaching. Neither of my parents had been to D.C.

I don't remember the places we visited except for the Capitol and the Supreme Court. As we stood on the steps of the Supreme Court, incredibly, the Chief Justice and another member of the Court came out the door and walked down the steps toward us. They were Earl Warren and Arthur Goldberg. Dad had bought a hand-held movie camera at a garage sale. One of us had loaded it with film, and I took footage of the two famous men. Tragically, whoever of us had put the film in had done so backwards. It was in a huge tangle when we opened the camera and, of course, there was no movie of anything we'd shot to be seen. Technology has always been a challenge for me.

Because we could not afford a hotel room, we had to drive back to Richmond that evening. By the time we were ready to leave, it was rush hour. I was driving, and Dad was riding shotgun. I got trapped in the inside lane (of four or five) of the traffic circle at the Lincoln Memorial. I went around two or three times trying to change lanes. No one would let me in. There was a ramp that left the street and went underground to a basement entrance of the Memorial. There was a sign, "Do Not Enter" and a policeman standing by it. I drove straight into the beginning of the ramp. His whistle blew. I looked up at him and he demanded to know if I'd seen the sign.

"Yes, sir, but you're going to have to help me" and I told him my problem. He stopped five lanes of traffic and signaled me to cross in front of furious commuters to the entrance to Memorial Bridge so I could cross into Virginia. People were enraged. I looked into the rear-view mirror. My poor mother had a lighted cigarette hanging out of BOTH sides of her mouth!

I loved graduation. It was my second such ceremony and would be the second of four. Each time it happened I felt the thrill of accomplishment, survival, success and new beginning.

After the ceremony and my parents' departure, and Sidney wrapped up her teaching contract, we set out on a cross country car trip. Our first objective was the New York World's Fair in Flushing Meadows. My most vivid memory was seeing, inside the Vatican Pavilion, Michelangelo's "Pieta."

We drove to the west coast. Our pattern was to stay in roadside parks, sometimes in national park camping areas, using the tent, gas stove and gas lantern we'd bought with the money from the dentist in Greensboro. We drove all the way to San Francisco and back, in that used blue Chevrolet I'd bought in Richmond. I don't remember all the parks we visited, but one of them was Rocky Mountain National Park. It may have been there, or perhaps another, one night, after I pitched the tent, it got dark and began to rain. I had hung the lantern inside so Sidney could take her sponge bath and dress for bed. Meanwhile, I was struggling with the supper. The tent had a flap over the front and only door which I had extended with ropes to a tree to keep the rain off the stove. There was enough room for the stove and my head under the flap but not for the rest of me. As I cooked whatever it was, my backside got soaked. I remember asking myself what was I doing, what was I thinking and why was I there? It was the only cross-country camping trip we ever did! Every third or fourth night we would rent a motel room. Blessed assurance!

Chapter 10

Smyrna

Smyrna was and is a very small town. It is about 14 miles southeast of Nashville, on the way to Murfreesboro. The town was named after the church which was established in 1820, a fact that makes it old for that part of the country. The church was named after the church at Smyrna in Asia Minor (now Turkey), one of seven to whom John of Patmos wrote in the book of Revelation, last book of the Bible. Of course, I knew that and eagerly looked up the text in preparing to preach for the first time. Here is what it says: "Do not fear what you are about to suffer." (Rev. 2:10a). I did not preach from that text.

The church was small, about 120 members; but there were other aspects to it that were most attractive. It was close to Nashville; the building was paid for and there was an endowment. The manse, next door, was lovely and spacious and pretty new. There was a large Air Force Base, Sewart AFB, that accommodated the famous C 130 cargo planes, and half the congregation were Air Force families. Even though the governance of the church was still firmly under the control of the old timers, there was a good relationship between the two groups and a growing acceptance of the outsiders, a very transient group, into the life of the congregation.

My salary was $4,800 annually; but we got housing and utilities and Sidney had a teaching job. The kitchen had appliances. We bought a bed, washer and dryer from Sidney's uncle, George Castles, who owned a furniture store in Wichita Falls. There was not a stick of furniture in the living room, but a nice carpet and a fireplace. When it got cold that winter, we'd sit on the floor in front of a roaring fire. We lived on my salary and saved Sidney's so we could buy furniture. It never occurred to us to borrow money for furniture purchases.

My study and the church office were literally next door. I got up each day, put on suit and tie, walked next door to work, and came back for lunch. Sidney used the car to get to school except when I needed it to make pastoral calls, and then she often got a ride with another teacher.

I was examined by Nashville Presbytery on July 18. It was a rigorous oral exam, far more so than any I've witnessed since. I had difficulty with three issues which conservatives among the ministers and elders thought problematic. I could not subscribe to the entire third chapter of the Westminster Confession of Faith (on "double predestination"), I had misgivings about the virgin birth of Jesus and I really did not accept the notion of infant baptism, but was willing to administer it as it was the tradition of the denomination. There was a motion not to accept or sustain the exam. It did not pass but there was a lively debate before it failed.

I was ordained on Sunday, July 25, 1965 at 7:30 p.m. in the sanctuary of Smyrna Presbyterian Church by a Commission of the Presbytery. The preacher was the Rev. Milner Ball, minister of the Manchester Presbyterian Church.

I got into trouble quickly. The wife of the leading elder had established herself as the person in the church who found, arranged, and placed a large bunch of flowers each Sunday on the communion table, in front of the central pulpit. I had been taught, in seminary, that this was exactly wrong. The table symbolizes the Sacrament of the Lord's Supper. The only appropriate items, really, to be seen on the table when communion was not being served are a chalice and a paten (or a cup and a small plate, for wine and bread). Some Protestant churches also permit a Bible or a cross, maybe even candlesticks, but seldom flowers. I explained this and asked that the flowers be placed on an unused flower stand nearby but not on the table.

Trouble was, the lady was a Southern Baptist who had become

Presbyterian only because she married one, and was not in to such theological details. She did not like us. She once asked Sidney if we were thinking about moving on. There is a sequel to this story, however. When her daughter and only child was to be married and I was the officiant, her father asked me how much I should be paid to officiate at the service. I replied that as his daughter was a member of the church I could not accept anything. His wife, who'd been angry over the flower episode, was so impressed by this that she completely reversed herself. Years later, when we went back for an anniversary of the church, she and her husband treated us as long-lost friends. She told everyone within hearing that I had declined an honorarium when her daughter was married.

There were other issues. It was 1965, and Lyndon Johnson was busy creating the Great Society. He had browbeaten Congress into passing, among many other such things, the Head Start program. A group in Rutherford County, Tennessee wanted to start such a program. The public schools were not interested since most of the children would be Black. Someone approached me and asked if they could use a couple of classrooms in our building. We used these rooms only for an hour on Sunday. Of course, I had to gain the consent of the Session (nine ruling elders, all men) as this involved a use of church property. The discussion was long and hard. The vote was tied so there must have been at least one absence. As moderator, I broke the tie (the only time the pastor is allowed to vote). The opponents were not pleased. The children were precious, and so excited. The program lasted maybe one semester before they found facilities elsewhere. One of my proudest possessions is a photo of this group of children, all Black, standing behind me as I sat at my desk in the study.

Smyrna, 1966

Sidney taught the

fifth grade in the local elementary school. She was one of the youngest and prettiest teachers in town. Somehow, we got to know an Iranian national who had got a visa and certification to teach art. His name was Hossein Falahi and he called himself Shane. He gave us some of his work. It wasn't very good, borrowing heavily from Picasso. But he was a colorful and entertaining personality. Of course, he took to Sidney. He owned a red Mercedes sports car convertible. He took to collecting Sidney at the door of her school and driving her, top down, home. No such behavior by a pastor's wife had ever been seen. Later, he offered an art class in the attic of the manse. Sidney and a half dozen or so other women in our church were his students. There were at least two art shows in the church, when pictures painted by this group were on display.

The First Methodist Church was across the street. For a while the minister there was Roy West. We got to be friends. One day, Sidney got a call and the woman said, "Are you Brother Mrs. West?" Sidney hesitated and then said yes.  The woman launched into a tirade telling Sidney how much she disagreed about something that was happening in the church and how much she disliked the preacher. Sidney finally figured out the woman had the wrong Mrs. West.

There was a Black Baptist church about four blocks away. I got to know the pastor there. One day a man died and somehow, I was in the church for his funeral. It turned out that the man was a backslider, hadn't been in church for years, but was a member. The preacher did not believe his credentials were good enough for heaven. He was in a bind. He rose, walked to the pulpit and said, "Wherever Brother ____ is, he's already there!" and sat down. I swear it.

There was a woman in town who was not a churchgoer. Her name was King and she later became national president general or whatever the title for the D.A.R. (Daughters of the American Revolution). Her aged mother, who was a member of our church, lived with her and eventually died. Sarah King asked me to do the funeral, which I was happy to do. She was so grateful she gave me a check for, I think, $250. That was a windfall. With it I bought a stereo record player and a black leather chair (but not the matching ottoman). I loved that chair and sat in it to read or watch TV for years until Sidney, ruling that it was broken down and disreputable, ordered it discarded.

In the first year, we revived the church library and the senior high fellowship and held the first of three open houses at Christmas time, in the manse.

We bought furniture for the living room and dining room, from a very good place in Nashville. A woman whom Sidney liked helped us decorate. It was basically English Georgian, Sheridan and Queen Anne style, all reproductions, of course. Most of it was made by Baker, considered a very good maker then. We still have the furniture. The sofa and chairs have been recovered three or four times. It's good stuff. It graced our house in Sherman and then in two president's houses and two vice president's houses.

I had two close friends, also ministers, who lived close by. Tom W. Boyd was pastor of the LaVerne Presbyterian Church, a UPC (northern Presbyterian) church halfway between Smyrna and Nashville. Don Reeves was pastor of the Jerusalem Cumberland Presbyterian Church, a large country church east of Smyrna. They would often come to my manse on Mondays. We would forage for whatever we could find to eat in our refrigerator and then talk about anything and everything. Wonderful conversations.

Boyd was quick, very well read (working on a doctorate at Vanderbilt and teaching theology part-time) and an articulate theologian. Reeves was smart, clever, often wise and one of the funniest people I ever knew. I called Boyd one day as I was preparing a sermon and said to him, "You know, I actually believe this stuff!" The church's part-time secretary, Evelyn Jane Lee, was in the next office and overheard and repeated the story many times.

I tried to prepare sermons carefully. I typed out every word and basically read them. I think I read them well, but I never learned, never taught myself, to be free of notes; I think that has always detracted from my preaching. I also wrote down every prayer and any other part of the liturgy. I tried to read, meditate, read the Bible and pray every day and I did most every day. I got in the habit of typing out the sermon and the prayers, etc. because there was a woman in the church, who attended every Sunday, a nurse, Lois Neel, who was completely deaf. She could read lips but not well from where she sat in the congregation. I'd fold and place the typed pages in the pew rack where she sat and she was very appreciative as were her sons and her husband. Walter, the husband, had a stroke and died. I did his funeral. Hibbett, the oldest son, became a very successful engineer. Roy, the youngest, became the Deputy Chief of Staff to Bill Clinton and entertained me for lunch in the White House, many years later.

I have saved every sermon I preached. They totaled 143. I also have recorded that I baptized 22, married people on 18 occasions, and conducted 12 funerals, during the time we were there. I also published a newsletter, "Presbyterian News" once each month but at the time of this writing I cannot find it. I have either discarded those files, or they are hidden somewhere yet to be discovered.

The budget of the church in January, 1966 was $13,255. My salary was increased to $5,100.

Sidney taught the primary class of our Sunday School, sang in the choir and, of course, was active in the Women of the Church.

In that second year, we began to sponsor a Girl Scout Troop while sponsorship of a Boy Scout Troop continued.

During July, 1966, we (Sidney and I) took most of July for our vacation and drove first to Texas to see her parents and my family. Mom and Dad gave us a dog, a miniature Dachshund, whom we named Woodrow Wilson West. He loved us but nobody else. He may have been one of the meanest dogs ever. I watched him attack a German Shepherd one day whom he thought too close to his territory and run the much larger dog away.

After seeing family in Texas, we continued on our road trip, with Woodrow in the car, to Canada, entering at Windsor and continuing to Montreal, Nova Scotia, New Brunswick and Prince Edward Island. A special thrill for me was to visit Campobello in Maine where FDR had a summer retreat. As we drove through Maine we stopped at an antique barn and bought a solid oak, pedestal type table, with three leaves, for $25. We used it for years as our breakfast table. It now lives in my study. I have written this book on it.

We also stopped in Manhattan to visit Sidney's great aunt, Jacqueline Castles, "Aunt Jack," a retired librarian of Columbia University. She lived with her widowed niece, Sydney van Leuen. While we visited them in their apartment, at 90 Morningside Heights, close to the campus, our car was broken into and three pieces of luggage were stolen, including my attaché. Police chased a man carrying all three who dropped our two suitcases, which we retrieved from the police station, but made off with the attaché. It contained my Bible with numerous notations and interlineations.

I tried to visit each family in the church and always called on anyone in the hospital. It was possible to do that as the congregation was small. We regularly took in new members but they were mostly Air Force families and as soon as they arrived, others left. It was discouraging to me that we could not grow larger numerically. Before we left in 1968 it was announced that the Base would be closed. That was a heavy blow to every church in town.

At some point in 1966 I applied for acceptance into a new degree program at Vanderbilt Divinity School in Nashville. It was called the D. Div. program, an earned Doctor of Divinity designed for parish ministers who wanted graduate work beyond the Bachelor of Divinity (then the standard professional degree for ministers). The program had required coursework, a reading knowledge of German, an oral exam and a dissertation. It was not a Ph.D. program, but it was not much less rigorous than that. I had no idea whether I could complete such a program, but I wanted to take advantage of the nearness of Vanderbilt; and I was encouraged by Tom Boyd who was then teaching there as a graduate assistant while he pursued his Ph.D. I began taking courses in the fall of 1966. I applied for and received a scholarship from the school and I commuted in for the classes. I loved it!

Unlike Union, Vanderbilt's seminary was on the campus of a major university and was far more ecumenical. There were faculty from several different Protestant denominations, a Jewish rabbi and a Catholic priest as well. Moreover, the offerings in ethics, systematic theology and historical theology were much stronger and more varied than at Union.

At about the same time Sidney began a master's program at Peabody College for Teachers, then across the street from Vanderbilt but not yet part of it as it is today. We both spent lots of time driving back and forth to Nashville.

I remember using the library at Vanderbilt, which I loved. It was large, comfortable, quiet. At home I set up a study in the manse, in an unused bedroom. Later, after our daughter Claire's arrival, I moved the study upstairs to the second floor, another large space we did not otherwise use.

I had excellent teachers at Vanderbilt. My adviser and dissertation supervisor was Jack Forstman. He and Peter Hodgson taught me systematic theology. My ethics prof was Jim Laney who would later become president of Emory University. Wilhelm Pauck was a visiting professor from Germany who was an expert on Calvin. Walter Harrelson was the Dean and an Old Testament scholar of great distinction from whom I took at least one class. There were others. It was such a joy to be back in an intellectually stimulating place again and learning so much more. I began to wonder if I had it in me to go on for a Ph.D. and try to become a scholar, teacher, writer. I loved the challenge; but I liked even more learning, thinking, writing papers, and reading.

At some point in the winter of 1967, I got a phone call from the principal of Smyrna High School. He explained that one of his young male teachers had apparently become discouraged about his teaching, resigned suddenly, left town and joined the Air Force. He was left in the lurch. He asked if I would fill in teaching 5 courses for the rest of the spring semester, in algebra, geometry and physics. I explained that I already had a fulltime job and so if he wanted me to teach that was all I could do. I would arrive for a class, teach it, then leave. I could not handle a home room, taking lunch money, faculty meetings, coaching a sport or chaperoning dances – all the things teachers have to do while they are, by the way, expected to teach. He agreed.

I found that teaching the math courses was not difficult for me. I liked math and I'd taken so much of it at Annapolis that beginning algebra and geometry were actually fun to teach. Physics was another matter. I had to work hard to stay ahead of the students for that. I would get up very early in the morning to try to master the next chapter in the text! Moreover, when I went into the physics lab, a lovely new space, I found brand new lab equipment that had not yet been unpacked. And the kids in that course were seniors, headed to college the next fall!

I really enjoyed teaching those kids. I never had one minute of difficulty with behavior. Once, three students came into class 10 minutes late. I asked why. They explained they'd been in a P.E. class and the basketball coach hadn't whistled them into the shower soon enough. I told them to tell the coach that he was using up MY time and not to let it happen again. Apparently, they did just that. He was furious and went to the principal. Of course, the principal told him to back off. He knew I could walk, in a minute, if I didn't get my way.

On another occasion a mother came to see me in my study at the church. She was distraught. I had failed her daughter in algebra. The girl had never made a grade below an A. Also, the girl was a cheerleader and very popular, from a wealthy family in town. Trouble was, the girl had been missing class some and not doing well on her homework or tests. I told her more than once she was slipping behind. She explained that she had to miss my class because of cheerleading practice. I explained that was not an excuse. She didn't believe me. The failing grade stood, the girl was grieved, her family were outraged. The principal would not change the grade. It wasn't the girl's fault. It was the fault of her ambitious mother and the sports-mad, popularity seeking culture of the school. But, I have often thought, how sad this was. I got by with insisting that academics came first. Many teachers, probably most teachers, were forced to compromise to keep their jobs in such places.

Chapter

New Adventures and Parenthood

In the spring of 1967, I received a phone call from a minister I had known in seminary,

Tom Johnson. He told me of an office of the General Assembly of the "northern" church in New York which arranged exchanges between Presbyterian ministers in this country with those in Great Britain, mostly Scotland and Northern Ireland. He had agreed to swap with a minister in a small town in Scotland called Salt Coats and he and his wife Kirstin were set to do that the following summer. He said he knew of another possibility in Belfast, Northern Ireland. I got in touch with the folks in New York and pursued this and it worked out.

The man's name in Belfast was Alexander Crombie (over there they pronounced it "crummy"). He had started a new church development in a new suburb of Belfast. It was called the Monkstown Presbyterian Church. His wife was from a wealthy family so they lived in a very nice house overlooking the Irish Sea on the Antrim Road in Belfast. We arrived there on July 2 and stayed with them before they left for the States on the fifth. Until August 21 Sidney and I lived and worked there and Alex and his wife, whose name I do not recall, lived and worked in Smyrna.

The money I'd earned teaching school helped make this possible, of course.

The people in the church there were lovely to us. There was no building yet. We worshiped in the auditorium of a nearby school. There were two funny incidents as we prepared to fly to Ireland, our first trip abroad. I was told that Presbyterian ministers in Northern Ireland wore a black suit and a white clerical collar. I did not own a black suit. I went to a large department store in Nashville, Cain-Sloan, and into their discount basement. I'd seen an ad in the paper. I bought a suit for $17! The material was so thin I could see the skin on my legs through the trousers. But it was a black suit. I asked the clerk if they could install a watch pocket (I wore a pocket watch) at no charge. The man looked shocked and said, "Sir? For $17?"

Alex told me his name was pronounced "Crummy." I explained, as tactfully as possible, that that word had a bad connotation in the States. I suggested he call himself "Krom-bee" and he did.

I preached on Sunday (there was no church school), visited people, called on folks in the hospital; but there wasn't a lot for me to do. It was still a tiny group. A few families "had us to tea." I read some, worked on my sermons in their bedroom at a desk which I moved so that I could look out over the sea, and enjoyed their house and garden.

Sidney was pregnant. She'd learned of this on her own, but had not seen a doctor before we flew over. At one point, she saw a National Health Service physician, who charged us nothing; and he told her she was, indeed, pregnant and that she seemed to be getting on well. There were two issues with her. She was cold much of the time. The weather in Ireland in late summer is often miserable. And she was hungry. One day, as we were walking downtown we discovered a shop that sold American groceries. She became very excited when she spotted Bisquick on the shelf. She rushed back, baked 2 dozen biscuits and ate every one of them all by herself. Before our daughter Claire was born the following February, Sidney had gained 40 pounds!

On July 19, we took 12 days and crossed over to the continent by plane to Amsterdam.

There we rented a car and made a huge circle as far east as Prague and as far south as Rome and then north again through Switzerland

and France to Holland. I thought I had estimated carefully how much money we would need and how much should be saved for the rest of the summer. I placed a certain amount in a bank in Belfast. When we got to Amsterdam, I was required to make a substantial deposit in order to get the rent car. That I had not counted on. Then, the problem was that the money in the bank, left behind, was in a "deposit account" and could not be withdrawn except by me, in person. We completely ran out of money in Rome and had to wire Sidney's parents for a loan which they wired to us via the American Express office in Rome. Great embarrassment.

On the Autobahn, driving through East Germany to Berlin, we were stopped by a Volpo (East German policeman) who did not speak English. I knew few German words. I figured out he wanted a bribe to let us go. We had not broken the law in any way. I reluctantly gave him a few German Marks. After all he was holding an automatic rifle. I still resent having to surrender that cash as we were so short.

In Prague I was wild to climb the winding steps to the top of the bell tower in St. Vitus Cathedral. Sidney, in her expectant condition, dutifully trudged all the way. Later, when she had a very easy delivery at childbirth, I claimed credit for making sure she'd had plenty of exercise on our trip.

The car we rented was a Volkswagen "bug." The gear shift was on the floor in the middle. On several nights, to save money, we slept in the car. She would move to the back seat, change into her nightgown and rest pretty well. I had a harder time of it. I was curled around the gear shift. One morning, after doing this, it was Sunday and we were in Paris. And we were hungry. Someone had told me that the American Church in Paris had a free breakfast following worship on Sunday. Guess where we went to church that day.

When we reached Schiphol Airport in Amsterdam we were completely broke. I had just enough change left to buy a cup of coffee for me and a pear for Sidney.

But what an adventure! A madcap tour of Europe: Amsterdam, Berlin, Munich, Prague, Rome, Florence, Switzerland, and France in 12 days.

We returned to Belfast on July 30.

On August 9 and 10 we drove to Cork in the south of Ireland (the Irish Republic). There we met cousins of mine. When my grandmother's family left Cork in the late 1890s, they left behind one sister, Adeline Taylor, to care for an elderly relative. When the relative died, the sister did not immigrate to join the rest of the family in Galveston. She stayed behind, married William Moore, and had three children: Adeline, William and Francis. We met her three children, two men and an unmarried daughter.

Adeline Moore owned a knitting shop in downtown Cork. Her brothers, William and Frank, were married and had children. We had tea with all three in the garden of one of their houses. Lovely people. We exchanged Christmas cards with her for years then lost contact.

I preached for the last time on Aug. 20 and we ended our work there. On August 21, we departed Belfast by train for Edinburgh in time to attend the Military Tattoo that evening in Edinburg Castle. We toured Edinburgh and then went by train for London on the 24th. We were running seriously short of money and I had no idea where we would stay. On the train, we met a retired police officer and his wife who were returning to London from holiday. He had served in the British Army in India. She was very Cockney (working class Londoner with a distinctive accent). They invited us to stay with them in their apartment! They charged us some nominal amount, fed us breakfast each morning and we stayed with them for four nights while we toured London using the tube. As we dragged ourselves in each evening, tired from miles of walking, she would say the same thing: "Allow Duckey, are ye all wacked out? Come in and let me fix you a nice cuppa tay."

After that trip I began a habit, never broken, of preparing a scrapbook with photos and every scrap of paper saved from our trips. In this first scrapbook, there were only a few items so I cannot reconstruct our first visit to London. I do know we attended Matins (main Sunday morning worship service) at St. Paul's Cathedral on August 27, 1967, because I saved the bulletin. I also knew, when we left, that London would be among our favorite cities in the whole world.

We departed London on a train from Euston Station on Monday

evening, the 28th and arrived next morning in Dublin. We certainly were not on a sleeper. From Dublin, we took another train to Limerick, and thus to Shannon Airport for the flight back to New York.

What a summer! What an adventure, on a shoestring. But our appetite for travel was whetted. We knew we had to do more of that, though it was hard to imagine how we'd pay for it. We did not get outside the country again until 1970; but we knew we would somehow. The thrill of seeing places in Europe I'd read about for years, and the joy of having seen so much remained with us ever since.

Upon arrival, back in New York, we took a bus to a place in New Jersey where Alex Crombie had a cousin, a nice woman with whom we'd left our car on departure. Alex and his wife collected the car there, drove it to Tennessee and then on their way home left it again with this cousin. She alerted us to the fact that he was very unhappy about our stay in his house in Belfast. We were shocked. We thought we'd been careful and left everything just as we'd found it. It turned out that the housekeeper didn't like us. She had not come regularly during our stay, perhaps only once or twice to carry on some special projects that had been assigned. She told the Crombies, by phone I guess, that we had been profligate in burning up furnace oil by keeping the heat on and the thermostat way too high. The Crombies apparently were furious about this, and the cousin warned us we'd probably hear from him on that.

I began thinking about this and realized that as we were chilled much of the time we were there, we probably had used much more heat than they would. Apparently, though they were wealthy, they were also frugal; and the housekeeper may not have liked us anyway, for whatever reason. Alex had put thousands of miles on my car as he had driven not only to Tennessee and back from New Jersey, but had also made a number of road trips including at least one to Florida. But it must have escaped him that this was as much an imposition on us as our overuse of heat was on them. Anyway, I got this letter of complaint. I sent him some money to compensate for the heat and never heard from him again. Not a word of thanks for the use of our manse and car, or the hospitality of our people. So much for exchanges. I've never considered doing one again.

However, I wouldn't trade the experience of being in Northern Ireland that summer, just before "the troubles" started up again (violence between the Catholics and the Protestants).

It was the first of many trips we made abroad. Herodotus said, "I travel for the sake of inquiry, for the sake of learning." Travel has been a passion for both of us.

SMYRNA PRESBYTERIAN — The Rev. and Mrs. Dan West.

In early 1968, we looked forward to the arrival of our first baby. Elizabeth Claire was named for two people. "Elizabeth" was inspired by an across-the-street neighbor named Elizabeth Lowry, whom we loved. She was known by her family and close friends as "Ditty." She was single and a retired school teacher. She lived with her sister, Ann, and her brother-in-law, Knox Lee, in a large three-story house the two women had inherited from their mother. Their father had been the town physician. They were well off (they had inherited money and saved a lot). Ann was a librarian at Peabody. Knox had a good job as a salesman with a wholesale grocer in Nashville. They lived directly across the street from the church and from us. We were with them daily. Ann was the church treasurer and paid me each month. Knox was an elder. Ditty taught children in Sunday School. Knox was an alcoholic and tried to go to AA meetings each week. I went with him a couple of times to be supportive. He was also a wonderful gardener. He had a large plot, behind a white picket fence, directly across the street from the front door of the church. He assigned space in it to me and let me use his tiller, an ancient machine that vibrated so badly we called it "the toothshaker." On Saturdays, we would work together and then eat a huge lunch comprising stuff from the garden which we cooked ourselves.

Claire was also named after her mother and her maternal grandfather, Claire Carmon Childs. She was born on February 14, 1968 in Rutherford County Hospital, Murfreesboro, Tennessee. She was very healthy, weighed over 8 pounds and was the best baby anyone could hope for. When she was about 2 weeks old she would go to sleep at six and sleep until six the next morning. We were shocked, and very pleased. We were overjoyed to have her. Tom Boyd baptized her in the Smyrna Church on April 21. She wore a gorgeous long white dress that Ann and Ditty told us had been worn by each of them and their brother John when they were baptized. Ditty sometimes babysat for us when we had to be in Nashville.

Claire was always well behaved, eager to please her parents, and healthy. Such a beautiful child with fair complexion and wonderful blond hair. She was also a quick study and has shown herself to be very talented in many ways since.

In February, the garbage workers went on strike in Memphis. I later learned that that city was one of the most segregated and racist places in the country. I drove to Memphis, when King called for people to do so, and marched in a long demonstration of solidarity with the workers. In April King went back to speak and was assassinated by James Earl Ray. I drove to Memphis again to march in another demonstration, this one in his memory.

In addition to these activities which did not endear me to the conservatives in our congregation, I was an active supporter of the National Council of Churches, then, as now, a target of bitter criticism by religious conservatives in our country. I attended two General Assemblies of the NCC, one in Miami Beach and one in Philadelphia.

In August and early September of that year we visited relatives and friends in Mississippi, Louisiana, Texas and Missouri, showing off our precious new daughter.

After we returned in September I had a call from John D. Moseley, President of Austin College. He wanted to visit us. We were surprised, not to say shocked and very flattered. What could he possibly want to see us about? He flew to Nashville, rented a car and drove to the manse in Smyrna. I remember vividly seeing him get out of his car and walk up our sidewalk. Of all the people I knew, he was the one man I most respected and admired. After touring the manse and meeting Claire, we sat down in the living room; and he told me he wanted me to join the faculty and staff of Austin College. He said he wanted to set up a new position to be called Director of Church Relations.

I would also be able to teach, part-time, as an instructor in religion. I would travel the state of Texas, calling on churches and ministers in the Presbyterian churches of the state.

I would help recruit students, raise money, and try to maintain and strengthen the relationship of that Presbyterian school to the church. Of course, I was flattered, but I was also taken aback. I had not yet finished my dissertation. Sidney was still working on her degree. We had only been in Smyrna for three years and 2-3 months. It would be a big change. I had spent so much time and had experienced so much struggle to decide what, finally, I wanted to do with my life and now another huge redirection loomed. But John D. was very persuasive, very convincing.

I had imagined that after I finished the degree I would be open to a call from another church but I was in no hurry about that. We were very happy in Smyrna. I had it in my head that I would be a pastor of a church for the rest of my time. I liked that work and felt I was effective at it. I wondered what it would be like to go back to Austin

College where many on the faculty would remember us as students, or as the student intern at First Presbyterian. We thought about it, talked about it, and prayed about it. In the end, I called John D. and told him I'd do it. Of course, he wanted us as soon as possible.

John Maynard Keynes wrote, "The inevitable never happens. It is the unexpected always."

I preached for the last time on October 27. We moved to Sherman on October 29, with our baby girl and the dog Woodrow; the college paid for our move.

In my head, I thought it would be something I would do just for a while, a sort of interim thing for a year or three, but not a permanent change of careers once again. I had toyed with getting a Ph.D. and having a teaching career; but I knew that would take years and would be costly. With a new baby, I didn't think I should pursue that. And, I liked the parish ministry.

Smyrna had been interesting, challenging and fulfilling in many ways, but it was also frustrating. I couldn't get the church to grow numerically; but I knew I was too impatient about that. I couldn't get the people to look outside themselves and their own circle as much as I thought they should. But that was hardly a surprise or that unusual for a small, suburban church. The degree program, together with my work as a pastor, kept me plenty busy. I was not unhappy at all, but the surprising new turn seemed an opportunity that should not be declined.

Smyrna was a very happy time for us. It was not easy. Sidney juggled teaching, degree work, being a pastor's wife, housework, and then motherhood. She would say later that the role of a minister's wife with its unrealistic expectations and a lot of church activity that did not excite her, was something she did not miss. She was good at it, however, and people loved her in Smyrna.

I felt I had found my calling. I had learned the discipline of preparing sermons each week and editing bulletins and the newsletter. I had managed to place additional requirements for reading and study on myself with the degree work, so I had grown a lot in my thinking, and moved miles ahead in my spiritual journey. My faith was not only intact, it was stronger than when I began the work there. I truly loved the people and felt I had made some wonderful friends.

In retrospect, I wonder why it did not occur to me that I might not like this new job, or that I might fail. I'm sure I assumed that if John D. Moseley thought I could do it then …

Also, I had struck out in new directions before. William Safire said, "the only power that endures is the kind that takes its chances." Theodore Roosevelt wrote, "Whenever you are asked if you can do a job, tell 'em, 'Certainly I can!' – and get busy and find out how to do it."

Chapter 12

Austin College and Sherman

It was the third-time Sidney and I had lived and worked in Sherman. In spite of Thomas Wolfe's dictum, "you can't go home again," we had returned not once but twice.

We arrived in October and as we did not have permanent housing the College rented us a small, frame house it owned on the edge of the campus. It was later torn down to make space for the Cern Music Building. So, we moved in, Sidney and I and Claire and the dog, Woodrow, and lots of boxes that remained unpacked while we searched for a place to live.

After we moved to our new house we could not keep the dog; there was no fenced in area, indeed no back yard. We gave Woodrow to Sidney's father, Chick (nickname for Claire Carmon Childs), who loved him till he died and then bought another Dachshund and another, both of whom he also named Woodrow. Louise tolerated this. The dogs were sometimes allowed inside but mostly stayed in their fenced-in back yard.

The house we found was on Belton St. on the other side of the main highway that goes through the town. It had been built by the president of the bank during the Depression. It was well built with good materials. It was a two story, white frame, with a nice side porch and a double garage behind. The price was $20,000. The college loaned us enough money to make the down payment and the bank loaned the rest. The widow of the original owner sold it to us and then moved next door to a smaller house they had built as an investment and rental property. Her name was Mrs. Gardiner.

The house had a kitchen, breakfast room, dining room, living room with fireplace, and a den downstairs. Upstairs was a master bedroom with a dressing room attached and a walkthrough bath to one of the two guest rooms. The second guestroom with a bath across the landing completed the second floor. We were delighted. It was our first purchase of property.

While we were there we painted the place, inside and out, installed a central heating system downstairs, and used the den as my study; the upstairs dressing room was first Claire's and then our son Andrew's room.

I completed the Doctor of Divinity degree in systematic theology in 1969 and was granted it by Vanderbilt in absentia, in August. Sidney also completed hers, the master's degree in elementary education at Peabody College and also received it in absentia.

Sidney got a job teaching the fifth grade and we hired Marion Kimes, wife of a math professor at the college, to babysit Claire. In the second semester of that year, the principal gave Sidney the class filled with problem kids, discipline cases, and slow learners. She finished the semester and the principal asked her to return, but she declined. I didn't blame her. She had worked hard to get her degree and was a good teacher, experienced after five years of teaching the fifth grade, but she never bargained for that. I'm convinced that similar situations have ended the teaching careers of good teachers in many places across the country.

I jumped into my work at the college, which amounted to inventing a new position. The directorship of church relations was John D.'s brainchild. He wanted to protect, and, if possible, strengthen the relationship with the Synod of Texas of the PCUS; therefore, I was expected to find ways to do that. I traveled around the state, calling on ministers, sometimes meeting with church school classes or youth fellowships and preaching as a guest or a fill-in, when invited. Of course, I attended a number of presbytery meetings and each year attended the annual meetings of the Synod. I was asked to give two series of lectures or sermons, in Dallas and in New

Orleans. My records show that between October, 1968 and August, 1972, when we left Texas, I preached on 89 occasions in almost as many places in Texas and Oklahoma. Oklahoma wasn't in the Synod of Texas but the Oklahoma border was close to Sherman and I was asked to "supply" pulpits in that state several times.

I enjoyed meeting many of the ministers of the synod. Almost all were dedicated, sincere, and effective. I was met with friendliness and warmth. Some responded with invitations to speak or preach. A few were helpful with names of senior high aged members, and a very few sent money to the college as benevolence gifts from their budgets. The most friendly and helpful were the native Texans who had also attended Austin Theological Seminary in Austin, Texas, and thus had known of the college for a long time. Austin College was the only college in the state related to the PCUS (southern Presbyterian Church). Trinity University in San Antonio was a competitor for students in some ways and was related to the UPCUSA (northern church).

On campus, I worked some with Allen Smith, who by now had been hired as Campus Minister, wrote public relations materials, staffed two endowed lectureships, served on a committee or two, guest-lectured in religion classes, and taught, on my own, three courses in religion. Two of these were January term courses with travel in Texas and Oklahoma involved.

Sidney and Claire attended First Presbyterian Church and Sidney taught voluntarily in a pre-school program and a church school class of junior high kids.

Sherman was a pleasant place to live where one or the other of us had met a number of people. At that time, the population was about 30,000. Our closest friends became Allen and Lois Smith, Roy and Sherrie Custer, Bob and Candace Leslie, Stanley and Carolynn Cobbs, and Honey and Robert Minshew. There were others, and we socialized a good deal, often with faculty members and their spouses; but we knew non-college people as well.

During our second academic year there, 1969-70, Allen Smith took a sabbatical and moved to Berkeley, CA, with his family, for the whole year. John D. asked me to be interim or acting campus minister, in addition to my work in church relations. I moved across the chapel into his office and suddenly got very busy. A small group of students were active in the campus Christian ministry. I enjoyed working with them to plan weekly worship services in the chapel. Of course, I met with individual students for counseling, participated in the college's convocations, met with several committees, and kept up my work in college relations. It was a very busy, but fulfilling year. I remember especially three students with whom I worked closely that year: Don Cameron who was president of the campus Christian Council, Debbie Dodson who became a Presbyterian minister, and Nanci Duff who is now a professor at Princeton Seminary in New Jersey.

One of the most interesting and significant relations that developed during those years was that between John D. Moseley and me. He was full of ideas for new programs, new policies, new ways of educating students, and new expectations. He taught me to worry about the future, not just next week or even next year but far into the future. He was a planner. I saw him develop long-range plans for the college which he revised frequently. He worked tirelessly to inform, persuade, and inspire faculty and staff and trustees, trying to bring them into his way of thinking and then trying to enlist their help in implementing new programs and policies. He saw everything in a "big picture" way. He worked to influence and shape state policy toward higher education in the state and across the country. He was a very faithful church member, never missing church when he was in town. He was not a minister, but he saw his role as head of a church-related college as a calling and a ministry.

I figured out that he seldom asked people for money. He would call on wealthy people, try to get them excited about what he was trying to do and expect them to get the idea that they were supposed to help him and the college with a contribution or a pledge. He had recruited an impressive core of trustees and others, wealthy and influential people in Texas, whom he carefully shepherded. He once told me that "the care and feeding of trustees" were among his most important responsibilities. He was also good at staying on top of crises or potential crises on campus. He had a fine political sense and was very good at anticipating developments. As a public speaker, he was always well prepared. However, he was at his best when speaking ex tempore in a gathering or in small meetings or in one-on-one conversation. He was always passionate about his ideas. He was not terribly articulate, the words just poured out and sometimes, after meeting with him, I'd think, "What was he saying?" But there was no question about his intelligence. In some ways, he was brilliant. He not only put Austin College on the map, he gave it a character and a quality, a mission and a style, that have remained., He is, unquestionably, the college's defining president.

Of course, I am prejudiced. I have a degree from Austin College and I worked there for nearly four years. But I firmly believe it to be the best independent (private) small liberal arts college in Texas. Still, as I look back, from the vantage point of living and working in five other colleges and in five other cities in the country, I realize the college and the city of Sherman were, to some extent, isolated, parochial, and constricted in numbers of ways. I am sure the place was and is very conservative politically. By 1970, most people in Texas were Republican, and John D. had to live and work with that. He and the college were very dependent on wealthy people in the state and they were mostly conservative. In 1978, Sara Bernice was elected Moderator of the General Assembly of the Presbyterian Church, U.S. and proved herself progressive on most important issues; her personality and grace made it possible for her to move easily among all political and religious proponents.

Meanwhile Sidney and I were increasingly opposed to the war in Viet Nam. And we both had a growing sense that our politics and our religion were left of center. This was evident when occasional speakers or lecturers came to the college representing a progressive or liberal viewpoint and we found ourselves in agreement. At one point, I suppose it was the summer or fall of 1970, we got much involved in the campaign for governor of Texas of a woman named Sissy Fahrenholt. We attended the precinct convention, did canvassing and voter registration and worked in other ways. She lost, as a liberal Democrat, and later became president of Wells College in upstate New York. It was still a novelty then to think of a woman getting elected anything.

I taught a January Term course one year called "The Underground Church." We visited experimental church groups in Texas and Oklahoma. These were house churches or communal groups, some Catholic, some Protestant, and all fascinating. The students were intrigued.

I got interested in what is called the "theology of hope." A German theologian named Jurgen Moltmann had published a book, "The Theology of Hope." Another German, Wolfhart Pannenberg, published several books with much the same approach. A Lutheran theologian in this country, Karl Braaten, wrote books elaborating on this. The focus of these "systematic" theologians was the coming Kingdom of God, the Parousia (or end time, the end of the world, the coming of the Kingdom), what theologians know as "eschatology." I found this very exciting because of the focus on the future, the new, the different. This has influenced my thinking ever since. At the time, I preached sermons and taught classes using this theme and was often encouraged by my listeners.

When we moved to Sherman I had not yet finished my degree at Vanderbilt. I had to travel back to Nashville to sustain my oral exam and I had to write my dissertation. The latter is titled "A Working Conception of the Church for the Professional Minister." It is copyrighted and there is a bound copy of it in the Vanderbilt Library, but it has not been published per se. I suggest in it that there are four bases for conceiving and understanding the Christian Church: revelation, scripture, tradition and contemporary circumstances. I go on to offer a new understanding of "church:" institutional and societal, and suggest a different relationship to the culture and the nation. Then I suggest an emerging organization and a series of ministries that largely move beyond the current denominational structures we have known during my lifetime. It is interesting to me that some of the developments I predicted in that work, of 45 years ago, have begun to occur.

The thesis was accepted, after revisions suggested by my major professor, and I received the degree of Doctor of Divinity (earned) in May, 1969, in absentia. Sidney got her Master of Arts in elementary education from Peabody College for Teachers at the same time, and also in absentia.

After Allen Smith returned from his sabbatical in the spring of 1970, John D. gave me other responsibilities, naming me to an important committee or two, meeting with me occasionally to talk about one project or another, making me feel like a junior member of the administration and not just a development person and a junior faculty member. My role was always ambiguous, to others as well as to me. It kept changing. Some people did not know exactly what to make of my work there. What eventually became clear is that John D. was grooming me, preparing me for a larger administrative role. This was not unlike the way he worked with others on the staff and faculty. He would recognize potential, see someone he thought he could develop, and begin to work them in to his thinking and planning. It all seemed a little fuzzy to many and it was. It was the way John D. thought and worked.

My mind does not work that way. Part of me got organized by the Navy. I tend to think in more sharply defined ways. Ambiguity is not attractive to me. I am eager to try the new and the untested; but if it does not work I tend to want to discard it and try something new, but not to fold the new into the old and proceed with some of this and some of that.

John D. loved to think of the new, the experimental, the untested, the potential. He was very far ahead educationally. He seemed to like to grow his own leadership right there on campus, rather than importing folks though he did both, of course.

By the summer of 1970, we needed a vacation. Sherrie Custer offered to keep Claire. She had two girls with whom Claire loved to play, Audra and Alison, both older. Claire was a little over two then, and it was daring of us to go off and leave such a little one; but Claire was a good girl and healthy, and Sherrie loved her. Her girls were beautiful brunettes; Claire was as fair and blond as a child can be.

The Smiths, Allen and Lois, asked us to go with them to Mexico, for a week. We flew to Laredo on the 22nd of June and then to Mexico City on the 23rd and stayed till the 30th.

We had a marvelous time.

Mexico was very inexpensive then. We made a side trip to Cuernavaca to visit Ivan Illich, whose writings I admired. He was a

Catholic priest who got very interested in educational reform. He had been kicked out of the Church by the Vatican because his views were too progressive. He drove us back to Mexico City in his VW, talking rapidly, in good English, the whole way.

In Mexico City, we stayed in the Montejo Hotel, a Mexican as opposed to an American- style place. It was right on the Reforma, the main street, and close to the Zocalo, the main square of the City. We had wonderful meals at good restaurants, for pennies on the dollar.

Back to Sherman and work at Austin College. Then, a very important development. Sidney discovered she was pregnant. Andrew was born on March 10, 1971. He was healthy at over 7 pounds. Don Renfroe, Sherrie Custer and I had stood at the foot of Sidney's bed in the labor room, arguing about what the name of the new baby would be.

We knew it was a boy. We couldn't decide between Benjamin and Andrew. Ray Stephens, the obstetrician, shooed us out of the room. I settled on Andrew. Sidney agreed, but always claimed later that she'd had little to do with naming her own child. When we brought mother and son home from the hospital it was Claire's first look. Her immediate question was, "Mommie, why doesn't he have a mustache?" She moved to the front guest room; Andrew occupied the small room off ours. Claire had some adjusting to do. She'd been the center of our attention for three years. One day she said to Sidney, "Andrew has got to go!"

They grew up alternately enjoying and annoying each other, much as do most siblings.

Today they are among each other's best friends, extremely close.

In the spring of 1971, John D. assigned me to be something called "Coordinator of Research and Development." He was working on a project he called "Total Institutional Development." It was his plan to revamp, in significant ways, the curriculum, the teaching methodology, the educational objectives, and the outcomes of an Austin College student's experience. It was far too ambitious for most of the faculty who resisted and scoffed and smirked, "another of John D.'s brainstorms." But it was interesting to me and exciting to be asked to help with it.

The Director of the project was a wonderful man named Frank Edwards, a chemist, and a brilliant teacher, greatly respected by his colleagues, especially in the science faculty, and capable of persuading, inspiring and sometimes browbeating the reluctant dragons on campus into "getting with" the new program. John D. admired Frank, and knew he was the right man to lead the project, but he also recognized his shortcomings. Frank was a visionary and a dreamer, an eloquent talker and speaker, but very disorganized, not very practical, dismissive of detail, prone to expect things to fall together, inattentive to budgets. He was a heavy drinker and an enthusiastic partier. (John D. was a teetotaler and inept at small talk.) My role, some of which became clear after I got into it and only partly explained by John D. at the time he appropriated me, was to fill in where Frank left the blanks.

John D.'s plan to fund this new institutional project was to get funding from two federal agencies: The National Endowment for Humanities and the National Science Foundation (NEH and NSF). The trouble was that neither of these agencies had ever thought of jointly funding anything. Each had its own culture, funding requirements, criteria, and regulations. So, we had a project that faculty questioned, government bureaucrats were suspicious of, and the campus director was unable to reduce to paper. (I heard a man say once, "If it's not on paper, it's only vapor.") My role was to coordinate the preparation of a proposal including a budget (set down to satisfy two agencies), and to get all this done in time for the submission deadlines at both agencies.

If I hadn't been so young and so naïve and so eager (the wonderful thing about being young is that you don't know what you don't know), I would have despaired. But John D. wanted this done, and I wanted to please John D. I dogged Frank to get things done, met with faculty every day, worked till all hours to put together the budget and draft or edit the proposal. (John D. had to be the final editor, and I dreaded that, but in the meantime, I had to get copy past Frank, who loved to edit with a black felt tip and often rewrote long passages).

John D. lobbied relentlessly with the NEH and NSF staffers and got everyone he knew in Washington to pull strings, prod, and nudge. We got the proposal in the mail with hours to spare after working on it up to the last minute. To my amazement (I was pessimistic) NEH and NSF agreed to talk with each other and then to send a representative from each agency to Austin College, to make what is called a "site visit."

Of course, John D. had us all on full alert. In those days $1 million was a whole lot more money than it is now. The stakes were high. John D. had put a lot of his own time, prestige, hopes and dreams into this. The two men arrived, one a philosopher and the other a biologist. Everyone tried to impress them with how wonderful we were and how sure the project was to succeed. Frank Edwards, in his usual style, gave a glittering dinner party in his handsome house, followed by a late-night party that went into the early hours next day. If he was there at all, John D. would have gone home early. I gave up and went home at some point after midnight. But the problem was that John D. expected us all in the president's dining room at 7:30 the next morning for breakfast, before the Washington guys departed. It was to be the final briefing, the capping of the visit.

The biologist from NSF was very hung over. The philosopher only slightly less so. The scientist had his head in his hands, staring at his empty plate, unable to think about eating anything. John D. was perturbed. He said, "Are you all right? What can we do for you? Do you need an aspirin? Something stronger? How about an injection?" I was on the floor, laughing so hard I couldn't breathe. John D. wasn't a jokester. He was not a funny man. This was amazingly funny.

We got the grant, the first time in history those two federal programs had collaborated on anything. I wonder if they ever did that again.

Now that we had all that money coming we had to figure out how to use it. John D. asked me to organize a workshop for later in the summer that would train faculty to implement the new plan.

I set up the workshop. It went well. John D. wanted me to run one of the new programs, something called Policy Research.

Meanwhile another small drama was playing out in Arkansas. A very small and very struggling college in Batesville (northeast part of the state), had lost its president after just two years. The board was struggling to find a replacement. They had tried to hire more than one. I knew at least two of them. But the board had been turned down. One of the trustees was Marshall Huser of Oklahoma. He had earlier been a trustee of Austin College. He called John D. to ask for a recommendation. John D. gave him my name even though he knew I was too young, too inexperienced and right in the midst of working hard to implement his new plan.

I got a call asking me to come for an interview. I was shocked and asked John D. what to do. He disclosed that he had suggested me and then told me that he wanted me to go off somewhere to learn to be a college president so I could succeed him when he was ready to retire. He told me that! I was full of skepticism, but I went.

I was met at the plane by John E. Mays, Vice President for Development, who had been hired by the best president the college had had, Paul McCain, son of the beloved long-term president of Agnes Scott College, Ross McCain. Paul had spent 17 years relocating the college and building a new campus. When he felt he'd done as much as he could he accepted the post of Vice President for Development at Agnes Scott and moved to Atlanta. His successor was a mismatch, a man with no experience in independent liberal arts colleges.

I visited the campus, talked with a number of people, then met with three trustees in Little Rock, Shuford Nichols, Frank Lyon and Carter Jeffrey (chair of the search committee). I was sure they would not pursue the matter. I was far too green. And I wanted to finish what I was doing at Austin College. To my great surprise, Carter Jeffrey called me, after I got back to Sherman, and asked me to come for an interview by the entire Board, and to bring Sidney. I'm sure he had talked with John D. who had urged him to hire me!

We met with the board in the parlor of the First Presbyterian Church in Little Rock. Sidney sat in. She was so beautiful and charming. How could they not be impressed by her? I asked a number of searching questions. I had been well prompted by John D. His major concern was not whether the college was strong enough to survive or what my problems might be if I was offered the post and took it. He wanted me to know whether the Board would support me. My questions were so pointed, so direct, on this issue, that one of the trustees, Bill McMillan, said he thought I was arrogant. I think I even asked, if we could go around the room and get each trustee to say they would do everything they could to help. Again, that was John D.'s idea.

After the meeting, we went to Batesville so Sidney could see the place and I could meet with a number of folks. Later, I was offered the job and, at John D.'s strong urging, I took it. I was 33 years old. I had been in college work for four years. I had no business walking into such a situation and no right to succeed at it if I did. It took hubris and ignorance and a strong dose of naivete to do such a thing.

We prepared to move at the end of the summer. I gave the directorship of the Policy Research Program to Shelly Williams. We put our house up for sale. John D. met with me more than once; and now, after the fact, tried to tell me what he knew of the situation in Batesville, much of it not encouraging.

Our years in Sherman and at Austin College had been happy ones. I had learned a lot. If it had not been for those four years at Austin College, I would not have had a clue what to do at Arkansas College. But I had watched and learned from John D. and, of course, Sara Bernice was, as she had been for years, a strong example for Sidney. I had grown in my knowledge and understanding of higher education, again mostly by watching John D. I had learned to love being on a campus. I did not shrink from travel and meeting new people. I had learned to ask people for money. I knew how to plan ahead and I'd had the very valuable experience of putting together a proposal for government funding and then implementing a new plan for innovation in teaching and learning. I learned how to work with trustees. There were so many things I did not know, but I did have this much in my quiver.

Among the many things I did not know was how to be very political, how to relate to college faculty, and how to anticipate and deal with controversy and crises, often manufactured on campuses by faculty or students or both.

I think Sidney went along with all this because she knew I was ambitious; we are both hard workers, and she understood that John D. expected this of us. She was as loathe to disappoint him as I was. However, she had two small children, one still a baby. She was 30 years old. She knew nothing of small town Arkansas or of that state, really. But she bravely went about preparing for the move.

Leaving a place has always been wrenching for us. We make friends wherever we are and we don't give them up easily. We have moved so many times that we have a collection of friends all over the place. In Sherman, we had a circle of friends whom we had enjoyed and loved. Emily Dickinson said, "My friends are my estate." We loved our house. Life there had been pleasant. It was hard to leave.

I knew I was taking a big chance. I might not succeed. After all, my predecessor had not. The college was weak, small, and isolated. Several others had declined the job I'd taken. But I have always been what Sidney calls a "risk taker." I had learned to strike out in new directions. And, very importantly, I had not sought this. It had come to me unawares. Just as the Naval Academy appointment, and the call to Smyrna, and the job at Austin College had been surprise developments, so now this had come, out of the blue, and I felt it was intended, like the other strange turns in my life, as the next adventure.

In theology, there is a division of thought called "providence." It is not to be confused with "predestination." The latter has to do with salvation. The former is more a matter of intentional consequences. It is impossible, at the time of occurrence, to know whether something is happening according to plan, according to an intentional development in one's life. It is only by looking back, reviewing what happened in retrospect, that one can see a pattern. It is impossible for me to deny that a direction that became a pattern happened to me. Was this something outside me that was directing me? How else would I explain it? I could never have written such a script for myself! I remember Soren Kierkegaard's observation, "Life can only be understood backwards, but it must be lived forwards."

Chapter 13

Arkansas College: The Stormy Beginning

In August 1972, Batesville, Arkansas was one of the oldest cities in the state. Located on the White River, 90 miles north of Little Rock, it is in the northeast quadrant of the state and not far from the Missouri border. It is a beautiful, unspoiled and largely undeveloped part of a state which lags behind the rest of the country in many indices but is underrated in many ways as well. Batesville had about 10,000 residents; there were just 30,000 in the whole of Independence County.

Arkansas College was organized by the Presbyterian Church, in 1872, after Batesville lost its bid for the new University of Arkansas, as runner-up to Fayetteville. Thus, the college was the oldest independent college in the state located in one of the oldest cities.

In 1972 a four-lane, divided highway, ended at Beebe, just north of Little Rock. The rest of the way was a narrow, two lane road that had not been paved for very many years, I was told. Batesville was small. isolated, and relatively unimportant.

The city was arranged along three commercial axes. Main Street was the oldest and contained a number of preserved stately homes ending in a six-block-long "downtown." At a right angle was St Louis Street, also State Highway 167. Harrison Street bisected it and contained most of the rest of the businesses on its way east. There was no shopping mall or fast food places that were part of national chains. Main Street, after it crossed St. Louis going east, became Highland Road and ran to the college.

Arkansas College was located on its third site. Initially in the middle of town on a block bordered by College on the north and Boswell on the south, it had been relocated to a second campus just east of St. Louis where a large, empty Independence Hall stood forlornly, next to an abandoned gym. When the Masons closed an orphanage further east, the college had purchased a hundred-acre site from them. There, one of my predecessors, who still holds the record of presidential service, seventeen years, Paul McCain, erected a lovely Georgian chapel, dining hall, library, science building, physical education building, and dormitories around the three Masonic buildings which were used for classrooms and offices. The eastern most building of this three-building complex contained the President's Office.

The college was small, fewer than 400 students and fewer than 200 resident on campus. It had had an up and down existence for all of its 100 years. On the verge of extinction more than once, the Synod of Arkansas at one point actually voted to close it. It had struggled with mission, enrollment, retention, lack of church and community support, little endowment, low visibility and low reputation. Now, with the benefit of hindsight and distance I can see that it never had a population base from which to draw students and money. Even today the population of Batesville is about the same as it was in 1972.

Paul McCain had made a heroic effort to redirect and revive it, after a series of presidents who had mostly maintained its struggling nature. He had raised money, but most of it had gone into buildings on the new campus, of course. At the end of seventeen years he had stepped down feeling, I am sure, he had done all he could against great odds. Pushed by a faculty member or two the Board had hired the wrong man to succeed him. Dr. Wygle was well meaning, energetic, amiable, good at faculty and community relations, but completely inexperienced in fund raising or small, liberal arts college work. After just two and a half years he had left suddenly to take the presidency of an obscure state- owned college in Oklahoma.

At this stage, at my age and given my experience and knowledge of higher education generally and small colleges especially, I should not have accepted the job. However, in 1972 I was 33 years old, ambitious, eager to rescue an institution founded by Presbyterians, and, above all, trying to please John D. Moseley.

It was an overwhelming challenge. The college had never been stable. It was not only tiny; it had less than a million dollars in endowment, a poor reputation, even in Arkansas, a budget of less than $2 million, just 29 full-time faculty members, only 17 of whom had doctorates, just 58,000 books in the library, an abandoned second campus, and a location in one of the poorest sections of one of the poorest states in the country. The situation could be summed up as follows: everything needed to be done at once. More students, more money, more visibility, etc. and etc.

Perhaps the most impressive aspect was a beautifully sited campus on the highest point in Batesville overlooking a wide valley to the north, with several relatively new buildings. It was bare because Dr. McCain had terraced much of it and thus removed a lot of old trees; but the buildings he had erected, especially the chapel and the dining hall, were lovely. And the old, Masonic buildings, along the north side of the Quad had a certain charm, especially the central one named for Isaac J. Long, founding president. The second most impressive asset was the Board. Headed by two remarkable men, Shuford R. Nichols and Frank Lyon, Sr., it included a dedicated core of locals: Carter Jeffrey, Sr., W. D. Murphy, Jr., I. N. Barnett and then a determined group of Presbyterians from across the state: W. C. Brown, Jr., Clark Barton, William Couch, Marjorie McCrary, Bill McMillan, Frank Sloan, John Trimble, Van Weathersby, and two from Oklahoma, Jean Abernethy and Marshall Huser. Others were to join them, some making an equal contribution, but this was the core and they made the difference in those first days.

I hardly knew where to start, but I installed my family in the modest but adequate president's house (built, with plans from a magazine, by the McCains) on the front of the campus and went to work. My office was in the south end of the easternmost of three Masonic buildings, a large room with an impressive bay window. I sat with my back to this great window and began trying to assess where we were. There were three very capable staff persons to help: Roberta Brown, the Dean, John Mays the Vice President for

Development, and Richard Thomas, the brand new, twenty-seven-year old Business Manager, just hired by Wygle only days before he decided to leave.

Where to start? Mays and I hit the road, trying to introduce me to people who could help. Thomas and I struggled to make sense of and balance the budget. I worked with Brown to set up an academic program-planning process. All of this began on August 1. As usual, when I took a new job, I jumped in to the work on the first day in town leaving move-in and set-up of house and family to Sidney.

Fortunately, the North Central Association, thanks to work done by McCain, Brown and Wygle, reaccredited the college for a full 10 years. That gave us breathing space. We set up twenty-two task groups to study, evaluate and recommend changes to every aspect of the college, but especially the curriculum. The outcome was to be called the New Plan and it was to be completed by Commencement. A very ambitious goal and an overly-ambitious time frame. Knowing what I know now I would never have rushed such a process. But certain factors pressed me. I knew the board had hired me to turn the place around. I knew there was no way we could attract more students with such a traditional, narrowly focused curriculum in an area and a state that had little tradition of liberal arts education. I knew I could not ask for large amounts of money without a convincing case to invest in something more and something better than the college had theretofore represented. I was fresh from a "total institutional project" at Austin College, daring, audacious and too ambitious in its scope and character; and that was my only knowledge of how to proceed.

Unknown to me at first, but soon to be evident, an entrenched group of faculty were not impressed and dug in to resist. Centered in the humanities and clustered around a handful who considered themselves the most influential and the most talented, they began the grumbling and the criticism that plagued me until I left sixteen years later. I should have known, and of course I do know now, that faculty are key to curricular innovation and usually conservative about change, especially if it affects them personally. The most serious issue was the governance system, overly cumbersome and overly tilted toward faculty override, that had been changed under Wygle to allow for much less presidential and administrative power, a reaction to Dr. McCain's style. I felt the governance, along with every other aspect of the college's operation, should be evaluated and changed if necessary. That was alarming to those who had worked hard to change it toward their own advantage. In the end, I won the fight by simply plowing doggedly ahead, but that left a bitter taste and the strained relationship with the core group of unhappy faculty leaders never was resolved. They were clearly relieved when I left in 1988.

As I arrived the college was only three months away from celebrating its centennial. A group of faculty had been planning this for months. Secretly I saw little to celebrate other than survival. But, we built a small marker and sealed into it a box of artifacts and held, on the original campus, on what had become the grounds of the First Presbyterian Church, a ceremony to observe the anniversary of the founding so long before. This was in late October.

We managed to sell the second campus including the abandoned Independence Hall to the Department of Housing and Urban Development. We got about $124,000 out of that and HUD built a low-cost housing development for needy people. We also sold the old gym on the adjacent site to a developer who converted it into cheap apartments.

One day as I worked in a carrel in the library, Richard Thomas rushed in to tell me an alumna, a retired school teacher in Honolulu, had died and left her apartment house in downtown Honolulu to the college. It was worth about $127,000. That was like manna from Heaven. We later learned that she had had no real connection to the college for many years but had once written for a copy of her transcript. Instead of sending it, Paul McCain had answered by saying it would be sent but first she had to send a check for $2.

The New Plan began to take shape. Some of the twenty-two task groups barely functioned and produced nothing. Many did incredible work and came up with creative and innovative new approaches. Roberta Brown coordinated all of that and did so extremely well. What emerged, as a proposal, was a new emphasis on "career preparation" for those students who wanted and needed it. For most of its life the college had offered a very traditional liberal arts program with the exceptions that it had a business department and an education (teacher training) program. Otherwise the usual departmental structure offered the same majors that could be found in thousands of other colleges, except there were fewer of them.

The conundrum in which the college found itself in was that students in that area desperately needed jobs; many emerged with a B.A. in one major or another and could not qualify for anything in the local industry or business. By starting, tentatively, to offer majors such as medical technology and "modern cultural institutions," we sought to offer some skills that would help our graduates compete with those coming out of the vo-tech schools, community colleges and state universities of Arkansas. With such an approach and great amounts of financial aid (mostly discounted tuition) we managed to inch the enrollment up a little. There was much pressure, mostly from the same resistant faculty, to slow down, be careful, rethink, etc. I insisted that we had to stay on schedule for completion by the end of the year. I felt we had to keep up the momentum and use the deadline set to get the work done. Otherwise, I was convinced the college would slip back into its old lethargy.

Inauguration, 1973

My inauguration was on April 12, 1973. There were attendant events (concert, ball, theatrical performance, luncheon) but the main ceremony occurred in Brown Chapel in the morning at 11. It was structured as a worship service, modeled after the installation of the pastor of a Presbyterian church, with hymns, prayers and scripture lessons. The speakers were John D. Moseley, Frank Lyon, then Vice Chair of the Board, who installed me, and Allen Smith, who offered prayers. Tom Boyd gave the charge to the President, Don Davis, President of College of the Ozarks in Clarksville, Arkansas, gave the charge to the college, Bill Fogleman, General Presbyter of the Synod of the Red River, gave the charge to the church. Fitzhugh Spragins, whom I had known at Union Seminary, chaired the Inaugural Committee. It was a lovely service. My parents, Sidney's parents, my aunt and uncle, Hazel and Bernie Spatz of Tyler, Texas, and a number of friends from Sherman and even Smyrna came. I was deeply honored by all this, more attention than I had ever received in my life. So many offering support and hope. I dared to think we might be able to succeed, somehow. I still did not understand how great were the odds stacked against us.

Sidney, as ever, was magnificent, entertaining, welcoming, radiant, beautiful. She had long brown hair, past her shoulders. She was beautifully dressed, as always. I have a snapshot someone took of her congratulating me, just outside the chapel, with my parents standing just behind her and Marian Kimes, from Sherman, standing to my left. It was a magical few hours.

Almost exactly one week later, on Thursday, April 19, at about 11:15 in the morning, with no warning, a tornado, almost blew the place away!

I was in a meeting in the conference room of the Administration Building, one of the three old Masonic structures. We were in the north end or front of the building. My office, in the south end, had large windows that formed a bay behind my chair. They were blown into the room. Had I been at the desk when it hit I would have been sliced up badly. Instead, as we met, on student financial aid matters, as I recall, we heard a loud noise that sounded like a fast train rushing by just outside the building. We all took cover. Some in the meeting dove under the conference table. I ran across the entrance hall, just inside the front door and got down on the floor in Marge Dowzer's office. As soon as the noise subsided, I got up and walked to the front door just in time to see a small car stop in the street below; the student driving it leaped out and ran; and a huge Oak tree fell across the car crushing it. There was damage everywhere. Bricks, roof shingles, tree limbs, shredded insulation, etc. littered the campus. The rain continued to pour down. Of course, my first thought was for my family. I had no idea where Sidney and the children were or whether they were safe.

I walked west on the street toward the president's house and Sidney drove up and we hugged each other unscathed.

The three Masonic buildings were ruined. The westernmost of them was sheared in half with classrooms exposed and furniture scattered everywhere. The middle building, largest and most attractive of the three, stood intact but we found later that its roof had been lifted and when it came down it was several inches off base. More seriously, the iconic Brown Chapel had its beautiful copper-sheathed steeple in pieces on the ground. and two of the front columns were down as well. The Alphin Dining Hall had much of its roof blown away. Otherwise buildings, including the dorms, were not damaged. I don't remember when I knew it for sure but the miracle was that in the midst of all this destruction and chaos there was not a single injury, not a scratch on anyone. With all that debris flying around and with classes in session, how could that be? I still marvel at that and I still remain thankful. Had there been many injuries and had we lost students the college might not have survived. As it was we were greatly at risk.

I sensed the danger at once. I don't remember panicking. Indeed, I recall quite the opposite. I think this was a moment in my life when my military training stood me in good stead. I sensed not only that I must remain outwardly calm, but that I should take firm control and make decisions in a steady, clear, and very objective way.

The first important choice, of course, had to do with the safety of students and employees. I directed that the campus be closed and that students should leave. The next important choice was when to reopen. I knew that a long period of closure would imperil the survival of the institution. I therefore announced that we would reopen on Monday morning – without knowing if that was even possible.

As students, faculty and staff went home or to wherever they could find refuge we were suddenly aided by many volunteers who came to help us clean up the campus. The County Sheriff's Department routed sightseers away from campus. The National Guard posted sentries at the two entrances and at buildings exposed due to damage. The State Forestry Commission sent workers to clear away fallen trees off the streets. We found a roofer to effect temporary repairs to roofs that were open to the sky as the rain continued to fall. Many faculty members, staff persons and students who lived too far to go home began gathering scattered furniture and records and equipment from off the campus and getting these items under cover again.

Over the weekend offices and classrooms in damaged buildings were moved to those that were unscathed. Four house trailers were leased and moved onto campus and parked in the lot next to the Alphin Building. It was in one of those that my office and those of other administrators were placed. The man who found the trailers and handled so many other details through all this was Richard Thomas, as resourceful as anyone I've ever known and as creative and imaginary a thinker as anyone. He called on businesses and organizations far and near to help us. He did much without waiting for instructions from me. He was magnificent.

The college's own maintenance staff worked without stint. Many students and volunteers from the local area simply showed up and began helping with the cleanup without being told what to do. A lot of students participated.

Somehow, on Monday morning we were open for business. Breakfast was served in the patched-roof dining hall, classes began at 8 a.m. I am convinced that this quick, jury-rigged response that dared any naysayers to think otherwise, that announced to the world we would go on no matter, saved the college from almost certain decline and closure.

Everyone in the state heard about it, and all were startled by it and admiring of it.

Not only so but the "Evaluation and Planning Process" was not allowed to lag. It would have been very easy to say that, "in view of what had happened ..." We completed it on schedule and gave our report to the Board as planned in May.

One incredible sight is etched in my mind's eye. It was the day after the storm hit. For some reason, I was walking up to the front of the Administration Building. A car drove up and stopped at the steps. Out came a prospective student and her parents, visiting the campus for the first time. Dutifully and sorrowfully a member of the Admissions staff was there to meet them and show them about. The first stop was the porch at the top of those steps where they peered inside to see the damage. Whether that student later enrolled I do not know, but the sight of that happening brings tears to my eyes every time I think of it.

I felt I had to exhibit composure, calm and confidence. For days I worked on what seemed like everything at once. However, my efforts were not unlike those of a number of others; we were determined, literally, to save the college. We knew we had to work quickly and well. It was perhaps the greatest challenge of my life and I had many helpers. I am convinced it could easily have gone the other way. Days after the event I collapsed, at home and out of sight, into complete exhaustion, mental, emotional, physical. But, by then, I knew that even though much had yet to be done, the battle had been won and we were going to prevail.

Oliver Wendell Holmes once said, "Trouble creates a capacity to handle it."

I offer two illustrations of how we not just survived but went far beyond.: A visit by Dean Rusk, former Secretary of State under Kennedy and Johnson, had been scheduled for May 15. He was apparently making a tour of campuses as a national speaking tour. Though he offered to cancel or postpone, I was determined that his visit should occur. I remember visiting with him privately in my tiny office, originally designed as a small bedroom, in the trailer on the parking lot. He spoke to a large crowd - I don't remember where.

Was it the Chapel with its damaged roof? Surely not. Maybe the gym in the Becknell P. E. Building?

And another example comes to mind. We had no computer and in 1973 we had a handful of faculty and students who wanted access to one. Richard Thomas worked with the president of the First National Bank of Batesville, to place their IBM (about the same size as a large refrigerator lying on its side) in our Smith Science Building. Our faculty and students used it, with its thousands of punch cards, during the day; and the bank staff came to use it each night. Such creativity, necessity being the mother of invention, occurred a lot at Arkansas College in the seventies and eighties, often the brainchild of Richard Thomas or other clever faculty and staff members. Such is often typical of small, private, liberal arts colleges that cannot afford to waste money.

The Evaluation and Planning Process ended with the New Plan. It restructured our traditional division and department structure into five new "programs." They were community service, health sciences, business management, humanities and the core curriculum. We went forward with the clear intention of serving local students as well as those who came from across and outside the state. The strategy was to build our numbers, remain faithful to liberal learning, and stave off talk of a state community college in town, which would likely, or so I thought, put us out of business.

From that first year until the time I left there was never a moment when I was not worried about the enrollment. When I departed in 1988 it was the most it had ever been, but it was far from stabilized and it still isn't.

Chapter 14

Arkansas College Begins to Develop

From the Evaluation and Planning Process there emerged a new structure of academic programs that was part of "The New Plan." Within five programs, we began to develop new concentrations such as medical technology, sociology/social work and political science.

In 1973, we had 32 full-time faculty of whom 13 had doctorates. At least four of those who did not, were seeking them by taking courses or working on dissertations at other institutions. I managed to find some money for compensatory salary increases for women on the faculty who were, on average, being paid less than others at their rank. I appointed Ed Moseley as Dean of Instruction. Part of my motivation in doing so was to free up time for Roberta Brown, who was already directing the planning process, to spend more time in grant writing as we desperately needed federal funding.

We won a Title III grant of $125,000. This was an important initiative of the federal government, often considered one of the most effective, in which grants were made to struggling, small, under-funded colleges, to stimulate experimental programs and practices designed to make them more self-sustaining.

During the year, I preached in various places on 22 Sundays. This was taxing. I love to preach, but the preparation and travel time meant a whole day of work added to a demanding 5-6 days' week at and for the college. It was important, however, to gain exposure and visibility among the churches and communities of the area.

I managed to find funding for and hire a campus minister, the first ever at the college. I team taught (with two other faculty) a course called "Christianity and Society." These were two examples, along with the preaching, of my career-long effort to hold church and college together in my mind and heart, not an easy task.

An opportunity seemed to present itself for conversations with the College of the Ozarks (now named the University of the Ozarks) in Clarksville. This is a college related to the former United Presbyterian Church in the USA, commonly known as the "northern church" as opposed to the PCUS ("southern" Presbyterian church). There is some question in my mind about how serious these conversations ever became. It's possible I exaggerated this in my own mind as I saw them as so important. It seemed to me there was a chance, a slim chance, that the two colleges could be merged and a new campus built in Little Rock. The synod owned property on the western side of Little Rock, called Ferncliff, which had been a church camp and conference center for years. It comprised many acres and was in the path of the western development of the city.

I discussed this idea quietly with 2-3 trustees who encouraged me to make an effort to start a conversation. Dr. Don Davis, President of C. of O., was cordial and seemed interested and we talked several times till it became clear he did not have the backing or support of his Board. I reluctantly dropped the matter. I had plenty more to do. I have often wondered since what might have happened if the idea had come to fruition.

Presbyterian colleges across the country have suffered from their locations in small and rural communities. In the rare instance where a Presbyterian college has been relocated to an urban location (Tulsa University or Trinity University in San Antonio), they have flourished in comparison. Both Ozarks and Lyon continue to struggle for enrollment, handicapped by their setting in pleasant but small towns. Meanwhile, the city of Little Rock has grown out to and beyond the Ferncliff property and there is no strong private university in the whole state. Hendrix is considered the strongest of the private colleges and is helped by its proximity to the city.

I worked with the other private college presidents in Arkansas to organize the Arkansas Council of Independent Colleges. There was no such body and we needed to collaborate with the Arkansas Foundation of Independent Colleges (fund raising) and also try to provide common efforts in planning, public relations and lobbying of the legislature. With only one or two exceptions the group of 11 or 12 colleges were weak. The whole state was dominated by the state university system and there was little appreciation or desire for independent higher education. The colleges in that sector were perceived either as elitist and too expensive or too closely aligned with their sponsoring church denominations and therefore sectarian in character. The ACICU was modeled after ICUT (Independent Colleges and Universities of Texas) founded by John D. Moseley.

In addition to the 477 full time students we enrolled in the fall of 1973, a slight increase over the previous fall, we had about 500 continuing education (part-time) students of whom 400 took courses in real estate offered in some 17 locations around the state. We also had a federally funded Upward Bound program that enrolled 75 or so local area and underprivileged high school students, mostly in the summer with some school year activity on weekends. In these ways, we tried to gain income, add to the enrollment base and use our facilities at a seriously under-enrolled college.

Every year I was at the college, usually in August, I produced, with the help of many faculty and staff persons, a President's Report to the Board of Trustees. This too was modeled on the practice of my mentor, Dr. Moseley. It was a thick volume, typically 150 pages or more, containing narrative and statistics that detailed everything that had happened in the previous fiscal year (June to July). These reports make it much easier for me to compile this memoir. They have also proven valuable from time to time, as various people have sought historical data for grant writing purposes and accreditation reviews. On two occasions, they have been the principal source for historians. Diane Tebbetts wrote "The West Years: 1972-1988," which was a booklet issued by the college in 1989. And Brooks

Blevins wrote "Lyon College, 1872-2002; the Perseverance and Promise of an Arkansas College" that was published in 2003 by the University of Arkansas Press. Both were heavily dependent on the annual President's Reports.

In 1973-74 we undertook two important studies, one of the tenure system and another of the athletic program. Both areas are always sensitive and often controversial in college life. I have been conflicted about both of these aspects of higher education and remain so.

Tenure is usually defended as a bulwark against the violation of academic freedom and it has provided that protection in many cases. Ardently defended by those faculty who have gained it, it is also subject to abuse; everyone knows of tenured professors who continue vital and effective up to their retirement, as well as those who virtually shift into neutral as soon as they win tenure or at some point afterward. My principal concern, at the time I was a college president, is the severe financial stress it sometimes caused to struggling, small colleges. At a place like Arkansas College, it was vitally important that every faculty and staff person pull his or her weight. We were so starved for students that we needed creativity, imagination and a lot of initiative on the part of our faculty to attract and keep full-time students. We had a number of faculty who did just that, and we had others who were content to let others carry the load while doing the minimum to get their paycheck. It was not unlike every other college I have known. But it was still frustrating.

My misgivings have been borne out. Today, many colleges and universities have been forced to raise tuition, even in recessionary times, because they are locked in to heavily tenured faculties and the only way they can innovate is to add younger or more talented people to teach (rather than concentrate on research and publishing) thus adding to the fastest growing part of the budget, personnel costs. It is significant that as I write it is reported that only approximately 40% of the faculty in higher education now are tenured as colleges and universities increasingly turn to part-time, adjunct, interim, contract faculty members in order to avoid more tenured people.

The tenure system is entrenched. Any college president who dares critique it is virtually blackballed. That almost happened to me.

Along with the unhappiness caused by the previous year's Evaluation and Planning Process and the changes that ensued to curriculum and structure, a number of my critics on the faculty fomented the idea that I really wanted to fire virtually everyone.

This wasn't true but my proposal, which the Board adopted, to declare a year's moratorium on the awarding of tenure while we studied the policy and practice, easily led many to agree with this charge. The crisis was averted by taking ideas from some senior faculty members as well as from me and changing the criteria and procedure while imposing a quota of 65% of the full-time faculty that could be tenured at any given time.

In a way, it was an unnecessary crisis, manufactured by me, as I thought we must have more flexibility in hiring new faculty. But it was seized on by angry opponents as an insensitive, anti-faculty power grab or worse and it accomplished little in the long run.

In my report to the Board for that year, as I reviewed my own activities, I admitted that, "I am a relatively inexperienced administrator, and I make many mistakes both in my own work and in my attempts to develop more effectively the work of others." I have many shortcomings. One of them is that I did not always listen carefully to what others were saying and use their opinion as well as my own for decisions. This coupled with my relative youth and my relative lack of experience in the classroom gave lots of ammunition to those who either disliked me or felt I was misguided if not wrong about some important issues.

It is very hard, under the best of circumstances and with administrators far more capable than I, to change a college. Clark Kerr (whom I knew) compared it to moving a cemetery. "It's a lot of work and there's very little in-house support." What is clear is that faculty are integral to a college and if they oppose a change or even if they are simply not enthusiastic about it, they can find numerous ways to stall or even end the innovation. A favorite tactic is to complain to students and win the students' opposition to the issue and their participation in criticizing the administration. Faculty are human, and it is unreasonable to expect them to take an institutional or long-range view of things, even if it might be in their own best interest, if the immediate development seems threatening or even disadvantageous.

On a more positive note we accomplished much that was impressive. We tore down the damaged Masonic buildings, all three of them. We obtained a loan from the Small Business Administration for $900,000 at 1% interest, to help us rebuild.

Let me turn aside for a bit and explain how this incredible loan of almost a million dollars at just 1% interest got granted. Richard Thomas and I met Shuford Nichols, our Board Chair, in Washington and went to see Senator John McClelland. The Senator, by then long in seniority, was a power in Washington. We were welcomed with great courtesy in his office and I figured out that Shuford was a significant contributor to his campaigns for reelection. As he listened to Shuford make the request for his help, he propped his feet on his desk and shelled peanuts, tossing the shells into his waste basket. In a few minutes he summoned his Legislative Assistant, explained what he wanted, and then engaged in light-hearted gossip about back home in Arkansas. Next day we met the L.A. in a conference room at the Small Business Administration office building and sat across from no less than six staffers. The L. A. said that "the Senator would like" this and "the Senator would like" the other and each request was met with quick promises that it would be done. It was over in minutes. The money came in one check, just weeks later. I learned how Washington really works.

We added effective new trustees from Texas and Louisiana, LeTourneau, Patterson, Hicks, and also a man who would become more and more important in the college's future, Robert Young of Ft. Smith. We bought modular buildings, two of them, to provide temporary dormitory space, we got important grants of $250,000 and later for $350,000 from the Mabee Foundation of Tulsa, to help rebuild.

With the help of Roberta Brown as Dean of Research and Development and John Mays as Vice President for Development, we aggressively sought funding from many sources. In 1973-74 we sought a total of $3,348,000 from 27 government agencies and won grants of $578,000.

The Annual Fund (unrestricted giving) reached $450,000, an all-

Photo of our family in early 70s

time high. And, we submitted 14 requests to as many private foundations and won grants of almost $500,000 from 7 of them.

The college had such a very small alumni base (about 5,000) and a weak tradition of alumni support, about 11%, and an average alumni gift annually of around $75. We had no choice but to look for funding among non-alumni trustees and other donors and from government and foundation sources.

Among the full-time enrollment of 477 in the fall of 1973 about 200 students were resident on campus.

The place was so small, as I look back, so struggling, but so many were working so hard. And, many beyond the campus believed in what we were doing. Somehow, we found the money to continue, but it was a struggle, often touch and go.

The mission was diffuse. We were basically a private, liberal arts college in a part of the country that barely understood that concept and in a state that had only scarce resources to support it. We were trying to attract paying students or at least those who could contribute something, but we had to welcome local area kids with few resources who needed job preparation desperately if they were to escape the poverty of their families. The Presbyterian Church in Arkansas and surrounding states, upper middle class as elsewhere in the country, sensed that we were trying to appeal to groups from two or three socio-economic groups and did not much respect us.

Almost everyone on the faculty and staff worked hard. Even those with limited experience or talent, gave their best. Each gain was hard won, but I never questioned the outcome. I was completely determined, optimistic, confident. More than I had a right to be. Why?

Part of my fierce energy was youthful exuberance and not

knowing enough to know how tough our situation was. Part of it was the torturous route I had taken to find my vocation and my place in the world. Finally, I thought, I have found my niche, my mission. Partly, I worked so as not to disappoint John D. Moseley, my family and friends, and so many who seemed to believe in me. I think another factor was my loyalty to the Presbyterian Church. Anything connected to it had to be better, more impressive and more effective than what I found at the college when I arrived. Finally, I fervently believed we could and were offering a better educational experience at that little college than students were receiving at the state universities and community colleges of Arkansas.

There is another aspect of this line of thought. The president of a small college holds a great deal of power in his or her hands, so long as the trustees continue their support and confidence. One in that position can make a great deal of difference, change things, improve things, make things happen. That kind of power is energizing, a kind of elixir that propels one on. It is a heady experience, in some ways, fraught with dangers such as overreaching, egoism, hubris, but also filled with promise and possibility. On a small scale, I experienced something of what it must be like to be lord of an estate in Europe, or head of a corporation, or mayor of a city.

This is what I think of when I try to figure out why I worked so hard, on so many different fronts, constantly moving about, seldom spending time with Sidney and the children, always thinking about the next step and the next.

At some point in 1974 or 1975 I received an invitation to interview for the presidency of Mary Baldwin College in Staunton, Virginia. This was the first of a number of times I was asked to consider another presidency. Sidney and I actually visited the campus, after I had been interviewed in an off-campus location which I do not remember. We were very impressed with the beauty of the campus and I was aware that U.S. President Woodrow Wilson's father had been minister of the Presbyterian Church there and that he, Mr. Wilson, had lived in the manse not far from the campus.

Subsequent to our visit the search committee offered me the job. We were tempted and it is fascinating to contemplate our career trajectory had I gone there. Sidney believes, to this day, that we should have done so.

I concluded that my departure, so soon after beginning at Arkansas College, would be a severe setback for them. I felt responsible for having led them into many changes and I knew we had not really recovered yet from the tornado. The college was still very weak. Perhaps I should not have placed so much importance on my own leadership, but, however much that was a correct assessment, I declined. Truth to say, in addition, I had some misgiving about whether it was any longer appropriate for a man to be the president of a woman's college. A number of years later, after the woman they had hired, moved on, they contacted me again about my interest and by then I was clear they should find another woman.

Since I made no mention in any report or document at Arkansas College of any conversation about another presidency I cannot reconstruct and it does not really matter, the actual years and months various colleges and I talked, but I can list the ones I remember. There were four that actually offered me the job: Mary Baldwin, Lebanon Valley in PA, Juniata College in PA and Carroll College, WI. At three others, I was the runner-up for the job: Davidson College in NC, Hampden-Sydney College in VA and Eckerd College in FL. I was interviewed by: Austin College, TX, Westminster College, PA, Westminster College, UT, Mt Union College, OH, Susquehanna University, PA.

Others, I can't remember just who and how many, called or wrote to ask about my interest and I simply declined to pursue it. I was also interviewed by a theological seminary which offered me its presidency, Louisville Presbyterian Theological Seminary in KY. In the last instance, I was very interested but finally concluded that a seminary is very different from a college and my expertise was in the latter.

Insofar as the three colleges where I was the second choice and therefore not offered the job, I believe I would have taken any one of the three had they been offered. Again, it is curious what might have happened had we gone to any one of them.

The most difficult decision was to take myself out of the running for the job at Austin College, my alma mater. John D. Moseley conducted the search for his own successor and came to Arkansas to interview me. I had three huge misgivings. It would have been the fourth time to return to Sherman for us. That seemed like testing fate. I worried that faculty and many staff would still regard me as a former student or, at best, a too young and still untried staff member. But, most worrisome, was our fear of disappointing or upsetting the Moseleys, our mentors and role models. Such a development seemed almost inevitable. I knew I was disappointing John D. but I felt our choice was for both his and our own good.

Chapter 15

The Mid-Seventies

In the fall of 1974 Arkansas College launched a capital campaign for $3 million. That seems like such a small amount nowadays, but it was more than the college had ever dreamed of raising at that point. The heroes of that effort were W. C. Brown and his sister Jean Brown of Hot Springs, Frank and Marion Lyon of Little Rock, Shuford and Laura Nichols then of Des Arc, and Clark and Mary Barton of El Dorado. These wealthy and generous Presbyterians stepped up and inspired others so that, including pledges from others on the board we had $1.2 million and then, by the end of June, 1975 we had $2.2 million. It was a thrilling and reassuring thing to raise so much in just 12 months.

I pause here to describe what became a firm policy and a career-long habit that I have urged on many other colleges. At the beginning of any fund-raising effort, I always made my own pledge first, and then I went to see the board chairperson. Once the chair had joined me in pledging I then solicited every member of the board insisting that we must have 100% participation. Once those commitments were secured, I always said, we were then ready to ask everyone else to help.

My strong contention is that if the trustees of a college are unwilling to pledge generously to a campaign, the institution has no business expecting anyone else to do so. The trustees know the most about the place, among all the constituents. They are the ones most privy to the inner workings, the problems and issues, and the real financial health of the place. They have to lead the way.

A development that I was extremely proud of was a total of $25,000 pledged by members of the faculty and staff.

There were other very heartening advances that year. Roberta Brown succeeded in obtaining over $800,000 in federal grants. The Arkansas State Legislature, for the first time ever, appropriated $700,000 for need-based grants to Arkansas residents attending independent colleges and universities of that state. The full-time enrollment of the college topped 500 for the first time in its history. We completed a beautiful annex to the library which became known as the Mabee Learning Resources Center, and a new administration building. Both structures replaced tornado-destroyed Masonic buildings.

These solid gains were off-set to some extent by serious internal problems that sapped energy and time and left morale slumping. An ineffective residence hall policy led to a relaxing of dormitory life rules and great instances of misconduct followed by angry reaction when the rules were tightened. Dissention and strife rose within the admission staff, and, a faculty member led an effort to protest and appeal to the board, over my head, what he considered inadequate faculty salary increases.

Somehow, we managed to survive these crises but the potential for misunderstanding, poor communication, controversy and strife on a campus is ever present and almost always damaging. A college is a complex organism comprising faculty, students, and staff, all with many needs and many agendas. Students are eager to engage in various struggles both as an expression of their emerging idealism and as an opportunity to exert themselves and learn leadership. Faculty are often suspicious of administrators whom they are sure do not understand their work or take their opinions seriously. Staff are often caught in the middle; unprotected by tenure and other faculty prerogatives, they have their issues as well and yet work more in a corporate structure that inhibits their free expression or outright opposition. The president and her or his immediate reports struggle to respect each group and to listen to their legitimate concerns. But there is often a good deal of immaturity and a surprising amount of unreality about campus crises. Students and many faculty have had no "real world" experience where much of their behavior would be dismissed as outlandish or offensive. Few people on a campus are able to obtain or maintain an overall, or institutional perspective that knows, for example, that unnecessary damage is being done to reputation and productivity by prolonged strife.

It is often extremely difficult to explain to alumni, donors, friends, and parents what is happening on campus and why. And, the lack of trust on the part of many toward well- meaning, if not always correct, administrators can be frustrating. And yet, argument and controversy are the stuff of academic life, and anyone who tries to quash it does so at one's own peril.

Students can be excused, much of the time, by their own lack of maturity and experience and by the way they are subject to heavy influence from faculty. Faculty behavior can also be explained, in part, by the less than adequate compensation they receive in most colleges, by the limited amount of influence they have in the society at large, and by the way in which administrators often do not share enough information with them about the challenges, especially financial, that confront the institution.

There is another ingredient that sometimes causes faculty unrest. Paul Fussell has written of "college teachers … ruined by convictions of inadequacy" (due to a lack of publishing or teaching effectiveness, or a failure to gain employment at more prestigious places) "who thenceforth devoted their lives to social envy and bitterness rather than wit and scholarship."

After an exhaustive search for a new academic dean we found Bob Knott. As part of the process, a really funny incident occurred. A student was sent by someone to collect a candidate at the Memphis airport. The student got lost driving back and went all the way to Little Rock and then north to Batesville. Upon arriving on campus, finally, the student wrongly took the candidate to a room in one of the dorms to discover the room untidy and the bed not made. Desperate, the student brought the candidate to our front door. By now it was 2 or 3 in the morning. Sidney, answered the door in nightgown, robe and slippers. Realizing what had happened, she said, "Come with me," and took the man to a room prepared for him in the guesthouse, just off campus. There, to his consternation, he found a tall stack of papers, brochures, and reports, intended to prepare him for the morning interview. He stayed up the rest of the night dutifully reading this material, but he did not get the job, poor man.

Robert E. Knott was at Mars Hill College in North Carolina. He proved to be a great find for us. He was a good listener, he had taught a lot, he understood faculty and they trusted him. The tone of the place changed after he arrived.

I spent so much time sitting in automobiles that we finally began to charter airplanes to fly me places, especially when I needed to be in more than one place in the same day. There were harrowing incidents, however. I always got in the back seat and opened my briefcase, taking advantage of the undisturbed time and absence of a telephone, to concentrate on work. One day I had to be in Little Rock for a morning meeting and then, by noon, I belonged at a lunch in the President's Dining Room on campus. We chartered a single-engine plane out of Jonesboro. The pilot picked me up early and flew me to Little Rock. I attended the meeting, returned to the airport, and we took off for Batesville. It was important that I be on time.

One of our trustees, Ferd Bellingrath of Pine Bluff, was flying a man named Bill Bellamy, up for lunch with me. We wanted Billy Bellamy to pledge $250,000 to start a new endowed professorship. Ferd had his own plane and piloted it himself. It was a sign of the dedication of some of our trustees that he would take the time and personally fly his friend up to lunch with me.

I took off, in the back seat of the small plane, and just north of Little Rock it threw a rod. There was a loud "bang, bang, bang" and then silence. Of course, with a twin-engine plane you can continue with power to bring it down safely. Much more difficult with no power. One struggles to keep the nose up and depend on what is called the "glide ratio" to come down but with no control over where to land. The pilot was good. He even had the presence of mind as we came down to turn and ask if I had my seatbelt fastened. I remember taking my glasses off, putting my work back in the attaché, buttoning my jacket. I looked down and saw a soybean field; it had been raining, and I decided we would hit the muddy field, which would grab the wheels, and we would flip over. I thought, "Well this is it. I'm going to die. It's been an interesting ride."

Beside the soybean field was a four-lane divided highway. The pilot told the control tower in Little Rock he was coming down and they told him to land on the northbound highway with the traffic. Drivers saw him coming down and pulled off the road. With no power, he landed on the highway. Incredibly, just after he landed, there was a place to pull off the road. I think it was a spot where the highway patrol could pull trucks off for checking them. He coasted to this place, pulled off the highway and brought the plane to a stop facing the highway, wings parallel to the road. Amazing.

Unknown to me the control tower had alerted the police. As I was crawling out of the door of the plane, shaken but unhurt, a state policeman stood there to help me down and said, "Well, I guess you'll go to church next Sunday." "Yes Sir, I will," said I. To my surprise this nice man put me in his patrol car and drove me to the county line where another state car and policeman waited who drove me to the Independence County line where a third car and patrolman waited. They called it relaying. The third man drove me to the college. I thanked him profusely, walked to the dining hall and was standing there, when Ferd Bellingrath and Bill Bellany walked in. Without as much as a hello, Ferd said, "Dan, you're not going to believe what we saw flying up here. Some idiot landed a plane on the highway." "Ferd," I said, "that was I!"

Thank goodness Billy Bellamy pledged the $250,000.

That night the TV and radio in Arkansas were full of the story about the President of Arkansas College landing on the highway. Sidney had been at a meeting in Atlanta. I tried desperately to call her. I knew she'd be frightened if someone recognized her and told her what had happened. Sure enough, as she walked through the Little Rock airport, arriving home from a meeting in Atlanta, Gov. David Pryor, walked up to her and said he was glad I was all right.

At Christmas, 1974, a very sad thing happened. One of the saddest of my career. A 30-year-old Nigerian student, Ignatius Udom, had a heart attack and died in the dormitory. He was a fine man, married and the father of four. He had made a huge sacrifice to leave his home and come to the U.S. for an education. I made strenuous efforts to contact his widow and repeatedly called the Nigerian Embassy in Washington.

To no avail. The Embassy never returned my calls. Nor did the widow. Local authorities insisted on an autopsy which told us why he'd died. Money was donated by various people to ship his body home but without the permission of the next of kin and no assurance that someone would claim the body upon arrival this could not happen. We held a funeral service in the chapel and buried him in a donated grave in the Batesville cemetery. We sent money, left over after funeral expenses were paid, to his widow but never got an acknowledgement. So sad.

At a 1974 meeting the Board authorized a "Planning Guide" which I had proposed. This was finished and presented to the Board for approval in 1975. It contained a 6-year budget, projections for enrollment, tuition, and endowment. There were plans and projections for faculty needs, housing needs, athletics, facilities, etc. I copied the idea from John D. Moseley. Such a document had never been assembled before at Arkansas College. Some of the trustees were very impressed. They believed, at long last, we were using modern management practices to guide the college. Ferd Bellingrath was so impressed, he subsequently asked me to join his board as a director of the Coca-Cola Bottling Co. of South Arkansas.

Among the new concentrations we added to the curriculum were several in the Community Health Administration program. These included "Community health administration," "environmental health," "health care administration," "medical office administration." Then there were two-year programs such as "environmental health technology," "hospital unit management," and "medical office assistant." We were trying to appeal to local area students who needed immediately employable skills as well as basic liberal learning. We were also trying, valiantly, to find courses of instruction that would boost our enrollment. And, in the back of my mind, was a strategy to head off the creation of a community college in Batesville or close by. Such a development would almost certainly have reduced our enrollment. This proved prescient after I left at the end of the 80s.

Our predicament was that the college was caught between the aspirations of two different audiences. There were the Presbyterians, on the one hand, who largely funded the school but lived in the larger communities of the state and wanted the college to become what it had always aspired to be, a "quality, liberal arts college." When we managed to recruit students from Little Rock or Ft. Smith or even Jonesboro they thought they were coming to such a place, and so did their parents. The same was true later when we managed to recruit kids from Oklahoma City or Memphis or north Louisiana. But such a vision seemed elitist to those closer by and to most in the small towns and rural communities of the state. It was also hard to compete with better established places like Hendrix or Austin College or Southwestern at Memphis (later to be renamed Rhodes).

This matter of being caught on the horns of a dilemma created a huge retention problem. Students from larger cities had been graduated from high schools much larger than the college. They came from families and communities that were more sophisticated. When they encountered students from disadvantaged backgrounds, smaller high schools, and rural communities, they were often, but not always, put off. It was a class divide of sorts.

There were many examples of experiences that occurred in just the opposite ways. Big city kids often made lasting friendships with small town natives. People from families who'd never heard of "liberal learning" were thrilled by inspiring professors who opened new worlds. But the divide was there and it still is. The stubborn inability of the host community, Batesville, to grow and expand its character and diversity, hurt the college's ability to keep many students.

There were also inherent in our structure and composition as a college, great challenges blocking what we were trying to do. Many in the faculty derided the experimentation and effort to be more creative in our teaching and learning strategies. I am sure that today, I would be accused of "throwing stuff against the wall to see if it would stick." There was some of that, I admit. But there was also a good deal of resistance to anything new, especially in the Humanities. The smug assumption that "we have what they need," and "we know better than those in the Administration what to teach and how to teach it," was strong. Faculty in the sciences and the social sciences tried, much more energetically, to reach for the new and the untried. I was to blame as well. I was so ambitious for the college, so eager for it to break out of its decades of lethargy and poverty, that I was too impatient, too ready to dismiss those who disagreed as foot draggers.

There was one fiasco, in 1974-75, that took the prize for self-destruction. As part of the planning process we had searched for a new calendar. The college already had a so-called 4-1-4 calendar when I arrived. That means two 4-month semesters with a one-month, January term, in between. I was hoping for something even more creative, something that would give us a distinctive recruiting angle, different from many other colleges. I was enamored of the Colorado College plan of 9 one-month semesters in which students took just one course and really submerged themselves in it, each semester. This was also being used by Cornell College in Iowa, but Colorado College had exploited it as a recruiting device. We also considered a 3-3-3 calendar in which, within three, three-month terms, students would take just three courses. Surprisingly, a member of the humanities faculty, proposed a compromise. We would have a 3-3-3 calendar with optional one-month courses within each term. So far as I knew, this would have been unique in higher education.

I might have known this was far too complicated to administer and later, cynically, I played with the suspicion that it was proposed as an idea doomed from the start as a sort of sabotage. Nonetheless, it was adopted by the faculty and we attempted to introduce it at the beginning of 1975.

There had been insufficient preparation. Faculty and staff alike were not ready to handle the complexity. Students were confused and those who saw their chance to undermine another experiment leaped at the prospect. It was a disaster. I beat a hasty retreat, and the faculty quickly reinstated the 4-1-4, and nobody ever imagined tinkering with the calendar again. Later, I remember telling people that the two things most difficult to change in a college are the calendar and the athletic program. I failed to change either at Arkansas College.

In January, Sidney and I knew we had to get away for a brief time. I had received an invitation to participate in something called the Institute for Educational Management at Harvard in the summer of

'75, but, as we were between deans, I knew I could not be gone for six weeks and managed to get the director of the Institute to allow me to postpone my enrollment to the next summer.

Sidney worked with a travel agent and booked us on a trip to Acapulco, a storied place we'd never been. We went for a week in January, '75. We were both exhausted. Because of the tornado, we had taken no vacation from August '72 until then. We hired a babysitter. I think it was Susie Seuberth of Moorefield. She was a good soul who loved our kids and they got along well with her.

The rest, the beach, the hotels, the sun, the good food in the restaurants were restorative. The city was very uncrowded in January. At first, we stayed at the famous Princess Hotel, in a "cottage" on the beach. The place had been made famous by the movie "10." We loved it. As we flew back we both knew hard work awaited us. I remember Sidney wept. She did not want the respite to end. As we drove up to the house on campus where we lived a crowd of students were gathered, in a demonstration, with posters and shouts, against the new calendar. It was late at night. Mrs. Seuberth and the children were frightened, inside. Sidney went in to reassure them and I confronted the kids. One girl burst into tears she was so upset. I promised them all I had heard their complaint and would take steps immediately to respond. They slowly calmed and finally left. Next morning, I started the process of abandoning the new calendar.

Meanwhile, many advances were being made elsewhere in the college. Improvements in management and administration often moved faster than those in teaching and learning. Under a new director of data processing, Gary Welke, all aspects of the college's record keeping were being rapidly digitized. Money was being raised. Grants were being obtained from foundations and government agencies. New trustees were recruited. The campus was looking better and better. New tennis courts went up.

And so forth.

Still, it was a troubled year, perhaps the most difficult of the sixteen we spent there. The crises and challenges of that year are illustrative of why Brooks Blevens, in his book, "Lyon College, 1872-2002," entitles the chapter on our years there as follows:

"Arkansas College in the Wild West Years." This is perhaps the most pejorative of all his chapter headings, but it reflects, I suppose, his evaluation of the struggle to find, through much experimentation and exploration, a new style and character for an old college, one that would work. It also reflects the difficulties of changing a college, any college. The irony is, almost none of the new ideas we tried came from me. Most of them, including the infamous calendar, came from faculty members.

Chapter 16

Smoother Sailing

I was fortunate during my time at Arkansas College to have three strong women who worked in my office as administrative assistant to the president. The first was Sarah Sheley. Of German extraction, widowed, plain spoken, somewhat salty, and nobody's patsy, she had served in the same position for much of the time Paul McCain had been president. She respected and liked him. She had also served in this job during the Wygle presidency. She knew everybody and everything about everybody, on campus and off. A wealth of information, she was extremely helpful to me on first arriving. She was always professional. She was close to retirement when I got there; she did so a couple of years later, and I missed her. I was very sad when she died a number of years after I left.

Her successor was a very young woman named Sylvia Spencer. Many thought her officious and accused her of taking herself too seriously. I found her smart, hardworking, completely loyal, discrete, and very efficient. Her husband was a local school administrator. They were active in a Pentecostal church nearby. She was ethical, totally honest, and very dependable. Later, I left for a whole year, on sabbatical, and she carried on, with an acting president, without a hitch. I knew she would. She left, in the early 80s when her husband was hired as a school superintendent in a small town in west Arkansas, maybe Altus. I don't think she'd had any college work, but she was so smart it didn't show. For years, we kept in touch at Christmas.

She was followed by Joanne Wilkes. She was the daughter of a physician who'd moved from California to a less hectic rural Arkansas and settled in Cave City. She was so good that I trusted her with my personal finances; she paid all my bills which created an enormous saving of time. I've never trusted anyone else to do that. I don't remember ever giving Joanne any instructions. She just knew what to do. She was excellent with callers and visitors. She handled donors and trustees beautifully. She sat in on meetings of the president's staff and took the minutes. Everyone liked her. Later, when I also hired an Assistant to the President, Helen McCallie, she handled what might have been a threat to less mature people, with equanimity and she and Helen became friends. I am sure that of all the talented people who worked for me and with me through the years she was at the top or close to it. She continued to work at the college through two more presidents and moved to development work before she resigned. She made an enormous contribution to the college. We still trade Christmas cards and occasional phone calls.

Great changes began to occur in the physical plant. The Brown Housing units, small group, condo-style units for 10-12 students each, went up, a loop road connecting Highland Road on the north with College Street on the south was finished, an irrigation system to keep trees and grass alive was installed. And, the beginning of construction on the Union building added to the excitement.

The endowment rose to $3 million, the Board grew to full strength at 33. and the executive staff was stronger than ever, comprising Dr. Brown, Dr. Knott and Messrs. Mays, Pochard (Admissions) and Thomas. Later, they were joined by Mr. Husband who became Director of Student Development.

That year, Shuford Nichols disclosed to me that, as he had been Chair of the Board for 10 years, it was time for him to step down. He agreed to remain on the board but was adamant about leaving the Chair. I was distressed. We all held him in the highest regard, and it seemed it would be impossible to proceed without him. Wisely, he was sure that Frank Lyon would prove a worthy successor. This proved true. They worked together very closely in the years to come. It was almost as though we had a co-chairmanship. They never disagreed with each other; they were always in sync. Their stewardship, over 21 years as perhaps the strongest chairs in the college's history, is an extremely critical piece of the success we had in the 70s and 80s.

Nichols was an unusual man in a number of ways. A native Arkansan and a Presbyterian, he had attended Arkansas College for one year before transferring to Washington and Lee in Virginia. He had married the daughter of a successful businessman, an insurance agent, named Campbell, in Little Rock. The union merged two wealthy families. His father had been a "planter." That's what people were called in Arkansas who owned so much land that their farming operations were conducted by others while they ran the business from an office. The Nichols enterprise was based in Des Arc and he and Laura lived there till relocating to Little Rock in the 80s.

Shuford was an astute businessman who managed a cotton compress, warehouse, real estate and various other investments as well as his farming operations. He lived in exquisitely decorated houses and maintained elegant gardens at each residence. He loved to travel and he and Laura often went to various parts of the world on several trips a year.

He belonged to a men's club in Little Rock called XV. They dressed in black tie once a month and met in each other's home for a gourmet meal, and enjoyed an invited speaker who would stimulate discussion among them. I was once invited to do this. It seemed like something out of the previous century.

Shuford was the most level-headed, calm, analytic, rational man I have known. At some point, his loyalty to the Presbyterian church, and to Arkansas, and to education merged into a determined and very focused commitment to Arkansas College. He could grasp the most complex issue instantly. He could see his way to a solution more quickly than anyone. He could think ahead and see ramifications easily. His memory was excellent.

His vision for the college was clear. I admired and revered him. He was not at all affectionate and he was not one to shower compliments or praise. But, I won his respect and confidence; I knew that, and I relied on him for support in many ways.

We tried to get Shuford to allow us to name the new

administration building for him. He declined. It was not like him to draw attention to himself. Years after he died, this was done anyway. It is a well-deserved tribute.

Sidney and I flew from Wisconsin to Little Rock for his funeral.

When his wife, Laura, died, his daughter asked me to conduct the funeral in Little Rock. At that point I was at Swarthmore and headed to San Francisco, with the president of the college, to ask a Board member for a large amount of money. I could not get loose to go to Arkansas. It is one of the biggest regrets of my life.

With the advent of Bob Knott as the new dean I redoubled my efforts to raise money and complete the campaign. I visited twenty foundations in a year. Pledges to the campaign rose to over $2.8 million

One of the grants we received was from the Exxon Education Fund and it included money that could be used for me to attend a six-weeks program at Harvard, run by the graduate School of Education but located on the campus of the Business School, and called the Institute of Education Management. I had been accepted for this the previous summer and postponed going while we searched for a dean. That delay proved fortuitous. The summer of 1976 was in the middle of the Bicentennial year of the United States.

The IEM program did not want participants to bring their families and required us to live in a dormitory on campus. I could not imagine leaving my wife and two children for six weeks. We drove up together and rented a floor in a house in Brookline where Sidney and the children stayed. I lived in the dorm all week and fled to Brookline on the weekends. It was the summer of the tall ships regatta in Boston Harbor and also of the visit of Queen Elizabeth and Prince Phillip to Boston. On July 4, we heard Arthur Fiedler conduct the Boston Pops Orchestra in playing the "Overture of 1812" complete with nearby church bells and howitzers. We saw it all and loved being there.

I could not believe the Harvard Business School. Located across the Charles River from "the Yard," it was larger and more impressive than many college campuses. I lived in the oldest dorm, Hamilton Hall, named for the first Secretary of the Treasury. The Institute began in June. Summer was a time of maintenance at Harvard. I swore I saw one door painted three times in 6 weeks. The place was immaculate and in perfect shape, old buildings as well as new.

I loved being a student again. The courses were taught in the "B School's" regular classrooms which were built to accommodate the "case method" of teaching. A case or example, written to simulate a real situation but often with names and locations disguised, had to be read beforehand. Then, the instructor would call on us, one by one, to comment on, answer questions about, or propose solutions for the case situation or problem. It was fascinating and I loved it. The best of the instructors was a woman who taught accounting at the B School; she did a course on college accounting. I learned a great deal. There was a lecture by the president of Harvard, Derek Bok, and another by David Riesman, the famous sociologist, who'd focused on higher education and somehow had learned about me and acknowledged me in his lecture. I was stunned.

It was such a thrill to be at Harvard, even though this was a non-credit, continuing education, "professional" program much like many others Harvard offered in the summer. I walked the campus, visited many of the buildings, and tried to imagine what it would have been like had I gone there as an undergrad.

Sidney and the children had a great time, often touring, riding the "T," walking about in Boston or Brookline, enjoying the sights and sounds of the big city. We loved every minute.

The tradeoffs between urban life and small-town living are of no concern to most people in the U.S. They live in either one situation or the other, prefer where they are, and never contemplate the other as an alternative. When we retired, we knew we had to live in a large city; we are urban dwellers for keeps. But, in retrospect, there were many advantages to life in a place as small as Batesville. One did not wait in lines. There was free parking everywhere. The traffic was never a problem. You could get wherever you needed to go in a matter of minutes. The cost of living was much less than most other places. It was safe; I can honestly say we never worried about our children's safety. Neither of our kids experimented with drugs. It was a clean, attractive, pleasant place to be.

In 1976 I began writing something called the "Highlander Memo."

It went out three or four times a year. I have a copy of each issue. It was meant for members of the Highlander Association, those who contributed $1,000 or more each year. I sent copies to the faculty and staff. It was a recap of Board meetings, important developments at the college, and my own and my family's travels. The first or second issue contained a review of our time in Boston that summer of '76. It was a way to stay in touch with donors, build interest in the college, cultivate more gifts and share my own experiences and impressions. The last issue I have is dated August, 1988.

By June of 1977 the capital campaign to raise $3 million, in private money, had exceeded its goal by about $250,000, and we had won another 16 federal grants that totaled over $850,000. I was especially proud of a grant for $123,000 from the National Science Foundation to fund interactive computer methods in teaching science. The endowment reached $3.6 million.

I spent a lot of time traveling, both for fundraising and also working on such organizations as the Council of Independent Colleges, the Advisory Committee on Postsecondary Education Planning for the state, the Association of Presbyterian Colleges, and the Institutional Coordinating Council of the Synod of Red River of the Presbyterian Church in the U.S. These activities and responsibilities took me away from home and family, consumed time I could have spent on college work and used plenty of energy, but I did such things for two reasons: I felt I needed to raise the visibility and respect of the college in the eyes of those outside its immediate family, and I thought that, in each case, I saw a chance to help the college, at least indirectly. Later, at the end of my career, I would question whether it had been worth it to devote so much time and energy to such things.

We finally received a settlement from the insurance company for the tornado damage to the various buildings on campus: a little over $600,000. That seemed and still seems too little to me.

I team-taught a course, with Dan Fagg and Dennis Wright, on "The Nature of Man." It was part of the Core Curriculum.

The Commencement speaker that year was Sen. Dale Bumpers. Steele Hays wrote a very favorable feature story on the college that appeared on the front page of the Arkansas Democrat.

The Teacher Education program remained the largest draw, enrolling 136 students. A grant from the Rockefeller Foundation in New York and another from the National Endowment for the Humanities financed the establishment of a new Folklore program and a new concentration in American Studies. These funds also paid for hiring two new faculty members to staff the new programs.

In spite of such creative work and so much success in all other areas the enrollment remained less than 500.

Chapter

The Hard Work Continues

The job was all consuming. I usually got up very early and went to my study. I had found an unused space on the second floor of the Brown Chapel. It was L-shaped, surrounding an electrical equipment room, but it had marvelous floor to ceiling windows on the west overlooking what became the Couch garden and windows as well on the north, so it was filled with light. I had shelves installed and used an old desk that had been in the basement, unused, of the destroyed Long Building, and set up a beautiful study. I've had a study everywhere we've lived. It has been in the house where we lived except at Arkansas College because, there, the place just wasn't big enough.

If I had writing and thinking to do it was usually in the early morning. When I was fresh.

I seldom got home before 6 or 6:30 in the evening. The only way I could ever relax was to leave town. So long as I was there, on campus, I was working, day or night.

The one thing that took my mind off the college was the garden. I had a large one in Batesville, the best I've ever had. I bought a used Troy-Bilt garden tiller and I established a vegetable garden just up from the house. Later, in front of it, I set up a Rose garden. I got someone to use bricks saved from the demolished old buildings to lay a low wall of old brick and I had red floribundas in the center surrounded by a border of tea roses. It was a picture, and I was very proud of it.

One day a woman drove up, as I worked in the garden, a person whom I knew somewhat, and asked if she could cut some of my roses for a party she was giving in her house. I consented. Next day I came out to find she had cut every single bloom in that large garden. There must have been two bushels of roses.

I added most of the leaves that came down each fall to the garden plot and turned them under. I grew lots of veggies, especially wonderful tomatoes. That part of Arkansas is a great area in which to garden. The weather is mild, there is good rainfall, and it gets cold enough in the winter to kill off most of the insects which love plants.

The thing is, when I worked in the garden I did not think about anything else. I went fishing just occasionally, but I never played golf or tennis, and I don't enjoy sports, so this was my thing. Everyone must have some pastime or hobby which takes you away from your work and that was and is mine. Everywhere we've lived, if there was room for it, I had a garden.

In 1978 the two greatest setbacks for me personally were the departures of Bob Knott and John Mays. Knott had calmed a disgruntled segment of the faculty, listened patiently to all their complaints, won their respect and trust, and led another revision of the core curriculum. He stayed barely two years. He was offered a post as VP for Academic Affairs at Gardner-Webb College in North Carolina and accepted. I felt left in the lurch. It had taken so much time and work to find him and I needed so badly to have someone of his ability to cover my flank given my need to raise money and be gone so much.

There was another kind of loss. His wife Brenda, and Sidney had become the closest of friends. They were soul mates. They had so much in common in their respective roles.

Sidney has always made friends easily and she had and has many, but in each place, we've lived she's had one woman, in particular, with whom she's become very close. Brenda was that person and Sidney was devastated when she left.

The other huge loss occurred when John Mays took a job as VP for Development at Oglethorpe University in Atlanta. He had been at Arkansas College for nine years, through three presidents. He was, by far, the best chief development officer with whom I ever worked; completely ethical, honest as the day, a former Naval officer, a huge man physically, with courtly manners and the strongest work ethic. He was a bit shy about asking but he made up for that in his organizational ability, and what he did was to make sure he got me in front of as many donors as possible and I then made the ask.

We had a disagreement over the effectiveness of one of his staff, and I insisted that person be let go. Either because he felt overruled or out of loyalty to the one separated, for they had become close friends, he felt he must leave. He sought and found another job. I knew at once that this would only increase my work load and that it would be impossible to find anyone nearly so good at his job.

My high opinion of him was confirmed later by Bob Knott who hired John at not one but two colleges where, Knott, subsequently worked.

By the time we retired and moved to Atlanta, John and Nancy Mays were already retired and living in Blairsville, Georgia. It was a joy to see them both again and a heartache when he died.

Another lengthy search, consumed scarce time and money, and then we found John Dahlquist at Kansas Wesleyan College in Salina, where he had taught and then was the acting or interim academic dean. John and his wife Diana were a godsend. By far, he was the best small college dean I knew or know. Smart, resourceful, a good judge of character, a splendid classroom teacher, wise to all the tricks faculty play, but also deeply committed to the profession and sympathetic to all their problems, he brought a whole new element of talent, experience and wisdom to our top leadership.

John and Diana went one better than the Knotts in reaching out to faculty. Because their three children were grown and gone from home and because they liked to do it and Diana was a talented cook, they often had faculty to dinner in their home, building morale and community. It made the college a different place.

Development was another matter. As it happened I had hired Dan Junkin, the minister of the Presbyterian Church in nearby Newport, Arkansas, as Assistant to the President before Mays left. He was John D. Moseley's son-in-law. After John Mays' departure, when Dan asked me to do it, I agreed and made him Executive

Assistant with responsibility for Development. Later I promoted him to Vice President. He was reasonably successful and we got on well, but he didn't stay long, deciding to move on to a foundation job in Oklahoma after a short while.

Turnover was a problem at the college. Too many people, good people, young and talented people, found the college and the city too small, the salaries too low, or whatever, and used us as a stepping stone in their careers. I spent far too much time recruiting and interviewing new faculty and staff. I insisted on meeting with anyone being hired on the faculty before they were offered the job.

There is a huge problem confronting small, liberal arts colleges in hiring. Most faculty and many staff candidates come from large universities, if not as undergraduates then as former employees or as holders of a graduate degree. Often, they are unaware of the characteristics of a small college and later discover, if hired, that they are not sympathetic and even frustrated. People in small colleges, faculty and staff, often have to cover more than one job or fill in when someone leaves or teach outside their specialty. Faculty have to help with the core curriculum, with advising or mentoring and with heavier teaching loads and often cannot find the time to write and publish.

One of the things I learned to do was try to determine how well suited to a small college situation a candidate was and how sympathetic they were to liberal learning.

Interviewing job candidates is an art not a science and I did a lot of it but I claim no special success at it. I hired my share of roaring successes and also my share of dismal failures. I finally determined that hiring people is a gamble and that you really don't know for sure until after the fact whether you did the right thing. If it was a mistake it takes three years to correct. A year to discover you were wrong, a year to make sure by giving the benefit of the doubt, and a year to work up the guts to separate. I am sure that selecting people was one of the hardest things I did and dismissing them was the most distasteful.

In the fall of 1978 we dedicated the beautiful new College Union, sent six groups of faculty and students off campus in January, and saw one of our trustees, Kaneaster Hodges, Jr., a lawyer from

Newport, appointed to the U. S. Senate to fill the unexpired term of Sen. McClellan who had died.

In January of 1978, Sidney and I led a group of students on a January term trip to England. It was part of a course I taught on "Historic London." I lectured for a week, on campus. We then spent two weeks in London. The conclusion was another week of classes on campus of discussion and evaluation and allowing the students to finish their journals. Grades were based on participation in class and trip and on their journals. We subsequently took two more groups abroad, one to Italy and another to Austria. Almost all of the students had not previously been out of the country; indeed, many had not been out of Arkansas. The groups were small, ranging from about 10 to maybe 15. I am convinced it was a life-changing experience for nearly all of them. We loved doing it though it was a lot of work and a huge responsibility. Sidney, of course, was a huge help, especially with the women, but really with all the students. I was trying to do my bit in teaching, but I was also trying to model for other faculty a way in which they could travel and teach. But, I knew, that since Sidney and I paid our own way, it would be hard for many faculty to finance the cost.

I spent a lot of time recruiting new trustees. After names had been submitted to the Nominating Committee I would call on persons approved by them and try to determine if they were willing to serve. We developed a list of expectations: regular attendance, advocacy of the college, help in recruiting students, help in fund raising, and willingness to contribute at least $1,000 per year. A number of people said they could not accept one or more of these expectations in which case I thanked them and went on to the next. I felt that if, after people were clear about what we wanted them to do, they said they could not, for whatever reason, we were ahead. Most boards comprise people who are not clear about what is wanted of them and there is much awkwardness and frustration on both the part of the trustee and the organization till someone who isn't effective decides to leave. By explaining in detail what we wanted before someone was asked if they would accept trusteeship we built a very strong and effective board.

The record shows that in 1978-79 I was a member of no fewer than eight outside boards, councils, committees, etc. This was in addition to speaking, preaching, and various other public relations events and activities. It was too much, and, as I have said before I'm not sure it was necessary to do that much. It took a toll.

We added more new concentrations (majors) such as health education, accounting, media arts, and political science, all in response to clues we got from market research on our state and regional target areas for recruiting.

During our years in Arkansas, the Governor appointed me to two state commissions and also to the Education Commission of the States. He appointed Sidney to the State Arts Council.

Sidney entertained several times a year each year we were there. Receptions and parties and garden fetes for new students and parents, graduating seniors and parents, faculty, staff, trustees, an annual Christmas party for faculty and staff, and numerous visiting speakers or other special guests. All of this in a small house not really suited to large scale entertaining but she managed. Often, because the college had such scarce funds she would drive into the countryside to gather wild flowers beside the road for beautiful arrangements. Sometimes she would use the beautiful Bevens Room in the Chapel and after the College Union went up we had a President's Dining Room, furnished by Marion Lyon, which was very useful and took much of the burden off our private residence and Sidney.

Often, when we entertained at the President's House, we expected Claire and Andrew to attend and help us greet guests. I am convinced that each of them learned their considerable social skills from such as that. They understood it was the family business and they willingly helped out.

Chapter

The Family

Being president of a college is a family business: one's spouse and children are inextricably bound up in the fishbowl of public life. I have been enormously blessed with a wife who is beyond outstanding and two children who are just as impressive.

I greatly admire Sidney's decision to shape her career path into an officially non-compensated partner with me in college work, a choice that is no longer popular or acceptable with many spouses of college leaders. Yet she did that without complaint and became very effective at it, to the point that everyone who knows us, including me, knows that she was a critical element in whatever success we achieved.

Sidney had the greatest responsibility for rearing the children because I was gone so much of the time. She had been graduated from Austin College with a major in elementary education, done graduate work at William and Mary, and earned a master's degree in education at Peabody College in Nashville. She had taught for two years in Richmond, three in Smyrna, and part of a year in Sherman.

But after Andrew was born, she had given up teaching to major in parenting and homemaking; however, when we got to Batesville, she did much, much more. Sidney was really an unpaid assistant to the President at Arkansas College. She was a one-woman public relations staff, hostess, greeter, friend to many faculty, staff, and students, counselor, confidant, and often a co-traveler with me on college trips.

Sidney's arena of action went well beyond the college. She was very active at First Presbyterian Church, Batesville: circle chair, officer in Presbyterian Women, and ruling elder. She served on the board of Ferncliff, a campground of the presbytery, and on Presbytery's Council. Later she became active on the national level: she was on the Board of Women's Work of the Presbyterian Church, U.S., before joining and later becoming chair of the Committee on Women's Concerns. These duties often took her to Atlanta, Louisville, and elsewhere. She attended the General Assembly of the PCUS five times.

Sidney, 1986

Sidney was appointed to the state Arts Council and served on the executive committee of the state branch of the AAUW. In Batesville, she was president of the Athena Study Club and served on a committee to study the Batesville school system. She was on the executive committee of North Arkansas Community Services, and the board of the United Way. She served on a committee of the Chamber of Commerce and on the executive committee of the Community Theatre. She was a founding member of the Batesville Arts Alliance, and on the board of the Batesville Symphony League.

Sidney and Marion Lyon collaborated to decorate the president's house, the president's dining room in the new college union, and the Alphin Building. She made many trips to Little Rock to meet with Marion and to other places, such as Dallas and New Orleans, to select materials and furnishings. Each space they decorated was elegant, tasteful, and lovely, a real credit to the college.

Not only did Sidney host several events a year in the president's house, she also entertained individual visitors, family and friends. She was often on campus, reaching out to visitors, speaking to students, staff and faculty, taking flowers or food to those celebrating, suffering or mourning. She was never paid a nickel by the college, but she earned the salary I got as much as I did, and we continued the practice, begun in Sherman, of dividing the salary I got from the business office so that part went into her checking account.

Little of this would have been possible without housekeepers and babysitters. They included Susie Seuberth, Ruth McCoy, and Gertrude Trinsher, all wonderful women. By far, the best came to us after we returned from Harvard, Betty Branscum, of Southside. Born and reared in the area, she had worked for years at the shoe factory before being hired by the college as part of the housekeeping staff. When she joined us at the house where we lived, in the early eighties, she made a huge difference. She was one of the smartest, most resourceful, hardest working people I've known. She prepared two meals a day for us, breakfast and dinner, virtually freeing Sidney from kitchen work. She cleaned and mended, made minor repairs, looked after the children, and even helped with bedding plants in the college's greenhouse. She was a marvel! And we loved her. Completely discrete, we knew we could trust her, and we depended on her greatly. She was never sick, never missed work. Sidney came to love her as a soulmate, and they remain in touch to this day.

As a family of four, we ate together in the breakfast area, between the kitchen and the den, every morning at breakfast and every evening at dinner. When one or both of us were gone, this schedule was maintained by babysitters who prepared meals. Later, after the talented Betty Branscum became our housekeeper, she came in early to prepare breakfast and prepared the evening meal before she left in the late afternoon. This was an enormous help to Sidney and ensured that we were together as a family virtually every day. I know this was important because I was so consumed with work and absent so much that when I was there it was often the only time all day when I was with the children.

Maybe this is one reason why they both look on Batesville as their hometown, and both still have a favorable view of it, even though they both left for school and college before we moved from there.

I prepared breakfast on weekends and we always attended church on Sundays as a family. I asked each child to make a pledge to the church as soon as they had an allowance with which to do so. I am pleased that each has continued, into adulthood, to be a regular churchgoer and pledger and that each gives annually to his or her college.

Gardening was an important part of life in Batesville. I had acquired a used truck, but there was no place to park it or store the tiller and other tools. I found some money to pay for it, ordered plans from a magazine, and had a shed, with pitched roof and cupula, built. In this "Carriage House" as we called it, all this was stored out of sight. Andrew set up a model train in the loft. One day, as I walked home from the office, Andrew called to me from the shed and asked me to step inside. He showed me the layout of the train set and said that he really needed three more cars, additional track, and a switch. I asked, "Son, do you know what all that will cost?" "Yes, Dad," he said, "and if you will buy it, I am prepared to set up a plaque right here that says, 'Contributed by Dan C. West.'" He is a quick learner, and he got the equipment.

In the early 1970s, Sidney and I established a pattern of traveling outside the country. By 1977, the children were old enough to go with us, and we took them to London. It was the first of three trips to Europe that they made with us. They were, by then, old enough to remember each, and I am sure it helped them with perspective, attitude, and viewpoint. They were good travelers, walking for miles, visiting too many churches, interested in most museums, and learning to try strange foods. Before the children grew up and moved away, we made trips with them to England, Austria, France, Bermuda, Canada, New York City, and Washington, D.C. I believe in travel as a valuable part of one's education, and I think these trips, together with others they made as college students, have made them more thoughtful and more open-minded.

Together, Sidney and I have been to England (8 times), France (7 times), Italy (3), Austria (twice), the Bahamas, China, Germany (4 times), Greece (twice), Turkey, Hawaii, Scotland, Spain, and Cuba. In addition, we have taken tours or cruises to Jordan and Israel, several of the Baltic countries, Scandinavia and Austria, Peru and Ecuador, and some of the Easter European countries. Sidney has made three trips without me, part of tour groups to the Mideast (Jordan, Egypt, Palestine, and Israel), in 1992 and to Vietnam in 2006, and to Haiti in 2011 (with a church mission group). We have been very fortunate to be able to afford these travels, and it has been a wonderfully broadening and informative part of our lives together.

Sidney and I are unabashed liberal Democrats and have been for years (in my case since high school days). Claire and Andrew are more moderate in their politics but are progressive in their thinking and especially in their attitudes to those less fortunate than they.

At some point in the 1960s, I began writing a "family letter" every Sunday. I think this came out of the habit I established in the late 50s, when I went off to college, of calling my parents every Sunday night. That evolved into a letter that went to them and then also to my siblings and later to nieces and nephews as the family grew. Gradually I added aunts and uncles and close friends, and then Sidney's family as well. Before e-mail, letter-writing was a good deal of trouble: typing, copying, stuffing envelopes, stamping. After e-mail arrived at some point in the 90s, it has been easier. I believe I have a complete collection of these weekly letters, and though I have never read through them, they do represent a detailed record of our family's life. In addition, each December, I have written an "Advent Letter," a theological statement appropriate for the times. It is enclosed with a newsletter as our Christmas card to family and friends.

Each time we have taken a trip out of the country and on some occasions when we have traveled domestically, I have kept a travel journal and shared that with those who receive the family letter. The travel journal, when printed out, goes into a loose-leaf binder that, along with photos, receipts, tickets, brochures, maps, etc., comprises a scrap book on each trip. There is now a collection of more than fifty of these binders in my study.

Since the 1960s, I have kept every calendar recording daily events. I have kept yearbooks, bulletins, speeches, articles I have written, and more. I have file cabinets full of letters received from others. Why do I record so much and save so much? I'm sure there is some psychological reason for it. It's a compulsion, a life-long habit, and I have been fortunate to have studies where I could accumulate all this paper. But it is clear to me that no one will be the slightest bit interested in doing anything except discarding all of it when I am gone. I am gradually sorting, re-filing, and discarding this mass of "stuff," but it is a slow process, and I do not let go of it quickly or easily at all.

I love books, have always wanted to be surrounded by them, and have a good collection. It is mostly concentrated in theology, Biblical studies, literature, history, and biography, but I do have a good collection of fiction and a smattering of things in other areas, e.g gardening and cooking. If left to my own devices, I usually gravitate to biography, theology, and history.

Today I am likely to give books away. I do not know how many books I owned when I retired and moved all this to Georgia. Thousands. Years ago, in Arkansas, I think in the 80s, I hired Claire, who needed a summer job, to catalog my library. She learned to use the Library of Congress system and did a good job of labeling and then typing a card for each book. When I retired, I managed to bring the cataloging of my library up to date, using the computer to log into the LOC site and get the call number of books I had acquired since Claire's work.

Sidney, too, is a book lover and has her own collection which is focused on philosophy, fiction, poetry and art.

Once, in Wisconsin, we visited a couple who had invited us to see their brand-new house. It was contemporary, minimalist in décor, interesting. After we left, Sidney said she was very uncomfortable in it. Why? There were no books. I agreed.

Chapter

The End of the Decade

In a report to the trustees of Arkansas College, in the late 70s, I explained that I had decided that I, as a college president, lived somewhere between where the college actually was, at any moment, and where I wanted it to be in the future when it had achieved what I envisioned for it. I went on to explain that I had learned that colleges, and many other institutions and organizations, have reputations that lag behind reality. Colleges either stand still or they move forward. And the public perception of them usually lags behind by years. Either they are cruising on images earned 20 years earlier or they are far ahead of where most people understand. That was a frustration at Arkansas College. I knew it to be a far better place than most of the public imagined and I was impatient for the image to catch up with the fact.

Nonetheless the college struggled much of the time I was there. I have already alluded to the need for more enrollment. In the 70s and early 80s there was also a chronic cash flow problem. We did not take in enough tuition at the start of the fall and spring semesters to carry us forward. There were and are few "full-pay" students. We were dependent on government grants, foundation grants, contributions, and fees, and such sources were not always within our control or received in a predictable schedule. The local banks were willing to lend us money at prevailing rates but that meant paying interest. It was always a concern to me, until late in the 80s.

The endowment inched up to over \$4 million, but at a 5% or 6% spending rate that was just \$200,000 and the budget was \$3 million.

The fact was our business model was not sustainable. It took too much financial aid to attract students and keep them since so few were able or willing to pay the tuition. So, we had to work hard to find money from many sources. That hard work included efforts to obtain federal grants, win state scholarships, seek foundation grants, and ask many for gifts. It was a constant, unrelenting scramble to get enough money to pay the bills and, all the while, the salaries were too low, the costs of operating continued to rise, and the need to compete with other colleges and the state universities required new investments in every direction.

At one point, we added over twenty maintenance, custodial and dining hall staff to the long-term disability insurance and retirement programs. It was unconscionable that they had not been covered until then. But each time that sort of decision was made it meant less money for other purposes.

Richard Thomas, ever the resourceful searcher for greater efficiency, began looking to buy an airplane to help me with my far-flung travels in search of donations. He discovered the government surplus property program. It is the case that after the federal government decides to replace or discard a piece of equipment it is offered first to other government agencies, and then to the state governments and, finally, is put on sale to the general public. In this way, Richard found an airplane that had belonged, I think, to the U.S. Forestry Service and then to other units of the federal and state government. It was old enough and used enough that it was cheap and he bought it. I used it to fly mostly to Little Rock (90 miles south) and Memphis (120 miles northeast) where the nearest commercial airports are. It was a life saver. I could start the day in my office, then fly to some place and see a donor or attend a meeting, and often get back before the work day ended on campus. It just multiplied my ability to get things done.

Occasionally Richard used the plane and we sometimes flew groups of vice presidents or faculty and students to meetings in Little Rock, etc. Later, Richard traded the plane for a newer Cessna twin-engine, but we never owned a new plane or even a slightly used one.

The pilot for 10 years or more was a man named Bill Upton. He was a retired U. S. Air Force pilot who had flown C 130 missions over Viet Nam. He was a native of Canada who had moved to nearby Heber Springs, AR, and wanted to keep up his license. We hired him on a part-time, as-needed basis and paid him by the hour for both flying and wait time. He was a colorful character with a salty style and wonderful stories to tell. I would climb into the back, cabin area, and, using a folding desk we had built for it, open my attaché and work away, seldom looking up till we landed. He respected this work time and we conversed little while in flight.

We often returned to Batesville late at night, after the terminal with its control desk in the office had closed. There was an arrangement for this contingency. The landing lights on the runways were turned off, but an approaching pilot could activate them by whistling into his microphone with the radio tuned to a particular frequency. Trouble is, Bill couldn't whistle. So, I would know when it was time to land when he would say, "Hey Doc," and hand me the mike. I would whistle into it, the lights would come on below, and we would land safely.

In June, 1979, I spent a lot of time on the first, and only, National Congress of Church Related Colleges. It was held at Notre Dame University in South Bend, IN, and it was the brainchild and creature of John D. Moseley, by then retired from the presidency of Austin College. He had asked me to help, of course, and I was never able to turn him down. I had attended planning meetings, served on one of the commissions, wrote the draft of one of the policy statements, served on the steering committee of the PCUS delegation, and was convener of one of the caucus groups. After the Congress met, I wrote an article about it for The Presbyterian Survey, a magazine of the church.

In some ways, this represented, in a symbolic way, a huge investment I made in protecting, strengthening, defining, and promoting church-college relationships. I have mentioned the frequent preaching and speaking in churches, the committee work in presbytery and synod, the founding of the Association of Presbyterian Colleges and Universities. Later I led the establishing of a General Assembly Committee on Higher Education. Why so much time and energy on this idea?

Once more, I was emulating my role model, Moseley, but I think I was also trying to remain faithful to the church and to my ordination vows. I really believed that it was important to have colleges, not just founded by the church, but still taking that relationship seriously. And I thought I understood that it was important to the church, especially the Presbyterian Church, to be related to higher education. Nowadays I have much less definite views about this.

I have had to conclude that other than acknowledging the historic significance of the church's role in our higher education system, there is little of substance to expect in the future of this relationship. The purpose, role, and mission of the two institutions, church and college, are simply too diverse. The church exists as an institution to promote the message of Christianity, to provide nurture and compassion to its members and those whom it chooses to serve in the surrounding community and to preserve and strengthen its own institutional structures. The college, on the other hand, must be far more open to ideas and trends that are beyond the traditional and the conventional. Its values are different. Its purpose is to seek truth, protect free thought and speech, and promote diversity within its own community. For many, in our society, the only real interaction with those different from ourselves, economically, culturally, racially, comes only during the college years. Most churches, by contrast, are far more homogeneous in their makeup.

The church has drifted away from the college, in part, because, as in the case of other institutions previously founded by the church, it can no longer control these organizations. Even among the more conservative denominations, there is a trend toward loosened bonds of policy and activity that previously limited the colleges to close conformity with denominational values and doctrines. The college, on the other hand, finds it hard to pay much credence to church groups which, less and less, provide financial and other support. Most colleges must now look to tuition, government grants and subsidies, private contributions from many sources, rather than churches for their maintenance. And so, the two drift apart. Is this inevitable? Perhaps. The record suggests so. Only among the most sectarian and separatist churches are there still strong ties to their colleges and many of those ties seem weaker now than earlier.

It is significant that, among Presbyterian colleges at least, it seems no longer important that the president and the predominant number of trustees be members of the parent church. This cannot be surprising given the fact that the main body of Presbyterians comprises, nowadays, less than 2 million people. The colleges in the U.S., who still refer to themselves as related to our church, must look to many other groups for students, faculty, staff, and contributors.

Years later, in the 80s, my misgivings about the future of the church-college relationship were borne out in the following way. I worked hard to found the Association of Presbyterian Colleges, and later, to obtain a part of the services of a staff member in Louisville (where the reunited Presbyterian Church was headquartered) to provide staff support for this. Still later, I worked, against significant opposition, to obtain a vote of the General Assembly (national governing body of the church) to establish a General Assembly Committee on Higher Education. Most of the national staff were opposed to this. After just 3-4 years of existence they used the first opportunity of a budget reduction crisis to shut it down. Higher education simply did not and does not hold any great importance for the church nowadays.

In addition to the factors I mention above, there is another important reason for this decline of interest by church people in being a college-related church. Most members and clergy who are

Presbyterians now are graduates of state universities. A shrinking percentage of U.S. college and university students attend independent or "private" institutions. It is difficult for most Presbyterians without any experience in and with a college founded and still related in some fashion to the church to attach any importance to that.

In the long sweep of history, it may not be tragic that this trend has developed.

Just as many hospitals, children's homes, schools, retirement communities and other social services agencies were originally established by the church and are no longer attached to the church in any meaningful way, so have colleges grown apart. Perhaps had I understood that in my 30s and 40s I would not have thrown so much time and energy into this issue.

Toward the end of the 1970s, at Arkansas College, there were many advances and accomplishments, but there were also grievous failures and challenges, some so severe as to be discouraging at the least.

I worked hard to persuade the governor and the legislature to set up a "Governor's School" in Arkansas, modeled after one I learned of in North Carolina. It was a way to provide summer enrichment, on a college campus, to gifted high school students and to encourage them to pursue college. I succeeded in seeing the school set up, but failed at having it located at Arkansas College. Instead it went to Hendrix College in Conway where it has remained. That was hard to take. It told me Arkansas College wasn't respected enough or prestigious enough or close enough to Little Rock or some such reason.

We continued to be hounded by sluggish student recruiting and attrition that was too high. We struggled to find a right approach to student development and staff persons for that part of the college who were capable enough to lead it. Our turnover in faculty was too high. Our financial struggles did not abate.

In spite of such chronic problems I do not remember really getting discouraged. I remained optimistic and confident. It was only years later that I began to realize how truly difficult it was and how hard.

I never doubted we would be successful. There was a sense, in my mind, that failure was not an option. Part of what was going on in my head was the certain fact that I had to remain positive in order to ensure morale did not sag among others. Part of my attitude had to do with fund raising. How could I ask anyone for money and not believe I was requesting support for a successful operation? And part of what was going on was that there was enough success, enough really exciting developments that they balanced out the discouragements.

In the late 70s the men's basketball team had a 23-8 record and got into the semifinals of the NAIA District 7 play-offs. The elementary education concentration won full accreditation from NCATE, the smallest program in the country to be so certified. Buddy Hughes led the Campus Ministry Board to resettle a refugee family from Viet Nam in Batesville. John Edwards, a retired businessman in Batesville, who had never been philanthropic, gave a large amount of money to build and install a fine pipe organ in the Chapel. Gaston Williamson, senior partner of the Rose Law Firm in Little Rock and a Rhodes Scholar, gave money to endow the Lamar Williamson Prize for Faculty Excellence and named it for his father. The endowment increased to $5 million and we decided to launch a new capital campaign in the fall of 1980, to raise at least $10 million.

In the face of such successes there was no time to get discouraged. It was clear, I thought, that we would overcome all obstacles and take our rightful place among the distinguished small colleges of the country.

Before the 70s ended we dropped certain academic concentrations (majors) that were under-enrolled: public administration, health education, political science, environmental health, as examples. We had set these and others up, hoping that they would attract student interest and then acknowledged they had not. Our main sources of income were government grants and private gifts, not tuition.

There were some real heroes among the staff of the college, in addition to those already mentioned. I shall recall two as among those who still hold extraordinary records of service for longevity and effectiveness. Marjorie Dowser was a native of Batesville who never married, lived in a house close to campus with her unmarried sister, and spent almost all her time working at the college. She was the Bursar when I arrived and kept that title almost until she died, working long past retirement age. In her last years, she spent nights, weekends and holidays calling students who had outstanding loans, cajoling them into making sometimes just token payments so they would not default. We had, for years, one of the lowest default rates in the country. The college was her life. There was no one more loyal or dedicated.

Jim Mitchum was another native of Batesville and graduate of the college who spent his entire career working there. He served in many capacities: guidance counselor, director of continuing education, and community service coordinator. He was selfless and totally flexible and ready to help in any way and he did. Everyone loved him. He was part of the soul of the place. I admired and respected him as did everyone else. He died too young, a loss to the college and to Batesville.

I could cite many others. There was so much talent and creativity, so much dedication. It was a collection of folks who could easily have taught and staffed a much larger college, and done so brilliantly. In this way, it was not unlike every other college, of course, but I felt fortunate to work among and alongside such people and remain convinced that this country is full of people like them, honest, well meaning, selfless, unassuming, ready to do their part. Without such as these this country could never have attained the exalted status it has in our world. As Casey Stengel said, "Ability is the act of getting credit for all the home runs someone else hits."

As the seventies drew to a close, I remarked in my report to the trustees that the 1979-80 academic year was probably "the smoothest of the nine years" I had been there.

Much of that was due to the work of John Dahlquist.

The endowment's market value reached $6 million. The budget went over $4 ½ million. We obtained the first two endowed chairs (in business and chemistry), meaning that restricted endowments of $500,000 each were established to support them.

But the challenges continued. Interest rates went over 20% and we had short-term debt of more than $900,000. Less than a third of our operating income derived from tuition. I remarked, in the report, that,

> We have been trying to increase the enrollment while, at the same time, increasing the tuition and the entrance requirements. In business, trying to increase sales while narrowing the market segment and increasing the price is not unheard of; it is sometimes done but not when overhead is rising dramatically, the price is way below cost, and one's principal competition is state owned, heavily subsidized and almost free to the consumer.

This is the situation many small colleges faced then and now. It is a business model that defies logic and market reality, yet it persists to this day. They stay in business because of what happens to the students enrolled in them. As I look back at the years at Arkansas College and reflect on the challenges and obstacles that place confronted then, throughout its earlier history, and since I left till now, it would be easy to conclude it was all for naught. Not so, however, because of what happened to so many students over the years. Even some who did not graduate there will say, now, that it changed their lives.

There were two categories of students I shall mention as illustrations. I have already alluded to the kid from the small-town Arkansas background who, seriously unprepared for college work, managed to catch up and take off toward real accomplishment because of patient, careful, and effective mentoring by faculty who labored largely without recognition or sufficient pay. Another example is the student who came from a more affluent family, perhaps a large city high school, who, maybe with strong encouragement from her parents, chose this small college in a small town and, without the distractions of big parties and football weekends, developed learning skills and expanded her perspective in many areas beyond her own or her family's expectations. As I said in my report, "Such is the heart of the college and the reason all of the struggle for funds and fixtures is worth it."

The three most important vice presidents, Dahlquist, Brown and Thomas, continued their extraordinary work. They were now joined by John Thompson (Admissions), Dennis Wright (Student Affairs), and Ralph Graham (Development).

In the midst of continued frustration with our admissions effort, I turned to a consulting firm in Atlanta, Dagley and Associates. We actually outsourced admissions. They took it over and managed it, and the director they hired was Thompson, who proved effective. Wright had been a biology professor and then acting dean of students. He became, at last, the mature, steady, wise and unshakeable head of that part of the college that we had needed for years. Graham came from Trinity University in Texas. He was a Presbyterian minister, an expert in planned giving, and he succeeded Dan Junkin.

Of the nine or ten boards, committees, etc. I was on that year, one was the Arkansas Advocates for Children and Youth. It was a board on which Hillary Rodham, wife of the Governor, also served. She was very active on this. I had already become acquainted with her as she was in active practice at the Rose Law Firm in Little Rock.

Because the college was too small to have legal counsel on staff whenever there was a legal issue that required a lawyer I would call Gaston Williamson, senior partner of the Rose Law Firm in Little Rock. I'd describe the issue, and he would then assign one of the lawyers in the firm to us. In this way, I worked with Hillary Rodham on at least a half-dozen occasions. I was impressed with her from first to last. She listened well, asked great questions, thought of all angles and contingencies, and prepared thoroughly for each meeting or conversation. She had the most extraordinary talent for solving complex problems. She would break them down into parts, and solve each piece, one by one; then the whole thing would be done. Another thing. She always delivered on her promises. She did not take forever to do so. And, she was always on time.

I have believed, for years, that Hillary is smarter than her husband. I like him, too, and I know he is probably the most talented politician we've ever had in the presidency, but she is a better person and even more talented than he. She would have made a great president and I was excited about that prospect as I believe it is high time we had a woman president. I supported her until Barak Obama won the nomination. I was disheartened and discouraged when she lost out again in 2016.

After nine years in college presidency I reflected, in my report for 1980-81, that those nine years had been, "at once the most difficult and the most interesting ones I had ever experienced."

Chapter

20

Sabbatical

I was tired, physically and mentally, and I was out of new ideas. I knew that nine years was longer than the average college presidency and nothing had been offered to me that I felt ready to accept. I imagined a sabbatical. I discussed it with Frank Lyon, who had become, not just my boss, but a trusted confidant and another father figure. He was encouraging. I told him I could not do it unless the college kept me on salary, but I said I would commit to stay at least another three years if they would do that. He was actually enthusiastic about the idea. He checked with a few other trustees and reported back to me that it was all right to proceed. I never knew how much of their early support was their own and how much they acceded to his strong approval.

Frank Lyon was an exceptional person in a number of ways. In a deeply conservative state where even the Democrats were right of center, he was a political liberal, far more than his friends or family. As a successful businessman, he had strong misgivings about the business practices of many whom he knew well. He told me more than once that it was wrong for anyone as successful and wealthy as he to oppose being taxed at a fair level. "Why shouldn't I pay a lot more tax?," he would say, "I ought to do that because others who are not as wealthy cannot." Amazing. He was also progressive in his thinking, ready to entertain a new idea, and more open to new approaches and innovation.

Every time someone suggests that the wealthy are usually conservative in the sense of always opposing change and always protecting their own interests, I always remember a man who was no such thing. Jane Austen, in "Emma," said, "It is very difficult for the prosperous to be humble." Frank was, nonetheless.

There was another important decision to be made were I to leave for a whole year. Who would be in charge? I came up with an idea that seemed to many of my friends in the college presidency to be daring if not risky. I suggested to Frank Lyon that we ask Bill Dunklin of Pine Bluff to be acting president for a year. Bill was a Princeton graduate, a wealthy planter whose sons were almost old enough to run his farming operation, and an individual who had the time to stay in Batesville for those months. Edith, his wife, chose not to move to Batesville with him though she came on special occasions. He stayed in the president's house and used my office, of course, and he was great.

He told me more than once it was like a dream. He enjoyed the whole thing. He said he thought he was like Walter Mitty in James Thurber's short story. He tried to keep everything on track just as he believed I would do were I there. He called me every Sunday night I was in Massachusetts and gave me a report. He did a terrific job. I knew he would. I never worried. I had enough confidence in the policies and systems we had in place by then, and I was so sure of the people in the vice presidencies that I knew it would work, and it did. Friends at Harvard and college president friends said they were impressed. Some said they'd never leave that long for fear the trustee would want the job for keeps or that things would unravel, etc. Not at all.

When Bill Dunklin died, in 2014, at the age of 92, I told his widow, Ethel, that he had done me and the college a great favor, for which I remain grateful.

I decided that in order to make the most of a sabbatical I needed to be part of a serious degree program with courses and grades, deadlines and requirements. It would have been fun to go to a great university library and hole up with long reading lists and many have done that, to great profit. But I knew myself and I believed I would accomplish much more in a structured situation. I did some research and I concluded that there were three graduate schools of education in the country that had degrees or at least concentrations in higher education management that would be worth my seeking entrance. They were Stanford University, Harvard University, and the University of Michigan. I applied to all three and was accepted at each.

It is interesting, as I reflect on it, the process of elimination that took me to Harvard. Stanford has and had an excellent program, but it was quantitatively oriented. It was heavily dependent on statistical analysis and business principles. None of that was bad and I was interested in such an approach, but I worried that it might limit my thinking. Then, there was my prejudice against the west coast. I'd never lived there, but I'd made many visits and also served as a consultant to a small private college in California once and I did not like the west coast as much as other areas.

Truth be told, the program at Michigan was probably the best of the three; it may yet be so. But I worried about the bitter winter in Ann Arbor and I was also up against my prejudice against state universities. I knew that Michigan was a different kind of place from the University of Arkansas or even the University of Texas. But it was still a state-owned place, and I worried I would not be happy there.

My heart was with the east coast. I had done three years at Annapolis, I loved visiting Washington and Philadelphia and New York, I relished the six weeks our family had spent in Boston, and I remembered how excited I'd been at the brief prospect of going to Harvard when I was in high school.

There was another factor. A man named Stephen Bailey was a new professor there. I had admired him when he had earlier been a vice president of the American Council on Education. His speeches and articles were excellent. John D. Moseley knew him well and agreed that if I could study with him it would be very advantageous. So, I chose Harvard and we prepared to move to Boston in the summer of 1981.

We sent Sidney ahead as a scout to try to find a place for us to live. She flew to Boston and rented a car, but was not impressed with any of the places we had heard of. She did think that one place, recommended to me by the Graduate School of Education at Harvard, might work. A Harvard professor named Patricia Cross planned to be on sabbatical the year we were there. She had leased a house in Lexington and wanted to sub-lease it while she was in California for the year. We took the lease.

We traveled to Massachusetts in August 1981 with a rented trailer behind us carrying all our clothes and other things we'd need for a year away.

On the way, I received a phone call as we were stopped for an overnight somewhere, that Miss Jean Brown of Hot Springs, AR, had died, unexpectedly. Of course, I would have to return, for the funeral. The family dropped me at an airport in Ohio. Sidney and the children drove on to the next two stops. They collected me at an airport in Connecticut two days later. I had gone to Hot Springs, attended the funeral of that gracious and generous lady who would mean even more to Arkansas College than she already had, and returned to my family, to continue our trek east.

I don't remember the rent, but the house we had was amazing. It was a very old farmhouse, once in the countryside, on Hancock Street in Revolutionary Lexington. The owners had retired to Florida and rented it as it was too valuable a property to sell. It was a two-story, white, frame house with a large barn in back.

I took some of the furniture out of the living room, dragged a wooden picnic table in from the porch, for a desk, and that became my study. Each of the children had their own bedroom upstairs. There was a large kitchen, family room and dining room. We were very comfortable.

The house was within walking distance of Lexington Common, where the very first skirmish of the Revolution occurred in April 1776. Midway between the Common and our house on Hancock Street was the parsonage where John Hancock's father, pastor of the church, lived. It was to this house that Hancock had come after he fled Boston.

And it was to this house that Paul Revere rode up in the middle of the night, waking Hancock and telling him to flee further west as the British were coming.

Claire and Andrew both enrolled in local public schools. Claire was in the 8th grade and studied for a year at an excellent school with fine teachers. Even today she says it was a year of inspiration and stretch learning for her and it gave her an idea of how exciting and broadening a good school experience could be.

We were not as fortunate with Andrew. He was in the 5th grade. The school he attended may have been just as good, but, for some reason, he was placed in a classroom of problem kids. Whether slow learners or miscreants or just newcomers, we were never sure. In retrospect, I blame myself for not moving quickly to insist he be moved or, perhaps, placing him in a private school, of which there were many in the area.

I walked to Lexington Green each morning, took the bus into Cambridge, got off steps from the "Ed School," and loved being there, in the heart of Harvard. The Graduate School of Education at Harvard is located in what used to be the campus of Radcliffe College, across Massachusetts Avenue from "the Yard." It was sited in three buildings on Appian Way, one of which was Gutman Library. Most of my classes were in Gutman and the older building, earlier used by Radcliffe, before it was absorbed by Harvard, called Longfellow Hall.

I was often asked what it was like to be a student again after nine years of being a college president. I was the only college president in the student body and thus something of a curiosity. I would reply that it was humbling, and very different. On the humbling part, I remember one day walking up to the main circulation desk and asking if I could sharpen my pencil. I could clearly see a sharpener on the counter behind the attendant. I was told that students were not allowed to sharpen their pencils.

Later, in a history course, I think it was, we took an exam. It was essay type and I was eager to get reliable critique as I strove to focus on my study and writing methods. When the paper came back the remarks in the margin were sophomoric. I marched to the professor's office and asked if he had graded the paper. The answer was no. It had been done by a graduate assistant. I told him I was too old and I was paying too much money (I paid full tuition without any scholarship) to have anyone less than the professor grade my work. If that were not possible, I said I would have to drop the course and take another where it would be. He promised me he would grade papers from then on.

One of my strong prejudices against large state universities can also be directed at some large private universities. Much of the teaching is done by graduate students rather than full-time faculty. That almost never happens in small, private colleges.

I loved being at Harvard. The whole idea of being a student again was positively delightful. I had worked so hard, for nine years, multi-tasking, responding to crises, and working long hours, under terrific pressure and up against great odds. Now I was simply expected to attend class, read books, take exams and write papers. It wasn't child's play, but I would say that compared to what I had been doing it was easier. So focused and intent had I become in my work, so developed had become my powers of concentration, and so used to finding new ideas and workable solutions to problems had I grown, that this was really quite fun.

There was another aspect to it that was fun. I had learned a lot about managing a college, but most of it was experiential learning, trial and error experimentation, and on-the- ground, front-line struggle. Here I was, now, learning theory and rationale for what I already knew to be best practice. Fascinating. And the opposite of the way most others learn such things.

I struggled hard not to be a "show-off" in class or seminar, though I knew that, on occasion, I knew as much as the professor. The professors were good at not putting me on the spot by asking what I had done in a situation similar to that under discussion. Part of what was going on was that though I was the only college president, there were many more very accomplished people. There were school superintendents, experienced teachers, professors of this or that, business people, politicians, etc. Harvard is full of talented people and doesn't get awed easily by any sort or kind. That was good. Indeed, the whole Harvard attitude, of quiet and unassuming awareness of the rich mix of talent in which one finds oneself, was positively thrilling.

Things got off to a bit of a rocky start. I went to see Stephen Bailey, my advisor, and told him of my plan to complete a doctor of education degree in "administration, planning and social policy" by spending just 12 months in residency there. He said that was impossible. I said I had no choice as I was on sabbatical from my job, obligated to return, and did not want to have nothing to show for the work. I asked him to approve my taking an "overload." That meant five courses instead of the usual four. The degree requirements included two academic years (four semesters) of 4 courses each or 16 courses. I planned to take 10 of those between September and June, four more as independent study in the summer (there was no summer school) and the last two as directed study after I had returned to Arkansas. He said that was impossibly ambitious, no one had done it before and he could not possibly agree. I asked if he would allow me to attempt 5 courses that fall, see how I did, and look at options at that point. He very reluctantly agreed.

It was the last conversation I had with him. It was reported that he had been taken ill. Later we learned he had cancer. He died before Christmas. I was very sad, not just that I had lost my advisor, but that I had barely come to know him. I was reassigned to David K. Cohen, a historian of education. He was a very bright, very knowledgeable man. He later co-authored (with two others) a book called "The Shopping Mall High School," which I read and appreciated. After I had finished my degree at Harvard he left and took a position, I think, at Michigan State University.

At the end of the first semester I received my grades for the five courses I had taken, an overload. I got five "A's." I was too old to share this with my parents. I felt obligated to Arkansas College, so grateful was I for the year off and the continued salary, and I knew this could never have happened without Frank Lyon, Sr. I decided to send the grades to him. Little did I imagine that he would tell everyone he knew and moreover, send them to Bill Dunklin at the college. Of course, Bill shared this with the executive staff and anyone else who would listen. I learned this had happened when Bill called me the next Sunday and congratulated me. I was embarrassed.

I spent lots of time in the library between classes, read many books, wrote many papers, prepared for exams, revised notes, and did all that during the "work day," seldom studying at all on weekends or even in the evenings. It was easy, first, because I enjoyed it and was interested in everything I was learning, and second, because I had had to learn to use every minute, juggle many tasks at once, concentrate on the issue at hand, and meet deadlines. I watched classmates struggle with one or more of these tasks, and I realized that my long days of work at the college had prepared me to handle this.

I made a number of friends. We were assigned to "study groups" in some of the classes and I met people that way. My best friend turned out to be a woman named Barclay Bennett, with whom I often ate lunch in the student cafeteria. She was the daughter of a diplomat, very well educated, and descended from a paternal grandmother who was extremely wealthy, with an apartment on Park Avenue. The other grandmother was also wealthy and lived in Georgia. Barclay was single, often unhappy, certain she would fail, but funny, smart, and interesting. There were others, equally interesting, a native American school superintendent, a college admissions director, a woman who was on leave from her college in the Boston area where she was a vice president, and another woman from Maine who had worked as a consultant to help small colleges obtain federal grants, just to name a few.

My two greatest challenges, in the coursework, were: computers and statistics. I had never used a computer and I had never had a course in statistics. With the former it was sink or swim, somewhat like my situation at Annapolis. There were computers on the second floor of Gutman Library and I struggled (as I still do) until I somehow managed to get one of them to work for me. I don't remember ever taking an actual computer course or having any instruction, except from fellow students who would occasionally help out. Statistics was a required course. I hated it. To this day, I do not understand the "null hypothesis." I somehow got through it. It was the only course in which I did not receive an "A"; I got an "A minus."

Other courses were much more interesting. I especially enjoyed the history of education courses, and those in the sociology of education, decision making, strategic planning, and organizational theory, to name just some.

We remained in Lexington for Thanksgiving and Christmas. We had company: Sidney's parents, Claire's friend Ann, the Nelms family from Batesville, and others.

Andrew had a paper route and played soccer. Claire had a close friend, Maureen. Claire and Andrew both learned to ice skate and Andrew learned to ski. Sidney took a course at an art museum and visited many galleries and art museums. We took weekend trips to places like Gloucester, Cape Cod, New York City, and Washington, D.C. and spent lots of weekends on all sides and in the center of Boston.

We mostly attended worship at the Hancock Memorial Church (United Church of Christ) in Lexington. Occasionally we visited a church in Boston. I especially liked Emmanuel Church, Episcopal, on Newbury Street, where, at the conclusion of Matins, the choir and a small orchestra would perform a Bach cantata, every Sunday. I remember attending a service in the "mother church" of the Christian Science Church where there is a magnificent organ, and at Trinity Church where Phillips Brooks had once preached. During the week, I liked to go to the chapel service (held daily) in the Memorial Church in the Yard or the communion service at the nearby Episcopal Seminary.

Sometimes Sidney and I would go to the Kennedy School on Friday afternoon. There would be free beer and pretzels and a visiting speaker, often famous, would declaim, after which the questions were lively. We frequently took the kids to plays and concerts. There were many in Boston.

It was a year of rich experience, great city activity, interesting tourism, and unusual time together as a family, without the constant strain of work and responsibility.

Inevitably the academic year drew to a close in May. I had three months to complete four more courses by "directed study." This meant working out a syllabus with a professor, reading and writing on my own, without lectures or classroom time, and submitting a paper to show what I had learned. It went quickly and I completed that, leaving two more courses to take as "independent study" after I returned to Arkansas.

It would have been easy to break off the project at that point, go back to work, and consider the 12-months odyssey a great success. But, at that point, I had too much time and money invested and was within sight of completing the degree. The program I was enrolled in was designed to begin with two years of residency-based coursework, another year or two of thesis writing, and an oral exam. I was told that some people took five years or more to finish, others never did, and no one finished in less than four years.

Back in Arkansas I finished the two remaining courses by remote direction, with one or two trips back to Harvard to meet with faculty, and wrote the thesis, after getting the proposal approved and sustaining the oral exam. I did this while jumping back into my work at the college. I got up very early most mornings, sometimes worked in the evenings and often studied on the weekends.

My thesis was entitled "Additional Resources for Financing Small Colleges in the 1980s." It was inspired by our work with Aberdeen (the brainchild of Richard Thomas) which enjoyed the enthusiastic and crucial support of Frank Lyon and Shuford Nichols, and also by what I had learned about similar projects at such places as Grinnell College in Iowa.

Professor Cohen was my mentor and advisor and I'm glad of that. He was an exacting critic, often made me rewrite, and taught me a lot about research, analysis, organization, sequence, and writing style. I finished the book, it was accepted, and I received the degree in June 1984.

Chapter 21

Back in Arkansas

We left Lexington in mid-August, 1982, to drive back to Arkansas and the college. Awaiting us was a remodeled house. Marion Lyon had taken it upon herself to do that, and Sidney had made three trips back to work with her on the project. She had moved the front wall of the living and dining rooms to give more space for entertaining.

She had done a new entrance with a columned porch and a circular drive off the street. She had closed in the garage and installed a door. The interior of the place had been refreshed with new paint, refinished floors, window treatments, and furniture, all selected, paid for, and installed by Marion. It was a magnificent gift and we loved everything she'd done. The children, for example, had new furniture in each of their bedrooms. Later, when we left the college, Marion produced saved receipts documenting the value of what she had given to the college, and I set up an installment-pay arrangement so we could purchase the furniture from the college. It took several years to pay it off, but we finally did so.

During my absence, the college had learned that Miss Jean Brown had left a bequest of about $16 million! Bill Dunklin actually received a check for $14.3 million one day, more money in one check than anybody had ever seen. The addition of this much money to the endowment was a huge boost for our finances. For several years, all scholarships were fully funded, as opposed to being discounts. There was no more cash flow issue. Our balance sheets were great. The feeling of relief and gratitude and confidence this gave me was enormous. Not to have to worry constantly how and when and from where we would get funds to pay for things was a huge development.

But still the enrollment was not where it should be. I had thought long and hard about this, of course, while I was away. I knew that the sabbatical could not, in the end, be just for my benefit, just for winning another degree. I had to return with a strategy to move us forward.

The overall strategy, largely unwritten but firmly in my head, included first, I had to do what I could to delay (the eventual outcome was inevitable) the advent of a state-owned community college in Independence County. This meant continuation of our part-time, adult and continuing education program, aggressive recruiting in the local area, and generous financial aid for full-time students. It also meant aggressive lobbying with state agencies and officials. Secondly, we had no choice except to continue the blend of career education and liberal learning we had worked so hard to establish. Third, we had to resume aggressive fund raising. I knew the infusion of Miss Brown's money would provide only temporary respite for us. That meant another campaign as soon as possible and, meanwhile, aggressive annual fund, capital and planned giving efforts, as well as active efforts to win federal, state and private foundation grants. In short, much more of the same as we had done from 1972 to 1981. Fourth, we had to step up efforts to establish an additional, innovative, income source. This meant expanding the Aberdeen Development Corporation. Finally, we had to find a way to increase the enrollment.

Let me pause to explain Aberdeen. It was the brainchild of Richard Thomas. It was a for-profit, wholly-owned subsidiary of Arkansas College. It was intended to pay federal and state corporate income tax when it made a profit, and its after-tax profits inured wholly to the college. We had learned that such structures existed in a few other places in the country. We had worked with lawyers at the Rose Form to incorporate it. We had six directors, three of whom, Messrs. Lyon, Nichols and Bellingrath, were also trustees of the college. Another three were friends and supporters, but not trustees. I was president of Aberdeen. Richard Thomas was vice president.

For the most difficult challenge, expanding enrollment, I had borrowed an idea which was already in place at two other small private colleges I knew about: the cluster college idea. This meant establishing separate and distinct programs, within the same institution, for full-time, resident undergraduates; part-time, adult, non-traditional, continuing education students; graduate programs (e.g. in education or business); and a high school academy that would act as a feeder.

I introduced the idea to the executive staff, the Education Committee of the Board, a faculty committee or two, and finally the entire Board. My concept met with polite attention but no enthusiasm. The Board was cool to the idea. The faculty representative to the Board, in a dismissive way, said it simply wouldn't work because the college was "too small."

I think I was not surprised, but I was nonetheless discouraged. As I look back I believe that was the beginning of a slow evolution in my thinking that led to the eventual conclusion that it was time for me to move on. It took another five years (instead of the three I was obligated for) before that happened, but I knew it had to occur. The problems of limited enrollment, a business plan that did not work, and a market that was unresponsive to our product in an environment that did not really want what we had to offer, were too intractable.

So, I directed energy to the parts of the strategy that were already in place plus Aberdeen, which did not require faculty approval. And, we were successful. When I left, in 1988, there was yet no community college, enrollment, including part-time students, was at an all-time high, Aberdeen was successful and had the potential to do much more, and the budget was balanced.

A highlight of the year in 1983 was the appearance on campus of former President Jimmy Carter as the Hodges Lecturer. Kaneaster Hodges, Jr., an attorney (and also a Methodist minister) in Newport, AR, was a trustee of the college who had been appointed by Gov. David Pryor to fill out the unexpired term of Sen. McClellan, who had died.

Sen. Hodges set up the Hodges Lecture Series in memory of his father and brought, first, Sen. Edward Kennedy, and then President Carter as the first speakers in this series.

That year, 1983-84, was also a pivotal one for the Aberdeen Development Corp., the for-profit subsidiary we had established to try to earn additional income that would inure to the college. Aberdeen purchased almost 1,550 acres of prime real estate on the eastern edge of Batesville. Also, the capital funds campaign to raise $6 million exceeded its goal and was concluded in October. The college attracted media attention and was the subject of an article in The Wall Street Journal, among other newspapers. It was the most successful year ever for the college athletics program. Men's basketball reached the semi-finals for the NAIA play-offs in Kansas City. A concert band was organized in September.

On the other hand, there were discouraging shortfalls. The enrollment remained small, despite our contract with Dagley and Associates to recruit more students. We continued to argue about Independence College (that's what I called the proposed continuing education program) and a graduate program in education. The faculty opposed both and there was little support among the board either. North Arkansas Community College attempted to establish an extension center at Batesville High School. We were unsuccessful in strenuous efforts to recruit leadership for the Business Management Program.

I had completed my doctoral thesis for the Doctor of Education degree at Harvard and was awarded the degree in June, 1984. Not only were Sidney, Claire and Andrew with me in Cambridge, but also Frank and Marion Lyon. The latter two flattered and surprised me with their attendance.

I had the satisfaction of finishing the degree program in three years instead of the usual four or five many took to complete the thesis and course work. Of course, I did not have the luxury of remaining in residence at Harvard for four years and I had pressing duties at the college which made it important to complete the work and get the degree, which I was determined to do. It was a great thrill to go back to Harvard for Commencement, surely one of the most colorful and tradition-filled such ceremonies in the country.

Sidney purchased a Harvard gown and hood for me to wear. I remember riding the T (public transport) from downtown to Harvard Square and, after seeing the family and the Lyons to their seats, I walked out to Mass Av, as it is called, and around the perimeter of the Yard to the place at the right corner of the platform where the Ed School grads were. As I walked I remember being absolutely elated. Could it be that my dream of earning a degree at Harvard, first formed in 1957, was now to occur? What an amazing turn of events had me there at that moment! My fourth earned degree. Such a moment.

In the fall of 1984, the headcount enrollment was the largest ever in the college's history, 724, but, of course, about 300 of those were part-time students. The social work concentration won national accreditation, the endowment grew to $33 million and the Synod of the Sun, Presbyterian Church, U.S.A (comprising the states of Arkansas, Louisiana, Oklahoma and Texas) met on campus for the first time.

Harvard, 1984

The major disappointment that year was Richard Thomas' decision to leave. He was hired away by the president of Mercer University in Georgia. According to Richard, the man did not bother to ask him what we were paying him, saying that whatever it was he would double it. How could Richard turn that down?

He'd been hired by Arkansas College just before I was in 1972, still a very young 27. He'd worked tirelessly for 13 years, stretching dollars, understaffed, always searching for new ideas to save money or enhance revenue. He'd created the Aberdeen Development

Corporation, overseen the construction of all nine new buildings, acquired Lock & Dam #3 on the river for Aberdeen, secured low interest loans from three federal agencies and much more. His loyalty to me and to the college was never in question. So valuable had he made himself that one trustee urged and won trustee approval to take out a life insurance policy on his life with the college as beneficiary. His departure was a huge setback for me and the college.

He moved to Atlanta to be president of Penfield Corp., a for-profit subsidiary of Mercer University, copying Aberdeen. However, the man who hired him had not told some of his trustees what he was doing and the corporation, president of the university and Richard all ran into stiff opposition. He left after only a year and joined Merrill Lynch, where he has had a very successful career ever since. He managed the largest portion of our personal investments until he retired in 2017. Such a talent.

Meanwhile I personally took on far too many outside responsibilities. I was a member of the national Presbyterian Church's Mission Responsibility Through Investments Committee. I was Vice President of the Association of Presbyterian Colleges and began working to establish a new General Assembly Committee on Higher Education. I was given an honorary doctor's degree by Buena Vista College in Iowa. Sidney and I began a series of summer seminars at Troutbeck, NY, sponsored by a foundation in New York City and comprising college presidents and their spouses, discussing the great books and contemporary issues. I was on the board of the Council of Independent Colleges and was elected to the Board of Directors of First National Bank in Batesville. I was also elected to the board of the Batesville Area Chamber of Commerce and chaired a project called "Independence 200 – Goals for Progress." I was part of the faculty in two workshops, sponsored by the National Association of College and University Business Offices, on developing new sources of revenue for colleges.

All of this, as well as other involvement I continued from previous years added up to too much. I stayed away from campus and family a lot. Of course, every involvement gave me valuable exposure to wider worlds of religion, education and business. They added greatly to my knowledge bank and management tool kit. But, in retrospect, I am sure it was too much.

Then why did I do all that? I desperately wanted the college to be better respected and more widely known. I needed the intellectual stimulation. I needed the interaction with other venues and groups than just the college. I must have imagined that I needed greater exposure, personally, if I was to be noticed for a future career move. And, overall, I think I imagined I was making a contribution to each organization. My final observation on this, in retrospect, is that it made it possible for me to stay in Batesville and at the college for another five years after returning from sabbatical, before moving.

In the spring of 1985 we finished remodeling the Alphin Building. Originally the dining hall, built during Paul McCain's time, it was a lovely Georgian structure, at the northeast corner of Brown Chapel. With the help of the Truemper Architectural firm of Little Rock, we installed a second floor, converted the first to classrooms, art gallery and studio (where the kitchen had been), and made the second-floor faculty offices with a lovely faculty lounge that had a balcony overlooking a garden. The Alphin Room, on the ground floor (a perfect double cube) became the board room and the meeting place for the faculty. Donors were honored with plaques on nearly every door. Robert Young's Arkansas Best Corp. donated the furniture. Sidney and Marion Lyon worked tirelessly on décor, furniture and design. It was beautiful, one of the most elegant academic facilities I have seen. Thanks to Elizabeth Bowe Sims of Hot Springs the east end (a blank brick wall) had attached to it a wonderful garden with a fountain surrounded by a vine covered pergola, inspired by the cloister of Mont Saint Michel in France. I was very proud of all this.

Our physical plant really had become the most attractive campus in Arkansas and among the most beautiful small college campuses in the country.

Chapter

Children

Claire and Andrew grew up in an unusual – if not somewhat rarified – environment that often resembled, or at least felt like, the proverbial fish bowl. I am happy to report that both not only survived the experience but have come into adulthood in stellar fashion.

Claire was only 4 ½ when we moved from Sherman to Batesville. The next year she started elementary school in Batesville and was graduated from Batesville High School in 1986. Always a good student, active in the church, an enthusiastic tennis player, with several close friends, she had a happy childhood and youth in Batesville, free of the problems that challenge so many young people and their parents. She seems so well adjusted today, so secure in herself, confident, talented, always multi-tasking, a great mother. That must have been a good time in her life. She remains loyal to Batesville and has returned for all of her school reunions.

Despite Claire's overall good experience, Sidney and I worried about the quality of the schools in Batesville. There were no private schools in town and no private boarding schools in Arkansas. In addition to summer trips to other parts of the country and three trips to Europe, we arranged for her and Andrew to do a two-week computer workshop in the Hockaday School, Dallas. Another summer, she was chosen for the Governor's School at Hendrix College. One year she was chosen as a Presidential Scholar and went to Washington, D.C. as part of a program for high school students. We sent her to Choate Rosemary Hall, a prestigious private boarding school in Connecticut that had a six-week summer program.

She and I flew to LaGuardia and drove over to Choate. The campus was beautiful, she enjoyed the classes, and she made some friends from elsewhere whom she enjoyed. But, unluckily, she drew a very poor excuse for a roommate. The young woman was from a wealthy family in New York City and probably did not want to be there. She acted not only as though she was superior to Claire, but also as though she was offended that she had a roommate from Arkansas! Claire was also offended, could not wait to come home and was appalled that anyone could act that way.

I have often said that one of the attributes of both of our children that I am very proud of is the absence, in them, of any snobbery or pretense. They are both able to talk easily with persons of any class, race, or level of accomplishment, without a trace of condescension. Maybe this experience drove that home to Claire, but I think she had that trait already.

She is very bright, a quick study, sensitive, resourceful, and has a great memory. She has no reason to take second place to anyone her age, and that experience in the east discouraged her from any serious thought of private school away from home. She was glad to get back to her family, her own school, and her friends in Batesville. She was graduated from Batesville High School in 1986.

During Claire's senior year, she and I drove to Washington University in St. Louis, which she really liked. She applied and was accepted. She also applied to Rice University, and was accepted. I had applied there and been rejected. I had always respected it as probably the best private institution in Texas. Claire applied, at our suggestion, and was accepted.

We drove her to Houston, pulling a U-Haul full of her clothes, and helped her move in. It was very difficult to leave her. I remember thinking it could not be possible that eighteen years had flown by since that joyous day in Tennessee in 1968. We were very proud of her.

Claire lived in a freshman dorm and made some friends, but it was not a happy year for her. There were two huge problems. She wanted to major in the humanities, but majors in the sciences, math, and engineering felt superior. Rice had been Rice Institute through most of its existence. It was not yet as comprehensive a place as it is now. She felt out of place, over her head, not really "part of." Also her roommate was incompatible. Claire wanted to come home at the end of the first semester. I urged her to stick it out till the end of the year, which she bravely did, and then we would help her transfer elsewhere.

She said she'd be happy to come to Arkansas College, but we knew that was impossible given my position. What she really wanted was to find a small college in a big city. We thought of Agnes Scott in Decatur which is really a suburb of Atlanta. She transferred there, became a history major, did well, made two lifelong friends in her roommates, Jennifer and Tracy, and was graduated in 1990. I think Agnes Scott can be credited with teaching her independence, building self-confidence, and helping her to be well read and broadly exposed to the world of ideas – all the things that women's colleges say they can provide and all the things that small, independent, liberal arts colleges make available to their students. Claire was already poised, loyal, smart, friendly, and well-travelled. To these traits, she added a fine education and plenty of confidence. She was ready to make her own way, and she has.

Another characteristic of both of our children that I am immensely proud of is their work ethic. When each of them went off to college I promised them we would pay all of their expenses, including travel, tuition, boarding, books, and fees, but we wanted them each to have a part-time job and earn their own spending money; they each did that, every year. Once, while Claire was at Agnes Scott, she got a job as a messenger for a local attorney. It was in the day before faxes and e-mail or even Fed Ex. She drove all over Atlanta. She learned the multiplex well and, to this day, she is almost never lost.

Andrew, too, had a happy childhood. He had a small number of very close friends; he is still in touch with at least one of them, David Nelms. He loved sports, especially Little League baseball, tennis, swimming, soccer, and football. He and David built forts and clubhouses down the bluff from the house where we lived. He knew lots of people on campus, where he often played. He was active in the church, was in the Boy Scouts and loved organizing his friends into such things as football teams and a summer baseball league. He was always busy. He had projects and plans and schedules.

Claire's wedding in 1995

As he entered junior high school, we became aware that his grades were not particularly good; he didn't read much, had trouble spelling, and wasn't able to write as well as he should.

During my sabbatical year 1981-82, Curtis Baggett, the Director of Admission at McCallie School, Chattanooga, Tennessee, asked if perhaps Andrew would be interested in going there. He suggested a summer school to "try it out." So, one of the summers after we returned to Arkansas, Andrew attended, took courses in English and geometry, and loved the sports program. Later, when we asked him if he'd like to apply there, he already knew the place.

In junior high, Andrew wanted to play football. We worried about that. After he got hurt a bit, we insisted he drop off the team. I think it was a huge disappointment for him. Sports, for boys at least, was everything in Batesville, far more important than academics.

He applied to McCallie, was accepted, and entered the tenth grade there in 1986, at the age of 15. I am sure the hardest thing Sidney and I ever did was driving him to McCallie and telling him goodbye. There was no tradition in either of our families of a child going away to boarding school. We were a very close-knit family. Claire had already left to go to college and now suddenly, too early, we were without either child. And what about Andrew? He had left his friends and family and the place he loved and, once again, after being uprooted in 1981, moved to a new, strange place where he had to start all over. We worried about him mightily.

But the most amazing thing happened. He called one night, not long after he had enrolled. He had a young English teacher, a man who may have stayed there only one year, who had inspired and motivated him. He was writing papers, reading, spelling better. We were elated.

McCallie was not easy for Andrew, but he handled the structure and the discipline and the emphasis on study and learning well. Though he had no chance to meet girls, he was popular with his classmates. He thrived on the sports program (especially soccer) and he had several teachers who lit up his imagination and built his curiosity. He learned to write, and he became a reader, like the rest of the family. He did well and when he was graduated in 1989, we were all three enormously proud of him. He had already been accepted for admission to Emory University.

Andrew, too, remained loyal to Batesville and has returned for reunions of his class, with whom he did not graduate. Indeed, this brings up another trait both of our children have, of which I am proud. They are both intensely loyal, to their families, friends, schools, hometown, church, employers, any organization with which they have become associated.

Andrew is extremely well organized, careful in his dress and appearance, happy to talk with anyone he meets, ever respectful of everyone around him, scrupulously honest, works hard at whatever he does, is creative and inventive in his work, and always operates with great integrity. I believe that much of this was developed at McCallie and then at Emory, where he took on leadership responsibility in his fraternity, the Kappa Alpha Order.

In 1990, as Claire approached graduation from college and she told us that she wanted to stay in Atlanta, we purchased a condominium in Decatur, borrowing the money from the Waukesha State Bank, on whose board I served as a director. It was an investment; we knew it was wise to own some real estate and begin building equity, something we didn't have because we had always lived in college housing. Claire and various friends lived there and rented from us. Andrew did also during his senior year at Emory and then when he was graduated from Emory.

We sold the condo and bought a house in the Winona Park area of Decatur. Claire and Andrew both lived there as renters with various roommates until Claire moved out to get married and Andrew eventually got his own place.

Claire and Andrew have chosen their own different careers for themselves. I think Sidney and I did not try to influence or guide them in this at all. I have sometimes looked at others whose children "followed" them into their own profession or occupation and wondered about that. Of course, I am certain that either of our children could have been very effective either in the ministry or in some part of education and maybe that might have happened had circumstances been different with one or both of them. I am pleased, on the other hand, that they have made their own way and stood on their own feet.

Claire worked as a nanny, a secretary, an administrative assistant, and finally settled into the technology industry. She entered that field when she got a job as a technical writer with a programming company called Radiant Systems. She worked as an account executive in the Hospitality Specialty Retail division of NCR in Atlanta for seventeen years. She is now a Business Analyst for Revel Systems.

Andrew began working for Emory Healthcare as a part-time file clerk while still a student. Later, his first full-time job was with Wesley Woods, the geriatric division of Emory Healthcare. He has continued to work for Emory since, except for two years when he was a consultant an accounting firm in Atlanta., BDO Seidmann. After Emory, he earned two master's degrees at Georgia State University in Atlanta, an MBA and an MHA (Master of Healthcare Administration). He is now Senior Administrator for the Georgia Clinical and Translational Science Alliance, at Emory University School of Medicine.

In 2000, at the age of 29, after earning a B.A. and two master's degrees, he volunteered for the Marine Corps Reserve. He went through basic training at Parris Island, South Carolina, and has remained in the USMC Reserve since. His billets have been Embarkation Specialist, Logistics Chief, and now First Sergeant. At the beginning of the Iraqi War, he was activated for six months and stationed at Miramar Marine Air Base, near San Diego. He was in charge of loading airplanes with equipment, ammunition, armaments and Marines. In 2013, he was activated for a year, and, for six months, he was stationed at Camp Leatherneck, Helmand Province, Afghanistan. On this tour, he was part of the effort to load planes and trucks with Marines and their equipment in retrograde movement from the country. He has been promoted several times and is now a First Sergeant, assigned to Marine

Artillery Battery M, 3rd Battalion, 14th Marines, 4th Marine Division, in Chattanooga.

He is single and lives in a high-rise condo in downtown Atlanta.

Claire married Peter Paddock in 1995. They divorced, amicably, in 1997, without children. She married Chuck Jones in 2001. They have two children, our grandchildren. Shelby Louise Jones was born June 18, 2002. Dalton Ellis Jones was born December 3, 2004. They were divorced in 2018.

Andrew, 2010

Claire, 1986

Chapter 23

Arkansas College: The Final Years

The teacher education programs, both elementary and secondary won national accreditation from the National Council for the Accreditation of Teacher Education (NCATE). I'm sure we were one of the smallest programs in the country to be so approved. Helen McCallie, whom we had met when we were at McCallie School to pick up Andrew from summer school, became my Assistant to the President. This was a new, much needed post, and she made a huge difference, almost immediately. Dick Valentine became Dean of Admissions and the enrollment began to inch up. Johnny Mitchum had taken over from Richard Thomas as vice president for finance and executive of Aberdeen Development Corporation. He managed to float a $3.5 million bond issue that made almost $2.5 million available to us for much needed repairs to campus facilities. He became very active with Aberdeen, selling a Kroger store we had bought in Alabama, at a good profit, and negotiating with Independence County officials on the hydroelectric power project we wanted to start with the two dams we now owned on the river. Most impressive of all, he managed an audit by the Internal Revenue Service, of Aberdeen, that ended in a "no change" letter.

In another surprising bit of affirmation, the college appeared in an issue of U.S. News and World Report among a ranking of "smaller, comprehensive colleges in the south." We were ranked eighth, and we were the only institution of any kind in the state of Arkansas to be listed in any ranking.

There was another grant from the Title III program ("developing institutions") which brought the amount received by us from this source to a total of well over $3 million.

U. S. Senator Dale Bumpers was the commencement speaker. We appeared in a very favorable feature story in the "Baltimore Sun" which highlighted our management practices and our innovative finance activity. And, I was asked to co-author a book published by the National Association of College and University Business Officers on capital formation and capital management for colleges and universities. The book contained five case studies, including Arkansas College, and was modeled on my Harvard dissertation.

I also wrote a chapter for a book published by D. H. Dagley on professional renewal for the college president (based on my sabbatical experience) that went into a book on small college administration called "Courage in Mission."

We finally hired a Barton Professor of Business to head the Business Management Program, Bill Weber, who came from Agnes Scott College, to teach economics. The endowment reached a market value of $40 million. We launched the quiet phase of a capital campaign that was intended to raise $50 million. I hired a new Vice President for Institutional Advancement, Darrell Loyless from Centenary College in Shreveport.

We reorganized the administrative structure of the college into five "service components:" academic, marketing, student, support, and Aberdeen, with a vice president heading each and reporting to me.

As I entered what would be my final year at the college I could see dramatic gains in almost every area, every aspect of the college. Aside from the chronic shortfall in numbers of full-time students, the quality and reputation of the place was far greater than at any time in its past. The faculty was far stronger and better. So was the staff and the top leadership. The campus, physically, was modern, attractive and in excellent repair.

The institution was financially viable.

Personally, I knew it was time to leave. I had fulfilled by more than a year my commitment to stay past the sabbatical. I felt I had accomplished as much as I could. A certain repetition in the events and issues of each passing year began to appear. I knew I could leave with a strong sense of accomplishment, and no one could gainsay the advances that had been made. I longed to be in a larger and more dynamic place, and a different location. Both of our children had gone off to school.

I began to see that the longer I stayed the greater the danger that, on the one hand, the college might become too dependent on me, by then its second longest tenured leader. And, on the other hand, I worried that I might become less flexible, less creative, trying to protect my ideas and policies (some of which had already been rejected), and treating the place as "mine" in some sense.

There was another factor. I had been contacted, or recruited, or interviewed, or even offered a job, by a number of other colleges. I worried that if I turned down another and another, I might not get asked anymore. I needed a new challenge and a new venue and, unlike the surprising new opportunities that had come my way before, nothing seemed to be coming up at that point.

Aside from Sidney, I confided to no one except for Allen Smith, a close friend and someone I knew I could trust. I should have gone to Sherman and talked things through with John D. Moseley, by now retired, but still vital.

Our final year at the college, 1987-88, was the 116th year of its history, and my 16th as president. I had lived there longer than anywhere else in my lifetime.

The most important event of the year was the resignation of Frank Lyon, Sr., as board chairman. He had wanted to follow the example of Shuford Nichols and step down a year earlier, after 10 years as chair. I begged him to stay and he relented and served one more year.

I cannot recall if I knew at the time what impact this had on me psychologically, but I am certain it was not positive. First Shuford Nichols and then Frank had been my staunchest supporters, my rocks of stability through many tempests, and my mentors and chief advisers. Even though both men would remain on the board, I felt,

I'm sure, less secure, a bit more vulnerable. This important transition must have strengthened my growing conviction that it was time for me, too, to depart.

Frank had become another father, closer in every way, than I had been to any other male before. He seemed to treat me as a second son. I felt his respect, affection, and trust, as a solid base, an anchor of confidence. I would learn, in the years ahead, just how important this had been, and how difficult it would be to manage without it.

I have already commented on his character and personality and wisdom. I will add just this. He never displayed anger or irritation with me or about anything I said or did. He never refused or failed to do anything I asked him to do for the college. And, he unfailingly demonstrated for me, an example of strength, wisdom, civility and honesty.

For my part, I never took him for granted. I never presumed on his friendship or generosity. I never misrepresented anything to him. And I never questioned his authority or judgment. Our trust of each other was complete. Our dealings were always above board. Our conversations were direct, plain, and guileless. It was a rare, even unique, relationship. It was similar to what I had known with John D. Moseley and Shuford Nichols, but it was more so, deeper, better.

The mentorship of Moseley had made possible my entrance into higher education administration. The mentorship of Nichols and Lyon had made possible whatever I accomplished at Arkansas College. Ironically, those 20 years of working for and with three exceptional men made me vulnerable and, in an important way, weakened my ability to deal with less principled, less honorable superiors. This insight has come to me, as I write. It is another example of the way constructing this memoir has driven me into introspection and clarity about what events occurred and the significance of what happened.

The trustees and I settled on Robert Young as our choice for the new chair. Fortunately, he agreed to do it. I had first recruited him to the board years before. I remembered asking him for his first gift of $1,000. He was a graduate of Lawrenceville School in New Jersey and Washington and Lee in Virginia. He had inherited the presidency of Arkansas Best Corporation, a trucking firm, from his father. He had married the granddaughter of a governor of Arkansas, the daughter of a graduate of the college. He was an active Presbyterian elder in Ft. Smith. He took hold, as chair of the board, quickly and well.

We lost two stalwarts on the board that year: W. D. Murphy, Jr. and Nels Barnett. They had been part of the Batesville group of trustees who had guided and held on as the college struggled through the hard years of Spragins, McCain and Wygle. They were admirable men. My esteem for Murphy was great. I knew no attorney who was more honest or selfless or smart. Barnett was equally impressive. Both were not just respected; they were loved by many in Batesville. Both were devout Methodists, serving a Presbyterian college all those years out of civic pride and vision, and also because it was the alma mater of each. I remember both with great affection.

In October 1987, the stock market plunged. Unlike many who feared for their personal fortunes, I thought only of the effect on the college's hard-won endowment. It reminds me of the way in which, during 20 years of college presidencies, I worried far more about the institutions I served than my own career or welfare, or even that of my family. That was a mistake.

Fortunately, because of the skill and prescience of trustees who oversaw the management of the endowment (I think particularly of Holloway, Dunklin and Nichols), while we lost market value (about $3.5 million, in fact) we had moved money into cash equivalents and bonds and averted even greater losses. There was some rebound, and within seven months or so we gained almost a million back. But, that taught me two things about investing. You cannot make money without taking risks and some speculation. But, you have to be diversified and balanced enough to avoid disaster if there is a big correction.

At some point, I was contacted by a search consultant who asked if I would consider the presidency of Carroll College, in Waukesha, just west of Milwaukee, Wisconsin. That happened because Bob

Cramer, the president of Carroll, who was retiring, knew me from our common membership on the board of the Council of Independent Colleges. I said I would talk with them.

The chairman of the Board came to interview me at the college. He was an alumnus, and a close friend of Bob Cramer. Later I was invited to interview at the college and then, a second visit, with Sidney, was arranged. They offered me the job.

Sidney did not want to go. There were two "red flags" for her. First, she did not like or trust the Board chair. And she has always been a better judge of character than I. Second, there was a point, in the meeting on campus between the search committee and the two of us, when the question of my clergy status came up, and it was clear that some on the faculty saw that as a problem. (two presidents just before Cramer had been ministers and one had had a short tenure). Sidney saw that as a problem. I should have listened to her. But, I'm reminded of something Richard Bode said, "We see only what we are ready to see when we are ready to see it."

I wanted to go forward for the reasons I've already mentioned. I was intrigued with the idea of heading another Presbyterian college, with no enrollment problem, in a large metropolitan area. I saw a chance to experience another part of the country, another culture and political climate, in a respected state with a prosperous economy and a progressive tradition. It was time to leave. I might not get offered as good an opportunity again. I'm a risk taker, and, as Beverly Sills once said, "You may be disappointed if you fail, but you are doomed if you don't try."

Nonetheless, it was a hard choice. My father, for one, simply could not understand why I would leave, after working so hard to get where we were at the college. So many things had gone well, and, in that year, more good things were happening. So much had been gained, at a huge cost. Surely there would be other offers. What would happen to Arkansas College? How could two Southerners bear to live in such cold winters? What kind of adjustment would it take for us to live in a very different culture?

I decided to go, in the face of Sidney's reluctance. She acceded, bravely and loyally. But, two of the hardest things we've ever done together, were calling first on Laura and Shuford Nichols and then on Frank and Marion Lyon to tell them of our decision.

Sidney found it especially hard to tell Marion. They had become very close. Motivated, I think, largely by her love for Sidney, Marion had made the college her project. She had worked without stint, paying for much of what she did out of her own pocket. After we left she built a beautiful president's house. Fittingly, she was awarded an honorary degree, after we left, in recognition of all she had done.

Frank and Shuford, in a last-ditch effort, to retain me, called me to Little Rock, days later, to meet with just the two of them, and they tried to argue me into staying. In my mind, though, I'd already left and though I promised to rethink, and did, I chose to leave.

Although it turned out not to be the right decision, at least in the choice of the place where we went, it was ultimately true that it was time to leave. I have spent no time wondering what might have been had we stayed. I know of a handful of small college presidents who had stayed too long and I did not want that for the college or for me. Also, my career, though sidetracked for years by what happened at Carroll, ultimately ended far better than either of us could have imagined at the time.

I don't remember any relaxation of effort, after the March decision to leave at the end of August. There was no lessening of our interest in or dedication to Arkansas College.

In April, the board approved a $50 million universal campaign. By the end of June, we had $12 million in pledges (including $5 million from the Lyon family), mostly from trustees. It was folly to expect this to go forward and it didn't, but I naively expected it to do so.

John Dahlquist returned from a well-earned fall sabbatical, in England and Massachusetts, and resumed his duties as academic dean. His substitute had been Bob Carius, a retired rear admiral in the U.S. Navy, and an assistant professor of physics, who had done a superb job.

We hired the first Black faculty member, Clara Jennings, as R. C. Bryan Distinguished Professor of Education. She stayed one year.

That year the faculty included twenty-nine people with earned doctorates, a record. (There were 13 when I arrived in 1972.) The number of endowed faculty positions, professorships and chairs, reached 15 (from zero in the early seventies).

Roberta Brown retired after 44 years of service to the college, working with four presidents. She had more institutional memory than any person then alive. She had worked tirelessly and very successfully to obtain millions in federal and private foundation grants. She was among the kindest, most gracious, most selfless people I knew. She remains a huge figure among the college's panoply of heroes.

We finished redecorating all of the dormitories. We firmly established a mentor program for students and set up a fitness center in Edwards Commons.

Johnny Mitchum and I worked together and managed to persuade Arkansas Power and Light Co. to donate Lock and Dam #2 on the river, to the college.

Gaston Johnson of New York City, a native of Ft. Smith and a graduate of Dartmouth College, left about $1.25 million in a bequest for an endowed scholarship, and named me as his co-executor.

Ralph Graham resigned and moved back to Texas. He had established the Scottish Arts Program, which continues even now. That year it attracted 4,000 to the campus. It was, by far, the most successful thing ever, in garnering local and in-state media attention and visitors from elsewhere. It has helped the image and brand of the college.

Marge Dowser retired, a milestone.

Helen McCallie, reached a peak of effectiveness and acceptance, as Assistant to the President, and became executive secretary for the presidential search committee.

Using the precedent set by Bill Dunklin and before him by Nels Barnet, another trustee, Graham Holloway of Dallas, agreed to take a leave from his company, and be Acting President, and move, with his wife Carolyn, to Batesville for six months!

There were two very hard funerals for us. The Holloways' son, Graham, Jr., was killed in an auto wreck while returning to the college where he was a student. I preached his funeral in Dallas. We'd become close to that family. I'd worked closely with his father, Graham, and grew to like him immensely. Sidney and Carolyn had traveled together, getting ideas for a new theater (the college's first), which she and Graham had agreed to pay for. The other funeral, in Batesville, was for John Edwards, a retired laundry and cleaners' owner, and a major stockholder in First National Bank.

Sidney and I, over years of friendship with John and his second wife, Bernice (also widowed when they married) had encouraged them first to pay for the organ in Brown Chapel and then to make the lead gift for the student union, and then to commit to a bequest. His estate, after death, paid for most of a new dormitory and left his house to the college. This from a man who had never given anything to anybody before we met. The total amount of his giving may still rank as the largest amount from a Batesville donor.

That philanthropy is one of my proudest accomplishments and one of the most dramatic "turnarounds" or conversions, if you like. Thinking about it reminds me of the huge satisfaction to be gained from leading people of wealth into philanthropy. It literally changes lives. John Edwards was changed. He discovered that giving money away was not only fun, but it gave him new purpose and meaning. He had no children. His first wife died. He adopted the college as his cause. He died knowing he'd done something far more important and lasting than just making a lot of money.

I once heard a preacher tell of a wealthy man who had died and after his funeral two of his friends stood on the street as the hearse drove by. One friend asked the other, "How much money do you think he left behind?" The other answered, "All of it."

The Lyon Family, Frank, Sr., Marion and Frank, Jr. agreed to build a new business building. They pledged $5 million. That was, at the time, the largest single commitment ever made to the college by a living donor. Shuford Nichols pledged $1.5 million to endow a new honors international studies program.

But that was not all that happened in a very eventful year. A new campus development plan was prepared and adopted. It proposed annexes to the Smith Science Building and Edwards

Dining Hall, the administration building and the Becknell Physical Education Building. It also projected new buildings for business, the social sciences, and education, a theater and four new residence halls.

Hillary Clinton was awarded an honorary degree at Commencement.

A record budget of almost $8.5 million was adopted for the next year. Marion Lyon and Roberta Brown were voted honorary degree recipients for commencement in 1989. A new dormitory, to cost $400,000, was voted, by the board. The headcount enrollment reached over 750, an all-time high (though the full-time count was just 440).

So many encouraging, even exciting things happened in that last of our years there.

In late May, Sidney and I attended another Troutbeck program, this one at a resort in Asheville, North Carolina. While there we met Roger and Annie Hull, then of Beloit, Wisconsin. He was president of Beloit College. We became friends with them. This presaged a most important development for us, years later.

In mid-June, we toured China, as guests of the Chinese Association for International Friendly Exchange. That happened when Harry Smith, president of Austin College, invited us to accompany him and his second wife, Etta, on a two-week tour. We visited Beijing, Hangzhou, Nanjing, Guangzhou and Shenzhen City. We also saw Hong Kong and Tokyo. While we were in China we visited three universities. It was just before the Tiananmen Square demonstrations. It was also our only trip to China. Fascinating. The Lyons gave us the money for the air travel there and back, as a going-away present. The Chinese government paid all our expenses, including car and driver and guides, while we were there.

Later, I learned something about the Chinese system. As president of Carroll College, I was contacted, then visited, by the man who headed the escort/guide team for our visit. He asked for admission and a full scholarship to Carroll, for his son. It was clear he expected this as a quid pro quo for our expense-paid visit to his country. I explained that his son would have to apply for both admission and financial aid and also told him that our funds to aid foreign students were very limited (neither federal nor state grants were possible), but I promised to see what we could do. I heard nothing further from him.

We left the college and Batesville in August, in a two-vehicle (our personal car and Andrew's) procession, for Wisconsin. Claire had a job and could not be away. Andrew got enlisted to help since he was out of school for the summer.

In the last president's report, I wrote, for that year, I expressed appreciation for what Sidney had done. I'd never done that before even though I'd wanted to do so. I said that there had been no harder worker, advocate, friend of the college than she, for the previous 16 years. She'd given heart and soul, all the while raising two great kids. She'd sacrificed a lot. She hadn't complained. Her work was clear for all to see and admire, none more than I.

I also paid tribute to all of the trustees with whom I'd worked. I said they'd been the key to whatever extent I'd been successful. And that their friendship and support had been at the heart of everything positive that had happened.

I also listed some "things I have learned" while I was in Arkansas. Since they are illustrations of my leadership style and approach to managing a college, I list them here.

People are happiest when they are busiest. We can all do more than we think we can when it is expected of us. The single most important thing to look for when hiring people is a positive self-image. It is cheaper to take longer and pay more and get a truly competent person than to settle for less than what is required. It is amazing the difference that just one person can make in a college if that person is truly effective and truly dedicated. It is incredible what can be accomplished if you don't worry about who gets the credit. It is unnecessary, no matter how difficult, to settle for less than the highest quality and the highest standards. A college is as good as its faculty.

In my heart, I knew that the college was stronger and better than ever. I knew that in every way there is to measure such a place we, Sidney and I, and our many friends and supporters, had accomplished much that earlier had only been dreamed of. It did not enter my thinking that much of what we left behind would be dismantled or left to atrophy.

The college airplane, which had made possible so much fund raising, was sold. Not long after arriving at Carroll College I had a call from Graham Holloway. He said they were projecting a deficit for the '88-'89 fiscal year and what did I advise. I knew that fund raising had slowed and I explained that aggressive solicitation of money, from all sources, government and private, was always necessary to balance the budget.

Three of my successors, as president, spent down the endowment. I was largely responsible for two unrestricted bequests, from Jean and W. C. Brown, that totaled $30 million. Every nickel of that and much more has been spent. It will never be recovered. Even today the endowment is, in market value, about what it was when I left, $40 million. It could have been and should be well over $100 million by now.

The campaign was allowed to fizzle. Staffing was reduced. Aberdeen was deemphasized and then dismantled. Its assets were sold off and then spent, for operations.

Dick Valentine, probably the most effective admissions officer the college had had, was fired. (He later became a college president.) Most of the curriculum that had been so laboriously built for "career preparation," enrollment building and service to small town and rural Arkansas, was dismantled in favor of "the pure liberal arts." The continuing education program was abolished and the college lost about 300 part-time students. The community college appeared and drew away students. The enrollment sagged.

Minority enrollment today is minimal. There is no minority presence on the faculty.

Mr. W. C. Brown, Jr., who was expected to leave as much or more money as his sister, Jean Brown, was manipulated into marrying his nurse, Mary Gee. Before I left I met with her and she solemnly promised me there would be no change to his will. She later hired her own attorney and rewrote Mr. Brown's will and coerced him into signing it, leaving little or nothing to the college, his life-long cause. When he died, the college declined advice from Gaston Williamson to sue her for alienation of affection and received about $14 million (compared to an expected $25 million).

All of this backsliding was partially offset by a magnificent new Lyon Business Building, a new president's house, a new dormitory and a new theater (all of which paid for with money that had been pledged before I left). Later, another dormitory, and a baseball field were constructed. Still later a gorgeous new science building was erected on the site of the demolished Smith Science Building. Much of what it took to construct it was either borrowed or taken from the endowment.

An honor system was established and the name of the college was changed to Lyon College.

All of these were great improvements. But at what price? And still, with little to show in enrollment gain. For years, the college remained alive only because of the dutiful subsidies of Frank Lyon, Jr., who was trying, admirably, to preserve his parents' and his family's honor. The campus is more beautiful than ever, but it is still under populated.

So, the aftermath has not been easy to watch, and it is clear that what is won does not stay won without constant effort.

The third president after me, Don Weatherman, a former professor of political philosophy, whom I recruited, was competent, hardworking and respected by the faculty. He was a good fund raiser. He seemed equal to every challenge (even the burning down of the Edwards Commons). His vision for the future was ambitious. He added football to spur enrollment and build support from the region and the local community.

The years we spent in Batesville comprised the hardest work I've ever done and the most satisfying and the most important. With the perspective of passing years, it is not surprising that all of the gains did not survive nor that many of the projects and ideas and programs I helped build were unsuccessful even while we were there. What is important is that a small college which has been of vital importance to thousands of students and residents of northeast Arkansas first survived and then grew stronger and better than any time in its history.

Lyon College is not unlike thousands of similar small,

independent colleges in this country, located in small towns and rural areas, where the population base and the limited wealth of alumni bodies and host communities holds them back from entering the ranks of those with stable enrollment and large endowments. Their business models do not seem sustainable to many outside observers. Many scholars of higher education (usually located in large private or state-owned universities) have been predicting their demise for decades. Yet they survive and help to form the most varied, diverse, dynamic system of higher education in the world. And they make a difference in the lives of millions of U. S. students and citizens.

They have enormous staying power. They are often led by trustees and presidents and deans who are true entrepreneurs. Their faculty sacrifice higher salaries and more prestige by staying with them. Students who choose to stay in their home state or who could not get in to larger places if they chose, are proud and appreciative of what they learn and experience. A combination of small endowments, state and federal financial aid monies, private philanthropy, and as much tuition as mostly middle-income students and often poor students and their families can afford, somehow keep them going. And that is a good thing for the country and the world.

Chapter 24

Family of Origin

This seems like a good place to divert a bit from "my story" and record at least some basic facts about my family of origin.

My mother died in 1986 at home in Lake Bonanza, TX. She was just 67 and she died of lung cancer, discovered in a late stage, and caused by excessive smoking since she was a teenager. Nan and Janet were both with her, along with Dad, when she died. I learned that the loss of a parent leaves you lonelier and diminished in some way. I had been so consumed with my work that she and I had not been in close touch, but there had remained a strong bond, and her death left me filled with sadness. Her funeral was at a funeral home and there was no casket. She had been cremated at her own request.

Dad sold the place in Lake Bonanza, and moved to Temple and rented a small house, to be near Bill, our brother. He became active in the Grace Presbyterian Church there and asked a widow, also a member, to marry him. She was Ruth Laramie and she was beautiful, gracious, kind. I grew to love her quickly. I performed the marriage at their church in Temple. Dad was immensely fortunate and he knew it. She owned a lovely house and had money with which to travel, and they did.

Dad became ill with esophageal cancer and died, at 78, in 1996. Again, I felt greatly orphaned and sad. His life had been tarnished by his parents' divorce and his mother's bitterness. He had been successful in business; he had risen to the top ranks of Blue Cross-Blue Shield of Texas, an impressive height with just a high school education. He was always kind to me and supportive of every important decision, and I felt his pride and confidence. He was a gracious, handsome, personable man.

Nan Gay West was born on February 27, 1961, in Galveston. She was graduated from Arlington Heights High School in Ft. Worth, Texas in 1961. She married Jack H. Huff in 1962. Jody Carl Huff was born in 1963 and Gayla Marie Huff was born in 1967.

Nan and Jack divorced in 1988. She married Harlan Barker in 1989 and they divorced in 2001.

She worked, for seven years, as jail administrator and dispatcher, in the San Saba County jail. Then she worked for nine years at the juvenile detention center that is part of the Texas Youth Commission in San Saba. She was a juvenile correction officer. She is retired now and lives in an extended care facility in San Saba. Jody Huff and his wife, Stephanie, live on their ranch nearby Cherokee, Texas. His son, Jack Huff, also lives in Cherokee, with his wife Rosie and their daughters, Bailey and Morgan. Gayla Hawkins lives in Sherman, Texas, where she is Grayson County Treasurer. Her son, Tanner Hawkins also lives there.

Janet Sue West was born on March 18, 1947, in Galveston. She was graduated from Westbury High School in Houston in 1965. She enrolled in Austin College in the fall of that year and left it in January 1967, having satisfactorily completed 3 semesters. Much later she enrolled at the University of South Alabama in Mobile where she studied, as a part-time, adult student from 2001 until 2005. That year she was graduated with a B.S.in interdisciplinary studies (sociology, psychology and communication).

In June, 1967 she married Edward S. (Ted) White of Daphne, AL. He had been a student at Austin College when they met. He joined the Navy after leaving college and became part of the Naval Engineers known as Seabees. He served two tours in Viet Nam, 8 months that began in August, 1967 and ended in 1968 and then another tour, later that year, that ended in 1969. He died of leukemia in 1982. They had two sons, Matthew was born in 1969. Patrick was born in 1971. Janet remarried in 1984, to Bill Penry. They were divorced in 2014.

She now lives in Fairhope. For several years, she worked for two different landscape companies, as a bookkeeper and payroll manager. She is a communicant in an Episcopal church in Fairhope.

Her son Matthew and his wife Tandy also live in Fairhope as do their four children, Sidney, Noah, Reagan, and Coleman. Matt is President of White-Spunner, a large construction and real estate company. Their oldest daughter, Sidney, married Gavin Willisson in 2018. Janet's younger son, Patrick White and his wife Ashley also live in Fairhope with their two children, Solon and McKinley. Pat works for the City of Fairhope.

William P West was born in Tyler, TX on August 16, 1950. I remember being overjoyed to have a brother to go along with two sisters. The first three of us were born in St. Mary's Hospital, Galveston. Bill was born in Mother Frances Hospital, Tyler. My mother, who was practically never sick was a patient in a hospital only to have her four babies.

Bill was graduated from Westbury High School in Houston in 1968. He married Cindy Lee Miller that same year. In 1969, they had his first son, William Troy West. They divorced in 1970. In 1974, he married Ann Green. They had two children, Kevin Howard West was born in 1978, and Megan Loraine West was born in 1982.

Bill worked for the Southwestern Bell Telephone company from 1969 until 1976, first as a marketing representative and then as a cable splicer. He then worked as a carpenter. In 1985 he went back to work for Southwestern Bell as a field technician. He retired in 2006. In recent years, he has worked as a systems technician for Southwest Telecom where he and Ann live in Belton, Texas. Ann worked for a number of years on the staff of the Belton Public Schools and is now retired.

Bill's son Troy lives in Austin. Bill's and Ann's son Kevin and his wife Courtney live in Washington, D.C., where Kevin is an accountant. They have two sons, Isaac Howard West and Jonah Tosney West. So, they carry the name into a fourth generation. Their daughter, Megan, lives in Belton, Texas where she is a teacher. Her son, Mason, lives with her.

Beginning in 1970, our family, my parents and siblings, have gathered at Thanksgiving each year for a reunion. Even after our mother and then our father and stepmother died, we have continued this. For many years, Sidney and I were far away from the rest of them and had to fly in order to have enough time to make it worthwhile.

Our group has rented condos on the beaches of Galveston, Texas and Gulf Shores, Alabama. We have rented church camps, state parks, and bed and breakfast places. We have been to Batesville, San Saba, Cherokee, and Daphne. Nowadays if everyone came, there would be 35 people in all! It has been a wonderful series to which we look forward every year. Both of our children have become devoted to all their cousins and now their children have come to enjoy their cousins, in what is now the fourth generation.

Chapter

Carroll College

In August, 1998, we drove to Wisconsin. Claire was working. Andrew helped us by driving his truck up, full of stuff, and pulling the fishing boat and trailer Dad had given me (never used the whole time we were in Wisconsin).

There had been a disquieting surprise before we left Arkansas. I had sent a list of questions about the financial aspects of the college to the Vice President for Finance.

Shortly after he resigned without answering me and took a job at a secondary school.

After arriving in Waukesha, a small city west of Milwaukee about 14 miles, I learned of other troublesome circumstances about which I was previously unaware. The college was badly in need of more dormitory space. Signs of deferred maintenance were everywhere.

There were troubled relations with neighboring residents. I learned that the capital Campaign, recently completed and advertised as having reached its goal, was full of smoke and mirrors. For example, one of the trustees had purchased a term life insurance policy with a large death benefit on his teenage niece that cost just a few dollars a year.

The previous president, my predecessor, had been arrested and charged with soliciting a prostitute (an undercover policewoman) in Milwaukee and yet the Board had allowed him to remain in his position until he chose to retire. (Years later I learned he had been granted "president emeritus" status.)

Dan C. West

CARROLL COLLEGE

April 1988

Dan West elected 11th president

The Carroll College Board of Trustees has announced the election of a new president, Dr. Dan C. West, who has served as president of Arkansas College, Batesville, Ark., since 1972.

West, 48, was unanimously named Carroll's 11th president at a special executive meeting of the Board of Trustees on Friday, March 25. He succeeds Dr. Robert V. Cramer who has announced his retirement effective Sept. 1, after having served the college for more than 17 years.

"We have found someone who is a scholar, an administrator, a strong proponent of the liberal arts and a superb fund-raiser, but above all else, West is a strong leader," said Pershing E. MacAllister, chairman of Carroll's Board of Trustees.

MacAllister chaired the 10-member search committee consisting of trustee, faculty, alumni and student representatives who selected West from among the 115 candidates. "After our initial remorse, surprise and shock about the retirement of Bob Cramer, we embarked on a thorough search that began last May and ended today," MacAllister said. "We believe that we have found someone best fitted to lead Carroll into its next phase."

West will officially assume the presidential duties of Carroll College on Sept. 1.

"I am honored to be elected president of Carroll College and grateful to its trustees for their confidence in me," West said. "My wife and I will leave Arkansas College reluctantly after 16 very happy years there filled with much accomplishment."

However, West said he was attracted to Carroll for various reasons. "It is a Presbyterian College of great strength, and I admire the work of Bob Cramer who has led Carroll into the front ranks of liberal arts colleges of the country," he said. "I am also impressed by Carroll's growth, its location, its quality and its great potential for further accomplishments."

Dan and Sidney West

Like Carroll, Arkansas College is a four-year, coeducational, undergraduate, liberal arts college, affiliated with the Presbyterian Church (U.S.A.).

During West's presidency at Arkansas, the college's enrollment has more than doubled from 350 students in 1972 to 750 students today. The endowment has increased from about $800,000 to $40 million, and money raised from private and voluntary sources for all purposes has averaged about $2 million annually during the past 10 years.

Last fall Carroll announced an all-time record high enrollment of 2,117 students, and its endowment totaled $10.7 million at the end of the college's fiscal year, June 30, 1987. Carroll is currently in the final months of a $14 million capital campaign and has raised $13.5 million towards the goal.

As president of Arkansas College, West has directed reorganization and expansion of the curriculum and the faculty into six

Nonetheless, Sidney and I threw ourselves into the work. We lived in the president's house, a very nice, three-storied Georgian style building, steps away from the campus. The college had it redecorated and a room on the top floor was remodeled into a lovely study for me. Sidney had a study on the second floor next to our bedroom. It was surrounded by high rise dorms so that anytime we stepped out into the back yard we were in full view of students, but we weren't particularly bothered by that and we were never troubled by excessive noise from those directions.

The vice president for development also resigned and I had to hire new people for that and finance. I asked the Provost (academic dean) to resign at the end of my first year and go back to full-time teaching as a tenured professor. It had become clear that he did not approve of the decision to hire me and did not enjoy working with me. So, I also had to hire a new academic dean. The dean of students had also been an aspirant for my job but he seemed to accept my arrival and we worked well together, so far as I knew. A history professor came to me and said she wanted to become an administrator. I appointed her vice president for planning. I knew that the college needed a great deal of re-envisioning, marketing, innovation and restructuring if it was to realize its potential. My dream was to see it become the outstanding liberal arts institution in the Milwaukee area. I did not understand why it had not already achieved that status.

The challenges were serious. My predecessor had been inactive. Fund raising was sluggish. The discount rate (based on the amount of unsupported financial aid subtracted from tuition to lure students) was too high. The faculty believed it ran the college because it had been doing so. One result of that: an alarming growth in majors. There was a history of two troubled presidencies. There was not enough space to house students or provide offices for faculty. There was loud demand for more faculty and staff.

In the first year, we spent almost $1.5 million in reserve funds to buy 13 houses, some of which were run down, an empty office building and an abandoned "coal yard," all on the edge of the campus and all unsightly, to give us breathing space. The Board decided to borrow enough, in a bond issue, to build a new residence hall/office building/conference space.

Compensatory salary increases to address gender disparity, a new affirmative action policy, and a women's studies program were implemented. Lower salaried staff were added to the retirement program for the first time. We worked to integrate the college with Columbia College of Nursing in Milwaukee. Along with the establishment of a master's degree program in education, this provided the basis for what would later (after I left) become the change to "Carroll University."

The athletics program was reorganized. We hired seven new full-time faculty. A merit salary review system was begun. We enrolled almost 500 new students, the largest number of freshmen since 1969.

Construction began on the new building in June and remodeling also began on the former commercial office building. Remodeling, roof repairs, painting and redecorating occurred in nine other buildings.

A five-year deferred maintenance plan was fashioned that would cost $4 million. We raised about $2.3 million that first year, for all purposes.

My inauguration was in the spring. The board chair asked to be the speaker. There were about 1,000 people in attendance.

As I had each year at Arkansas College, I compiled a thick "president's report to the board of trustees" on each of the three full fiscal years I was at Carroll. Thus, it is easy to recall the accomplishments as well as the problems each year.

The two greatest frustrations the first year were the adamant opposition from neighbors to the demolition of five insignificant houses on Charles Street (to make room for the new residence hall) and the refusal of the National League of Nursing to accredit the Carroll-Columbia Nursing Program.

At the end of the year I felt strong support from the board, a sense of momentum and progress, after years of inertia, quiet approval from most faculty and muted criticism from a few, and great confidence that we had moved the needle forward and could do much more.

Two friendships developed quickly, in the fall of that first year, that were to mean a great deal to Sidney and me, and which continued for years after we left Wisconsin.

Gordon Folsom, senior professor of English and long-time chair of the English Department, easily the most respected member of the faculty, adopted us. So did his wife Ellen, after Sidney ran to the sidewalk, as we were moving into the president's house, and insisted that he come in to tour the house and get acquainted. Gordon and Ellen were New Englanders who'd lived in Wisconsin for years after he earned his Ph.D. at Madison. They were interesting, cultured, very well-read people who had great integrity and charm. They introduced us to Door County where they loved to escape twice a year. She was well traveled. He refused to leave the country. He was a fine cook. We spent many hours with them. He supported me, not unquestionably, for he often challenged or criticized. But he recognized in me many of the qualities he had seen in his favorite Carroll president, Bob Steele, and he often defended me against faculty criticism. Sidney persuaded him to go with us to England. It was the first of five trips abroad they made with us, after we left Carroll.

Another great friend was Don Taylor, a trustee and president of Waukesha State Bank. He asked me to serve on his board. We became friends with him and Carol. He, too, supported me, way past the time when others had fallen silent. They, too, stayed in touch and we met them several times in various places after we moved from Wisconsin. I've often wondered how different the story would have been had he, Don Taylor, been the board chair, which could easily have happened.

Sidney was asked to join two women's clubs in Waukesha. She worked hard to complete the redecoration of the president's house. Marion Lyon flew up from Arkansas to help her. She quickly established herself as a friendly presence on campus, a popular newcomer in the city, and a great hostess at numerous events designed to entertain the campus and the community.

On the second try we won accreditation for Columbia College of Nursing by the NLN.

This was important to me for not only was Carroll's reputation on the line, but Columbia comprised an almost entirely female faculty and student body.

We hired faculty for the new Ed.M. program. We developed and voted a new strategic plan and a master plan for the campus. We completed the new residence hall and office building on Charles Street and finished one floor of the Barstow Office Building. We began fund raising for a new art building. We created 165 new parking places in what had been an ugly abandoned railroad property. We decided to change athletic conferences. We raised over $900,000 for the annual fund and added $500,000 to the endowment. Four faculty were granted sabbaticals. We increased the percentage of women on both faculty and staff.

Disappointments included a failure to hire any minorities in the still all-white faculty. The vice president for development resigned and the post was unfilled through midwinter.

At the end of the year I remained confident that though it wasn't easy and it was taking an enormous amount of energy to do so we were moving, we could succeed, and the potential for the college was great. Carroll's only competition for preeminence in the Milwaukee area was Marquette which had become a comprehensive university and was strongly identified with the Catholic Church. I admired Marquette and appreciated its role in Wisconsin which has a very large Catholic population. I felt there was an equal need for a non-Catholic, residential, mostly undergraduate liberal arts college. The other such institution in the state, which held status as the best, was Lawrence University in Appleton, far removed from the population centers. I felt Carroll, because of its uncertain progress, confusion about its mission, and uneven leadership history, had missed an opportunity to be the leading liberal arts institution in the state and I aspired to help it achieve that.

I think I was so excited about being in a place with a large population base and a large economy and great philanthropic potential, and on a campus where the critical mass of faculty, staff, students and hometown population was so much larger than either place I had worked before, that I was sure there was an opening for much improvement, growth and achievement. And there was.

I hired Helen McCallie, Assistant to the President at Arkansas College, to fill the same role at Carroll. She is the only exception to my avoidance of hiring people away from former employers, a practice which I have never liked. But she was practically part of the family. She helped with many tasks, freeing me to do more in many directions. I sometimes preached on Sundays, at Presbyterian churches in Wisconsin. I accepted board memberships in the Chamber of Commerce, the Boy Scouts, and the United Way. I was active in the Wisconsin Association of Independent Colleges, in the National Association of Independent Colleges and Universities, and in the Council of Independent Colleges. I published articles, co-authored books, spoke to civic clubs. All of this was meant to help me stay in touch with the higher education community and also to make Carroll more visible, locally and nationally.

At some point, I received three speeding tickets in ninety days and my driver's license was suspended for six months. I can truthfully say that each time I was stopped I had not been intentionally speeding. I had been thinking about many other things than the speedometer. What to do? I had to travel. Meetings and fund-raising calls could not go unmade. The solution was to hire a retired policeman as my driver so I could continue to use the college car. A mobile phone was installed in it. I sat in the back seat, working away, sometimes dictating on the phone to a recorder on campus. The driver would deliver me and collect me, door to door. I loved it! It confirmed to me that I disliked driving, always have, and that if I had been a rich man the part I would have enjoyed most is the car and the driver!

Chapter

Third Year at Carroll

I began my report to the Board on the 1990-91 fiscal year by writing, "In many ways it was an extremely difficult year." We had a record enrollment but with more transfer students and fewer freshmen, more local students and fewer out of state students (thus fewer residents). This meant less revenue from residence hall rent and dining services. This led to an operating deficit of $380,000 on June 30. Further, our recruiting effort did not go well, and it appeared we would have fewer students in September. These developments followed closely on the completion of the new residence hall, financed with a bond to be amortized with room rents.

I have reflected, of course, on why this happened. Evidently the increase in transfer and local students came, in great part, from the publicity we received on the many changes, improvements in the facility, and construction. However, the admission staff had not seized this opportunity by enlisting more new students from outside our immediate area.

In addition, we reduced the rate of tuition increase for the following year ('91-'92) and also slowed the rate of increase in the financial aid budget. Both of these decisions were reached in the face of persistent demands by faculty and trustees that our discount rate (the difference between tuition and the actual amount paid, on average, by students) was too high. The economy moved further into recession. It was a perfect recipe for enrollment decline.

A variety of complaints and criticisms rose: the condition of parts of the physical plant, the still incomplete conversion of the Barstow Building (due to lack of money), our inability to raise faculty salaries as much as was needed, the lack of parking close to residence halls and classrooms. Fraternity issues reached a climax in July when a student in one frat house set another frat house, across the street, on fire with a well-aimed Roman candle and the house burned down. Most seriously of all, the new chief financial officer and his staff were unable to report, in a timely and accurate fashion, on our financial condition.

Still, much was completed, improved, or accomplished. A new honors program, new policies on Greek life, adoption of smoke-free campus rules, married student housing, an English as a second language program, transition to a new athletic conference, a master plan for the physical plant, increasing the market value of the endowment to about $14 million, remodeling of another residence hall, and more.

New faculty were hired for eight departments. An environmental science major was approved. A major grant was obtained from the Keck Foundation in Los Angeles. An African American was hired as the new head librarian, and a high-speed computer linkage was established connecting five of the buildings on campus. Almost $400,000 in government grants were obtained. A CPA was hired as the new comptroller.

I mention all this improvement (not to mention more) not to brag but to illustrate that many people on the staff and faculty worked those three years to move the college forward on several fronts at once. It was happening. It could have been done. After years of stasis the college began to realize its potential.

But I had made some critical mistakes. An English professor came to me saying she wanted to be an administrator. I hired her as Vice President for Planning and tried to groom and mentor her. It was a way to staff an important missing element in the administration. Later she repaid me by engineering a grand scheme to force my resignation. Also, though I used a professional head hunter I hired two vice presidents, in finance and in development, who were not up to the challenges they were asked to take.

And, when I asked the provost I inherited (who'd applied for the presidency) to rejoin the faculty (he had been allowed to retain his tenure), he worked to undermine me. He told me he had committed to a young counselor in the Admission staff (whom he had supervised) that he would be director when that post opened. I unwisely agreed instead of appointing a clearly better qualified person, also on the staff, to be the director. The man I appointed was ineffective; recruitment suffered.

I listened to faculty and trustee critics and reduced financial aid not understanding how dependent we were on unfunded scholarships to attract and retain students. I spent too much time on church relations, board memberships, outside activities and commitments and not enough time on fund raising. I did not find a way to circumvent or supersede the ineffective methods in finance to provide me with accurate financial information, until too late.

In the middle of the year I declined to recommend a faculty member for tenure. I knew this would be controversial. He had been approved for tenure by his tenure committee, unanimously, even though, I learned later, that many faculty were dismayed, some even shocked, by this. He was undeserving they thought. My decision was not a mistake (the man sued but the college settled out of court, after I left, to keep him off the faculty). This, however, was very politically damaging to me. It set the stage for a coup d'état. A faculty board of inquiry was appointed and found in my favor, but several senior faculty, including the chair of this body, felt this was an unacceptable presidential use of power over faculty and could not stand.

As I understand the criticisms and arguments used against me in the following months, I know that the operating deficit, the enrollment decline, and the anticipated deficits in income and students were the most often cited. But, I believe the tenure decision was what drove the most opposition among several senior, influential faculty members. They saw it as a threat to faculty power and prerogative. It is not appropriate to go into detail on this tenure issue, but I could not bring myself to do otherwise without compromising my conscience. I fear I would make the same choice had I to do it over, even knowing the consequences.

In the Spring of 1991, I gave critical evaluations to four of the five vice presidents and withheld salary increases for them and myself. In two instances the evaluations were so negative it was clear the vice presidents were in danger of dismissal. They became defensive and angry and were enlisted in the cabal. It was during the summer of 1991 that a plot was hatched which was put in full operation that fall. The woman I had appointed vice president for planning, also a tenured professor, began scheming against me. She made common cause with the English professor who had been provost. They, in turn, enlisted the aid of a handful of faculty who felt threatened or simply offended by the many changes I had introduced and decisions I had made, including the one on tenure.

Exploiting the enrollment decline, the deficit, the anticipated deficit and a variety of other issues and problems the two leaders of the effort and their allies began blaming me for everything problematic, real and imagined. I did not know about this project, fully, for months and months. Indeed, the full extent of their behind-the-scenes activity was never fully apparent to me until after the January board meeting. Those who were close to me, on the faculty and staff, chose not to keep me informed, for whatever reason.

For example, the vice president mentioned above, organized breakfast meetings of those who reported to me (the "executive staff") without my knowledge. The two vice presidents, for development and finance, met secretly with a trustee in Chicago and convinced him to ask for my resignation. The vice president for planning convinced the board chair (with whom she had been in close touch for years and certainly throughout my time there) that I should be forced out. It is now clear that her main motive is that she wanted to be president of the college.

In October, the board met and by then four other trustees, in addition to the chair, were won over to my opposition. The Chicago trustee introduced a motion to fire me. It was defeated. He resigned on the spot and left the meeting. I was given a vote of confidence with no dissent, but a "study committee" was proposed and appointed by the chair to look into the dissatisfaction on campus. The chair appointed the trustees who were my critics and five others.

All but one of the trustees appointed had been on the board less than a year. Three of the eight were attending their first board meeting. The deck was stacked.

The two vice presidents who had met in secret in Chicago were allowed to resign, effective immediately, but with pay through January. The vice president for planning came to my office the next day and tearfully apologized for her actions against me, asked forgiveness and pledged support. I didn't believe her, but felt I couldn't dismiss her as vice president. That would, I thought, create even more turmoil. I was wrong not to send her back to the faculty. She quickly resumed her work against me.

There were two meetings of the faculty that fall when motions of no confidence in me were introduced. Neither was passed. Instead, a "Faculty Liaison Committee" was appointed. It was chaired by the former provost and the vice president for planning. The "Trustees Study Committee" met, without me, to hear complaints and criticisms from faculty, staff and students, most of whom had been urged to do so by the vice president and former vice president, now leading the coup. I do not know what the findings of either committee were. There were no written reports.

The board met in January, 1992. The board chair urged me not to attend. I should have done so anyway. They adopted a strangely worded motion, a copy of which I never received, requiring me to restrict my activity to certain areas (e.g. fund raising) and appointing a trustee who was a retired banker to mentor and advise me. I was given no reasons for this nor was I ever provided with minutes of the meeting. I cleaned out my office next day and wrote a letter of resignation. The point is I was not fired, technically, but it was clear I did not have the confidence of the board chair and a significant percentage of the trustees, so I left.

I had a contract which required the college to pay me for another 18 months. We left Waukesha on March 10 and moved to Atlanta. We owned a condo there in which Claire and a roommate lived as renters. There were three bedrooms and three baths and the master bedroom accommodated Sidney and me. Most of our furniture was stored in Milwaukee.

In the words of one faculty member at Carroll, what happened "was a tragedy." For us and for the college. Friends in Waukesha and Milwaukee assured us of their support, told us of their shock and dismay, used the word "scapegoat," and talked about a power struggle. Observers in other institutions of higher education in that area described Carroll as a troubled place and talked of three failed presidencies and an "impossible" faculty.

The board chair and his allies required me to sign a "no disparagement" agreement, and threatened to hold my pay, but I had already decided not to comment publicly or defend myself in the press. It would not have changed anything. My reputation was already in tatters and my career threatened and anything I said would have been furiously disputed by my enemies. I had invitations from civic clubs to give my version of what happened and a request from the newspaper for an interview. I knew that would intensify and prolong the drama unnecessarily, and damage the college beyond what had already occurred.

It has been 25 years, at the time of this writing, since those events occurred. That gives me plenty of perspective, but much of what I think about it has been formed by hindsight, disclosures by friends who were there at the time, and analysis of my own papers and records. I did not read what was written in the local papers, mostly quotes from my critics.

What do I believe happened? The short answer is there was a power struggle and I lost. The longer explanation is that an unprincipled, even ruthless woman wished herself to supplant me and, with shocking manipulation of others, turned a handful of faculty and, beginning with the Board chair, a small number of trustees into a vocal group of my enemies. They managed to panic the board into concluding I was a threat to the future of the college.

Why did this surprising turn of events happen? An outside observer might say that I should have been more astute politically, acted faster and with greater ruthlessness to overcome my enemies, or anticipate sooner what was happening and either outmaneuver or leave. They would be right.

The enrollment decline and the deficit were not the reasons I was pressured to resign. I think the real reasons are the following. I made too many changes too fast. I was naïve politically, too trusting of those around me and not alert to the risks to myself. For example, it never occurred to me until too late that the board chair would turn against me. Also, I failed to raise enough money soon enough. Faculty became frightened for their financial security. I made poor choices in hiring. I tried to do too much and did not delegate enough. I misjudged the culture of the place. I learned there is a strong prejudice against southerners in the Midwest.

What happened was a tragedy, for me and for Sidney and for the college. The college already had a history of troubled presidencies, including the two immediately before me. Another was to follow. It would take years to overcome the unfavorable parts of its reputation.

Neither of the people who led the revolt on campus became president. The woman who had concocted the plot eventually left the college. After a difficult search a man was found to be president but his time there was very controversial. He and a group of trustees tried to deemphasize the liberal arts and move in the direction of professional training. The faculty voted to organize into a union. Only after he retired and a number of trustees had rotated off the board, did things calm down, and under another president was progress resumed.

Sidney and I lived a few months in the condo in Atlanta. I interviewed for three presidencies, all small, liberal arts places. I withdrew from two of the searches because the situations were just as troubled as Carroll's. I was offered a post in a very conservative western state but could not bring myself to move into another, still more unknown culture.

My reputation (as a president) was greatly reduced. My future was uncertain. But I did not despair. I somehow remained confident a new way ahead would open. Sidney and I spent relatively little time discussing what happened. We are both forward facing people. We knew life is short and we had to move on.

In my heart, I know I did not deserve what was done. I also know that I worried far more about the college than myself and my job. And, I know I accomplished a great deal in a short time, much of which eventually helped the college survive through difficult years in the 1990s. I am not embarrassed or ashamed of my shortcomings as president or my failure to outmaneuver my enemies, politically. I know what I did and that it was honorable, open, and honest. I am convinced that the majority of people who were there at the time do not believe that what happened should have occurred or been done in the way it was.

In a curious sequel, years later, I returned to the campus for the memorial service for Gordon Folsom, at which his family asked me to speak. Afterward, the former vice president and provost whom I had relieved, came up to me and said, "We made a mistake. We should have remained a liberal arts institution." He was implying that such would have occurred had I remained in 1992. I remember my late friend, M. J. Williams, used to say, "The hindsight of an idiot is equal to the foresight of a genius."

Chapter

A New Part of Higher Education

In April, 1992, I had a call from my friend Roger Hull, the relatively new president of Union College in Schenectady, NY. We had known and liked each other while I was at Carroll and he was president of Beloit College, Beloit, WI. He had released the longtime vice president for college relations at Union, in the middle of a campaign. He needed a new vice president and he assumed I was seeking another presidency but he wondered if I would work for him in the interim and complete the campaign for him. I agreed to go for interviews.

I began work there in August. We moved our furniture out of storage in Milwaukee to a large college owned place in Schenectady. It was a fascinating new scene in another completely new (to us) part of the country.

New York is the "Empire State." We lived in the "tri-city" area, an urban complex comprising Schenectady, Troy and Albany (the state capital). Troy and Schenectady had been manufacturing cities and were now emptied of many jobs. Schenectady had been the headquarters of General Electric, since moved to Connecticut. Both cities were much diminished. Albany remained more vital because of the presence of state government offices and the legislature.

Union College had been founded in 1795, making it among the oldest institutions of higher learning in the country. It was named

"Union" because it was founded by an unusual cooperative effort among Presbyterians, Methodists, Baptists, and Dutch Reformed congregations in town (in other words the white, Protestant establishment). It never had a formal relationship with any denomination, but, interestingly, until the early 20th century, all of its presidents had been Presbyterian ministers. The most famous was Eliphalet Nott.

A graduate of what is now Brown University in Rhode Island, Nott was serving as minister of First Presbyterian Church, Albany, when, in 1804, Alexander Hamilton was killed by Aaron Burr in a duel on the Palisades opposite New York City. Hamilton's wife was from Albany. A large, city-wide memorial service was held at which Eliphalet Nott was principal speaker. His address was a diatribe against dueling. He demanded that Congress outlaw the practice. His sermon was published in newspapers all over the country; he became famous overnight. On the strength of that fame he was asked to be the fourth president of Union College. He remained in that post for 62 years. He still holds the record for the longest serving U. S. college president ever. He was an innovator. For example, he added engineering to the curriculum in 1845.

Close to the center of the city in what had become a mostly working-class neighborhood the college occupied a close-knit campus whose design had been the creation of Jacques Remee. I'm sure it must be one of the most beautiful small college campuses anywhere.

When Roger Hull arrived in 1991, from Beloit, the college had drifted into a certain quietude and complacency, with not much visibility in the list of eastern colleges and a lot of deferred maintenance in its physical plant. Roger set out to focus on two main initiatives: first, improving the quality of the student body while enhancing revenues, with aggressive recruiting and enhanced marketing; and secondly, fixing the threadbare condition of the campus. He was a good fund raiser. He was not much interested in curricular reform or academics generally. He'd been a lawyer and then a university fund raiser, not a professor. And, he was a loner in the sense that he did not join clubs or associations. His motto was "tend to your knitting." He focused his time on raising money and managing it well. He largely avoided conflicts with the faculty. He transformed the campus into a jewel. The enrollment and endowment grew. The college's standing and reputation swelled.

My office was in a former residence, a large three-story house, Lamont House, next to another former residence which housed the rest of my staff. Sidney and I lived two blocks away, across Lenox Avenue from the campus at the corner of Lenox and Avon. The house was part of something called the G. E. Realty Plot. It comprised acres of large, old (early 20th century) houses, east of the campus, built by the General Electric company as residences for its executives. The college had bought a number of these and rented them to faculty or the public, or, in our case, and for the provost and dean of students, provided housing with the understanding we would entertain for college purposes.

The house had three floors and a full basement. The top floor contained a ballroom, two bedrooms and a bath. The second floor had a master suite, and three bedrooms, another bath and a large room in back which became my study. The main floor had a large living room, den, dining room, kitchen, breakfast room, and pantry. There were four working fireplaces. The dining room had a fireplace and a plate glass window that overlooked a formal, English garden. Off the den was a screened side porch which Sidney loved. I spent many happy hours in the garden. There were beautiful, tall trees on the corner lot.

Once we gave a garden party, inviting 100 or so local friends of the college, as a development event. An older man, a bit of a toff, came up to me and, saying he admired the house and the garden, asked, "Do you have staff?" "Yes," I answered, "that woman (Sidney) is the housekeeper and I'm the gardener." "Oh," he said, somewhat disappointed.

The largest residence hall on campus, the freshman dorm, was called "West College." Funds to endow it or name it had never been secured so that it could be named for a donor. So, it was named for its location. Some people enjoyed telling me that it was nice I had it named after me.

My title was Vice President for College Relations; I was responsible for public relations, communications, alumni relations, and fund raising. The staff comprised thirty, many of whom were well experienced, and all of them talented. I considered several of them to be experts in their respective specialties. Among the most impressive were Kathy Quinn, administrative assistant, Deb Balliet, director of development, Vincent DeBaun, director of grants, Alice Marocco, director of planned giving, and Sally Webster, Mike Smiles and Mandy Mason, major gifts officers.

Before I left in 1999, we were moved to North College, a two-story building that was among the oldest on campus and, at one time, had been the residence of the academic dean. Unfortunately, part of the staff remained behind at 17 South Lane (next to where we were previously) and another part was moved to Fero House off Nott Street. I learned the challenge of leading and coordinating a staff housed in three places. Not good, but not unusual in higher education. Development and other external related functions are often given the leftover spots on campuses.

I remember one day, not long after arriving, as I walked to the house from my office along Union Avenue and then west on Lenox Road, I noticed a broken and bent place in the iron fence that extended around most of the campus. I thought, "That must be repaired at once," and then I caught myself. I remembered that campus maintenance was not part of my job description, that another vice president had authority over that part of the staff, that I could report what I had seen, to him, so as not to go over his head, but that my role was limited to development. For the first time in twenty years I realized I was not responsible for the entire college and all its parts and pieces. And, for the next 16 years of my career I was often thankful that I had only to worry about those functions and not all. It was a luxury, in a way, to be so much more narrowly focused. It was far less pressure too. And more fun. I enjoyed the work, and I enjoyed being liked again by those with whom I worked. I figured out that when you are not making decisions every day that are, by their nature, going to make someone unhappy, it is a different existence. In 6 ½ years at Union I had to fire no one. When I left, the staff was not only well organized and structured, but smooth-running and strongly cohesive.

The Campaign for $150 million, the Bicentennial Campaign, had been publicly launched in 1991, a year before I came. I think they had raised about $60 by the time I arrived, August 1992. It concluded in mid-1998, about 6 years later, at $151 million. The endowment increased to $200 million. Five endowed chairs were added to support faculty. Major renovations and restorations were undertaken for the Schaffer Library, the Nott Memorial, the Campus Center, the administration building, and Memorial Chapel. A new science building and a new theatre were built. New endowed scholarships, 128 of them, were started. That represented 40% of all endowed scholarships established at Union since the first one in 1874.

There were 23,362 gifts from individuals including 37% of $25,000 or more and 28 of $1 million or more. Grants were obtained from major foundations including G.E., Kresge, Hewitt, Calder, Keck and F. W. Olin. Four major grants were received from the National Science Foundation and the National Endowment for the Arts.

I took special pleasure in helping to raise funds for the library, the science building, Jackson's Garden, and the endowed scholarships. I learned that the last were my favorite thing to ask for, and the easiest capital (endowment or construction) gifts to obtain. What is more compelling than to set up a permanent fund the income of which goes directly to help a student with her or his tuition? It took a relatively small amount (at that time our minimum was $25,000 that could be paid over several years), and you could put the donor's name on it or anyone else's you chose.

There were a handful of projects I undertook almost single-handedly (so far as actually soliciting gifts). These included the restoration of Memorial Chapel, a beautiful neoclassical structure designed by McKim, Mead and White of New York City. I also worked on endowment to support Jackson's Garden, and endowments to support the Jewish and Protestant chaplaincies.

It dawned on me, one day, that whoever asks for money, has a good bit of discretionary authority and can choose projects, suggest restrictions to the gifts, and prioritize requests in ways that can help shape and change the college. I knew the president could do this. I realized the chief development officer can, as well.

Roger Hull and I divided the responsibility. He took personal charge for a handful of donors he thought might make the largest gifts. He was good at that, and quite successful. I solicited all of the trustees, annually, for the Annual Fund, for capital pledges, and also for planned gifts. Beyond that I had a long list of second tier prospects, including quite a few I cultivated "from the ground up" (from non-giving or small-gift status).

One of my major coups was the Olin grant for $9 million. The F. W. Olin Foundation in New York City was run by an engineer named Lawrence (Larry) Milas. Mr. Olin had left his fortune to it. It was set up for the sole purpose of building buildings on college campuses. It was unique in that it insisted on paying for the entire project. I had first learned of this in the 70s while at Arkansas College. I began a series of annual visits to Mr. Milas in his office in New York, but, after several years at Arkansas College, we never got to submit because we were too small. However, Larry and I became friends, and he started to call me "the Arkansas Traveler" when I showed up each year. I continued to see him while at Carroll (which did not have enough endowment). When I moved to Union, he became more interested. Among other things Union had an engineering program, unusual for a liberal arts college. It also had a strong science program, and it was in upstate New York.

Roger Hull was skeptical. "They won't fund us," he said. But I insisted we submit a proposal. To everyone's surprise (including mine), it was funded. It was the last building Olin did before shutting down and transferring all remaining funds to the Olin School of Engineering, next to Babson College in Massachusetts, in 1997. I am convinced that a contributing factor in Larry Milas's decision was my persistence, over 18 years, of calling on him, with hope and expectation, every year, on behalf of three different colleges.

Hull and I operated separately. He preferred to work alone and liked to keep his strategy and tactics close to the vest. He concentrated on a few individuals he thought he could move to principal (seven figure) gifts. I called on many more including those who gave major (five figures) and up. The two construction projects for which I raised the most money and the most number of separate pledges, were the Nott Memorial and the library.

I worked with two board chairs while I was there: Joe Hinchey and Norton Reamer. I liked them both a lot, and they liked me, a pleasant change from Carroll. I recruited several new trustees and suggested several possibilities for board membership who later got added to the group. I also worked as the staff person for the Trustee Board of Advisors, a sort of training or audition group for trusteeship. I worked closely with two chairs of this group: Cy Meisel and Frank Messa. The latter later became Chair of the Board of Trustees. All of these men were alumni of Union, successful in business, and outstanding persons. In my experience business people make the best college trustees and professional people (clergy, lawyers, physicians, academics) make the least effective.

During the course of the Campaign we built the Annual Fund (mostly small, individual and one-time gifts from alumni) to $3.5 million annually. We also added a large number of planned gifts (bequests, annuities, trusts) which we did not count in the campaign total.

It was, by far, the largest, most successful campaign in the college's history and I was very proud of the success we had in enlarging the donor base (the number of people and organizations who contributed some amount at some point during the campaign period).

During these years at Union, Claire was living and working in Atlanta. Andrew, at first, was attending Emory (until 1993) and then working at Emory and earning two master's degrees at Georgia State University in Atlanta. So, Sidney and I lived alone in that enormous house, but we entertained often - the Development staff, members of the faculty and other staff, friends, donor prospects, and family. We housed trustees when the Board met. Sidney was busy and, with only infrequent housekeeping help, entertained a lot. But, she was no longer a college president's wife and that made a huge difference.

For her, there were close friends, more time to do what she wanted, and much less pressure.

She made several very close friends, other women, not necessarily connected to the college, whom she met and liked. Her closest friend was Gail George, wife of a biology professor, Carl George. He had been on the search committee for the vice president when I was interviewed. They became soul mates. Sidney was invited to join the Queen's Fort Club, a women's group that owned a house for its meetings.

Also, because of Gail and Carl, both of us were invited to join the Fortnightly Club, a group comprising mostly retired G.E. executives and research scientists. This was a real throwback to another time. They had earlier met in each other's homes, but as time wore on and the membership aged, they met mostly in the public library building. It was black tie, men in tuxes, women in long dresses. A member of the club gave a presentation, followed by questions and discussion, and then refreshments. Once, dressed in the kilt, I gave a talk on "Scotland, It's History and Culture."

I remember three evenings, in particular, when we entertained groups at the house. The dining room was large enough to feed ten or twelve. Once we gave a dinner party and Sidney wanted a fire in all four fire places (living room, dining room, den, master bedroom). I spent most of the evening feeding wood into those fires. I understood why people who lived in houses that big needed servants. I also understood how much work it is to keep log fires going in a big house.

On another occasion, we gave a New Year's Eve party complete with dancing in the third-floor ballroom. We invited people to come in costume. One gay couple from Albany came in white tie and tails and top hat and opera cape. Carl George arrived as a sheik, with his wife as his concubine. I wore the kilt. It was a hoot.

After visiting some local (Schenectady) churches and after I'd transferred my membership to Albany Presbytery, we decided to affiliate with First Presbyterian Church, Albany. This happened because Sidney knew and had worked with Bob Lamar, the recently retired senior minister. They had served together on the Joint

Committee on Church Union that put together the plan for reunion of the southern and northern factions of Presbyterians. Located close to the state capitol, the church had a grand building that had seen better days. The congregation had shrunk, as was the case in so many inner-city churches, but the group worked valiantly to remain viable, and we liked it because of the diversity. There were blacks and gays, rich and poor (even some homeless), liberals and conservatives. It was just a more interesting mix than any of the Presbyterian churches in Schenectady. Sidney, already elected an elder back in Batesville days, was elected to the Session and became very active. This was good for us. It introduced us to others unconnected to the college and it took us over to Albany at least once a week.

Another delightful aspect of our years in New York, was our proximity to Saratoga Springs (we visited many times) and our closeness to the Massachusetts and Vermont borders. We especially enjoyed going to Lenox, MA (Tanglewood concerts, plays at Edith Wharton's The Mount), Dorsett and Manchester, VT.

For two Texas natives who had spent 16 years in small town Arkansas and then almost 4 years in the Midwest, this was another world. It was part of a richer (and older) history.

It was more cultured (the arts flourished in every direction). It was a different climate (gorgeous, cool summers, magnificent autumns). It was a wealthier area of the country. It was more secular, more literate, more closely connected to the intellectual heart of the country. We decided we were easterners and urbanites more than southerners or Midwesterners or small-town types.

My work took me often to "the City," by train (which I loved). Sidney went with me sometimes. She fell in love with New York. She wanted to live there. I pointed out we could stand neither the expense nor the frantic pace of it. It's hard work just to get around Manhattan.

Beginning in 1984 when I got my doctorate from Harvard I joined the Harvard Club of NYC. It's wonderfully located on West 44th Street, a few blocks from Grand Central (to the east) and Times Square to the west. Beginning with the time at Arkansas College I had travelled to New York every year, sometimes more than once a year. A third of all the major foundations in the country are in Manhattan. The Club became my base. Its public rooms were magnificent (the building was designed by McKim, Mead and White). Its bedrooms were basic but adequate. The food was good. The price was more moderate than midtown hotels. I learned, over the years, that prospective donors, including alumni, would meet me there. It was a prestigious address, it was a convenient location, and it was comfortable and quiet. By the time I retired from Swarthmore in 2008, I would often go to New York, check into the club, and meet with a half dozen people (over coffee, drinks, or a meal) right there. That was very efficient fund raising.

I still belong. It's the only private club I ever joined. Its membership is long since multiracial, multi-ethnic, and gender-neutral.

We met many fascinating, accomplished, talented people in the course of those 6 ½ years at Union. Many of them were extremely wealthy. We were in homes, clubs, apartments, restaurants, hotels, and offices (often extremely elegant) we never would have seen had we been in another place or another job. We met more Jewish people than we'd ever known anywhere. We learned more about investment banking, corporate management, eastern U.S. politics, Catholic culture, the arts (especially theatre and music) and "society" than we'd ever dreamed of doing.

The year Bill Clinton ran for President against George H. W. Bush, Sidney presented herself at the Democratic Party headquarters in Albany as a volunteer. Her accent was Texan but New Yorkers can't tell the difference between that and Arkansas-ese, so they put her at the front desk, inside the main door, to meet and greet everyone who came in. Everyone seemed pleased that a woman had been sent from Campaign headquarters in Little Rock. She was also asked to make a speech, on the steps of the state Capitol, supporting Clinton. When Clinton won, we were invited to attend the second Clinton inauguration (bitter cold) in Washington, D.C., and went to the New York State ball at Kennedy Center, all because of Sidney's volunteer work in Albany.

We both became (and have remained) avid readers of the New York Times. Nowadays I can't imagine not reading the Times every day. Nor can I believe the difference in quality between that paper and all but a few of the rest in the U.S.

Our lives were changed for the better in so many ways, culturally, intellectually, emotionally, spiritually, by the relocation to the northeast.

It wasn't all good. The winters were brutal. I realized that Schenectady is on the same latitude as Milwaukee! Gardening is more challenging than in the South. We learned that Northeasterners (and especially the denizens of Manhattan) could also be parochial. We worried about the decline of industry there (upstate New York is definitely part of the rust belt). We were dismayed at the state of public education. It was sad to see the rapid decline in mainline Protestant and Catholic churches. State and local governments were full of corruption. I used to think that places like Texas, Louisiana, Mississippi, and Alabama had the most corrupt politics in the country. I learned that New York State politics went further by several degrees.

But it was wonderful to be in a part of the country where higher education was not so dominated by state owned universities and football. It was great fun to be close to so many historical sites and museums. It was exciting to find such rich variety in theatre, music, religion, ethnic traditions. (We used to say, where I grew up, that there were more Baptists than people.) The level of intellectual discourse, the greater amount of information on which people based their opinions, and the liveliness of activity, was stimulating and moved us further away from our backgrounds.

People often asked Sidney, "Where are you from?" She loved saying, "Anson, Texas," and watching the mystified expression. I became aware that though I'd lost my Texas accent, I still spoke a whole beat or so slower than New Yorkers.

When the college's campaign ended in late 1997, I thought we should immediately begin work on another. The college still did not have enough endowment. There were more physical improvements needed. We had to continue to grow and that meant a larger budget.

But, what excited me, as a fund raiser, was the way we had expanded the donor pool, enhanced our staff effectiveness, and stimulated interest and commitment of so many alumni and friends toward giving to the college. I felt it would be a shame not to exploit this momentum in another large effort. There was little "donor fatigue," and, a greater feeling of pride and anticipation. This old college, which had become a bit sleepy, had awakened and now began to realize its long dormant potential. There it sat in an area of the country where there was great wealth and with an alumni body that had, at long last, been challenged to rise to a new level of support. Such intangible assets, however, soon dissipate if not exploited and reinforced. I feared just that would happen.

There was another reason I was eager to begin planning a new campaign. I had discovered that, given my experience of 20 years of fund raising, free of responsibility for other parts of the college's operation and thus to focus (specialize) in development work, I could do that well, and happily. I was less interested in seeking another presidency that would probably be at a small college in the south, struggling for students just as the three had for which I'd previously worked. I was in a far stronger college than before. I was being paid more than ever. I felt I was good at what I was doing, I enjoyed it, and I loved the college and the people with whom I was working.

But the president, my boss, had no interest at all, in this approach and attitude. It was clear, that there would not be another campaign anytime soon. I was disappointed and frustrated.

In 1999, I got a call from a search consultant, a "head hunter" in Boston. He was working for Swarthmore College in Pennsylvania. He asked for my resume. I sent it, not very seriously. I was still not that interested in leaving Union. We could have stayed another five or six years, so happy were we there.

The next thing was a request to visit with the consultant at his office in Boston. That was followed by an invitation to interview at Swarthmore, then meeting with the president, Alfred Bloom, in New York City, and then an invitation to return to the campus, with Sidney, for talks with the president and others, including trustees, on campus. I was impressed by the thoroughness of the search process, the number of people involved, and the seriousness with which they seemed to take this post. I learned later there had been an earlier search that was not successful.

One of the people who interviewed me was the long-time trustee, alumnus and former board chair, and the lead donor to the college, Eugene Lang, at his office in New York. Immensely wealthy, well known as founder of the "I Have a Dream" Foundation, and very knowledgeable about higher education, he asked searching questions. He displayed an unusually deep knowledge of how colleges work and what makes them successful. I told him I'd never met a trustee who seemed to know as much about the management and funding of private colleges. He accepted the compliment and told me it was much harder to find a good development officer than to find a college president.

Sidney was captivated by Swarthmore. While I was in interviews she roamed the campus, talking freely with students, staff and faculty. She said she felt she'd come home. She felt more attune to the feel of the place than anywhere we'd ever looked at or considered. She was far more positive than anywhere else I'd ever considered. I had learned that her instincts, her intuition about such things was far more reliable than mine.

I was flattered to be taken seriously, enthused about the feel of the place and greatly attracted to the location, the prestige of the college, the challenge of raising money for an already well-endowed school (approaching a billon in endowment), and the extraordinary compensation package. I accepted the offer and told Roger Hull.

He expressed surprise. He said he'd expected me to take another presidency. But I hadn't thought about another presidency after I'd been at Union for a year or two. I also hadn't thought about leaving Union. Now, the thought of working for one of the best liberal arts colleges in the country, one of "the little Ivies," and of living in the Philadelphia area, was amazing, and exciting. I told him they wanted to launch a campaign, they already knew how much they wanted to raise and for what, and they already had nearly $50 million pledged (toward a $250 million goal). It was too good to turn down. I'm sure he agreed though I don't think he wanted me to leave. I knew it was important to leave on an up-beat and with a positive relationship between us, and I did.

Our leaving was bittersweet. We were excited about going to Swarthmore, but, in a short time, we'd made many friends on and off campus and we'd been so happy at Union. Our departure seemed premature, in a way, our stay incomplete.

Gail George staged an elaborate party in the new Yulman Theatre, for our staff and off-campus friends. She assembled sets or scenes of various stages of our lives: gardening, fundraising, Sidney's clothes and shoes, etc. The staff performed skits and wrote songs and poems. It was amazing. Roger Hull hosted an elaborate reception in Hale House to which many members of the faculty and staff came. After Arkansas College and Carroll years I experienced actually having friends and fans on the faculty at Union. We were overwhelmed.

This reminds me of an important learning about development work. I found that reaching out to faculty and staff beyond the development ranks, building relationships, forming partnerships, involving them in fund raising and public relations makes for far more successful fund raising. I think it is an important element that most development types overlook.

We set out for Swarthmore on a cold January day in two old cars, relics from Arkansas and Wisconsin days, one with a trailer full of plants. On the way, the muffler fell off the Chrysler and we drove into the Borough of Swarthmore, noisily.

Our days and years in New York were some of our happiest. In addition, there was no constant worry, about money and enrollment, as there had been everywhere else I'd worked. There were no sniping critics. I no longer had the burden of association and outside board responsibilities. My church work (occasional preaching and presbytery committees), was much lighter than anywhere I'd worked before. We continue to look back on Union days as bright ones in our experience.

Chapter

Swarthmore College

Swarthmore seemed like a dream at first. Nine years later, when I retired after 40 years of college work, it stood as the apex of my career.

The campus facilities were unremarkable. Except for an impressive central building, Parish Hall, and a grand chapel, Clothier, the buildings were unimpressive. They were "Quaker plain," even, in few instances, ugly. It was obvious that, over the years, the place had scrimped on architectural fees. But the entire campus comprised the Scott Arboretum and that made it a beautiful place. Trees, flowering shrubs, perennial flowers, garden design, expert maintenance, labels on everything, made it a gardener's heaven.

Situated on a hill, the highest point around, in the midst of a square mile borough (township) it was about 17 miles from center city Philadelphia. Down the hill from Parrish, by way of a long walk and steps covered by great trees on either side, one descended to the Village or shopping district ("the Vill") and a train station! The SEPTA ran every half hour or so and took you to the city. I'd never lived anywhere where you could walk to the train station and ride a train anywhere! I knew people in Swarthmore who commuted every day by train to New York City!

Swarthmore, the borough, was a bedroom district filled with professionals: lawyers, physicians, college professors, investment bankers, a lot of retirees. It was a beautiful area of high property values, leafy, and well established, a haven of affluence and privilege, anchored by the college in its midst. It had grown up around the college which had been set down there in 1865. Walks through its streets were delightful. The college's playing fields, in the center of the borough, next to "the Vill," seemed a kind of village green. The public schools were excellent because of the high tax base. It was 15 minutes from the Philadelphia airport on nearby I 95. It was just off the "Blue Route," an interstate connector between I 95 and I 76, to the north. It was close in to Philadelphia but a world apart. Convenient to everything in the metroplex but detached in its quality of life. Blocks from the very large Springfield Mall and Baltimore Pike, but a protected haven of quiet beauty. It was a sort of paradise.

We lived in the vice president's house, on campus. Built in 1923 it had belonged to a geography professor who taught at both Penn and Columbia! It had a full basement and three floors. It had eight bedrooms and 5 ½ baths. We used one small bedroom on the second floor as a den and TV room and I used another as my study. Sidney had a study in what had been a spacious sleeping porch, since closed in. In addition to the master suite with its own bath, there were 5 guest rooms. We had almost enough furniture of our own to fill it. The college provided the rest, some of which was already in the house.

The ground floor had a large living room, with a working fireplace, a side porch, a large dining room, butler's pantry and kitchen with breakfast area. In the bedrooms above we had enough double and twin beds to sleep nine.

There was a very spacious garden in back (borders on both sides of a long greensward (perfect for garden parties) that extended down steps from a terrace immediately behind the house. It was a lovely place. We entertained a great deal and we housed trustees, parents, visiting prospective students, family, friends, and donors. Sidney really spent all of her time maintaining the house and yard and entertaining. She did have two part-time housekeepers and catering help, more help than she'd had since Batesville, but she still worked very hard. It was here, in Swarthmore, that she became interested in the garden for the first time.

The college had been founded in 1864 by the Hicksite branch (the liberal faction) of the Society of Friends. From the beginning, it was co-educational. The faculty included both men and women as did the Board of Managers. Indeed, it had been necessary to petition the State legislature to pass a special law allowing women to serve as board members because the Friends insisted on equal numbers of men and women to govern it and hold the property. It was the only institution of higher education to be founded by the Hicksite Quakers.

This part of Quakerism was "unprogrammed." That meant no clergy, silence in worship, universalist beliefs, and a more progressive stance than other branches. The college was named after Swarthmore Hall in England, the home of George Fox, founder of Quakerism.

There are twelve colleges in the U.S. that were founded by Quakers. There are only about 100,000 Quakers in the entire country. The Quaker tradition has had an influence on American culture out of proportion to the small numbers of its adherents. It includes non-violence, peacemaking, gender equality, service to the poor, the interconnectedness of all persons, antipathy to creeds, and personal empowerment.

Although the college has had no formal relationship to the Friends, since the early 20th century, these values and certain aspects of Quaker style and attitude still permeate the place. A Quaker meeting house, built in 1879, still stands on campus as a potent symbol. A small number of Quakers still enroll. By tradition, a handful of Quakers still serve on the board. There is a Friends Historical Library and a Peace Studies Collection, both housed in the McCabe Library.

In my file is a quote from the 1973-74 Swarthmore College Bulletin: "Quakerism: as a way of life, it emphasizes hard work, simple living, and generous giving; personal integrity, social justice, and the peaceful settlement of disputes."

I found all of this strongly congruent with my own values and somehow strongly affirming. It even felt like a vindication of sorts, in respect of feelings and attitudes I'd developed and held for years, at times within environments where they were not the dominant ones.

There was more. This was not a typical college, in other ways. There had been a president, Frank Aydelotte, who served from 1921 until 1939, who, building on the strong foundation of his immediate predecessor, Joe Swain, had transformed the place.

As a Rhodes Scholar he'd become enamored of the English tutorial system and, modifying it to the American environment, had introduced an Honors Program. It was much copied in other colleges later on. Small groups of students met in seminars. The faculty member acted more like an enabler, questioner, discussion leader, than as a lecturer. The Socratic method prevailed. There were no tests or exams, but lots of reading and lots of papers written. A thesis was required for graduation and an oral exam. The examiners were faculty from other colleges or universities, regarded as top in their fields. The Swarthmore faculty member could sit in but not speak in the oral. Thus, it was also a kind of exam of the quality of teaching that had occurred.

Many Swarthmore graduates in honors have said it was the equivalent of master's or even doctoral exams in graduate school. This program became the signature of the Swarthmore curriculum.

Aydelotte did more. He changed athletics. He said it was more important to participate in athletics than to be a spectator (another approach he'd learned in England). He instituted frequent faculty sabbaticals (as in every three years). Thus, there was no excuse for faculty not keeping up in their fields or doing research. He raised admission standards and faculty hiring standards. He insisted on limiting the mission to undergraduate instruction. He said the college should remain small, and elite. He raised faculty salaries, emphasized research and expected faculty to live close to campus so that students could find them. He reinforced consensual decision-making and Quaker-style egalitarianism. And, to support all this, he built eight new buildings, increased the endowment, and expanded the enrollment.

In short, Aydelotte, the defining president, had left a college that had a singular commitment to the life of the mind as its chief focus and highest priority.

In 1999, upon joining this community, I relished the discovery that such a place existed. Other colleges and universities I knew about, including those I'd attended or worked for, talked about academic excellence and education as their primary purpose, but many other objectives and priorities competed: athletics, social life, career preparation, the pursuit of grades and status, competition for students and money, rankings, socialization of students including pursuit of a spouse, and, in the case of faculty, research, publishing, career advancement.

Suddenly I found myself in a place where it was not only acceptable to be a good student, it was the norm! Geeks and nerds and "brains" were welcome. High school valedictorians and salutatorians were on every hand. Many students were the children of professors sent there from all parts of the country. It was what Burton Clark, writing about the college, called, "the glorification of academics."

It was a place, he said, where "fixing the leading student as the hero of the student body" was assumed.

There were fascinating examples of all this to be observed or heard about. There were entering freshmen who knew more about the subject of a course than the professor offering it. First-year students, used to being at the top of their class, year after year, in junior high and high school, suddenly found themselves confronted, on every side, by colleagues with exactly the same record. Students came to the realization, after a short time there, that they weren't competing with each other nearly so much as with themselves.

Students were charged a flat activity fee, and there was no admission charge for any event or activity on campus. No one knew, really, who was from a wealthy family and who came from a poor one. Most women dressed down and wore little or no makeup. It was important to signal that they were not searching for a man and that they were people of substance and independence. Faculty were never addressed as "doctor." Occasionally a faculty member might be called "professor," but mostly they were addressed by their given name. (Interestingly,

Quakers never used titles, not even "Mr." They called each other by both given and surname, i.e. Dan West.)

Athletes sometimes missed practice or even a game if they had a conflicting exam or an important paper. The library was full most evenings. The student newspaper, "The Phoenix," was full of good writing. I was awed.

In the development offices, we loved student workers. They would come to work, for an hour or two, between classes, and a staff person would orally give them a list of things to do. They would say, "O.K," and everything assigned would be done quickly and well, with no request for repeated instruction and no checking for accuracy needed.

There was an amazingly strong sense of community. Students genuinely cared about each other, helped each other, even defended those with whom they disagreed. Students of various national origins, racial heritage, sexual orientation, were treated as equals and, on rare occasions when this acceptance was violated, students rose as one to defend the criticized or mistreated and to reinforce the community ideal.

None of this was inexpensive. Keeping the place small, recruiting numbers of financially needy students, paying high salaries, offering frequent sabbaticals, supporting an expensive honors program, and providing the best in library, lab equipment, computers and all the rest, was very costly. I often said that if I wanted to devise the most expensive way to provide higher education it would look like Swarthmore. Therein lies another fascinating story.

A man named Tom McCabe had been head of Scott Paper Co. He was the first non-Quaker (he was Presbyterian) to be placed on the Board of Managers. He later became President of the Philadelphia Federal Reserve. During World War II, he served in the Roosevelt administration. When the war ended, he figured out that the U.S. was the only combatant nation not to have suffered destruction, and, that, because of the industrial expansion needed to win the war, its economy would take off into a long, sustained upward spiral. He convinced a conservative college board to abandon the standard rule of thumb, 50% of endowment invested in stocks and 50% in bonds, and, instead to place nearly three-quarters of its funds in big cap, blue-chip stock. When I arrived in 1999 the endowment's market value exceeded $900 million, and most of that was from growth, not gift additions.

So, three men took a small Quaker college, respectable but invisible, to national prominence and financial security. Swain, Aydelotte and McCabe had done what I'd dreamed of doing at four other colleges. And here I was, working as a vice president, at a small, private college of stellar reputation, secure enrollment, and financial stability, where the highest priorities were academic achievement, intellectual accomplishment, ethical integrity. Amazing!

Swarthmore, 2007

Chapter 29

The Campaign Launches

When I began work, as Swarthmore's Vice President for Advancement in January 1999, I had a staff of forty. They were organized into four groups: alumni relations, news and information, publications, and development (fund raising).

The most recent campaign had ended in 1986, the "Campaign for Swarthmore." It had a goal of $75 million and had raised $89 million. The board had talked of another campaign for several years. In an effort to encourage this, Eugene Lang, former board chair, had pledged $30 million, the largest pledge, at that time, ever received by an independent liberal arts college. Then, incredibly, my predecessor, Harry Gotwals, had died, suffering a heart attack in the driveway of the vice president's house. At first stunned into inaction and later recovering only slowly, the college had been without a vice president for two years.

Alfred Bloom had become president in 1991. He had degrees from Princeton and Harvard and had taught linguistics for several years at Swarthmore before becoming Provost at Pitzer College in California. Then, he'd been appointed president at Swarthmore and so he returned to a faculty many of whom he already knew.

The board had already decided they wanted to raise $230 million and they already had a long-range plan and a list of objectives developed. Co-chairs had been selected. The launch date was set for July, 1999. A campaign consultant had been engaged.

251

When I arrived in January of that year, I learned, however, that the college was not prepared for a campaign because it was at the end of a long period in which budget and staff had been stable, and attempts at increasing both had been resisted by the faculty; moreover, the previous vice president had adopted an approach in which focus and energy were concentrated on a handful of donors and prospects thought to be capable of very large gifts. The Development Committee of the Board and Board members generally saw themselves as overseers of development staff rather than enablers, partners and participants in fund raising.

Without a campaign staff, the Board took a leap of faith in setting a $230 million goal in May, 1999. Al Bloom, the president, made it clear to me I had a free hand to hire more staff and increase the budget. I estimated that we needed 15 more staff people and would have to spend an additional $10 million over 7 years beyond what the college was already budgeting for all advancement programs. The president decided the campaign would be "self-funding," i.e. these additional costs would come off the top of whatever we raised.

In addition to a lack of readiness in infrastructure, I found other challenges. There was little awareness on the part of anyone that the college needed to raise money. There was even a distaste for development among some. Did this come from the traditional Quaker bashfulness about discussing money? Or, was it complacency caused by the dangerous assumption we had plenty? Some of both. And there was another cultural challenge: Swarthmore had long been a place that emphasized social justice and social action. Many assumed that most of its graduates worked for non-profits or in public service occupations, and there were many teachers and professors among its alums. Some thought we had few alumni-ae who had gone into business and become wealthy.

We used the consultant for just one year. At that point I had been in college work for 27 years. She and I realized I knew as much or more than she. She and I came to the same conclusion; we did not need her. That saved time and money.

We raised $101.5 million during the nucleus or "quiet" phase of the campaign, July 1999 to September 2001. This exceeded expectations by $50 million. Then, the first set-back happened: 9/11/2001. Fortunately, the college had not lost alumni in the Twin Towers collapse, even though we had many in New York. I had been in those buildings visiting alums and others on a number of occasions.

We had planned an elaborate Campaign announcement, celebrating the success of our quiet phase and announcing our goal. We rented a large tent for Parrish Beach (the greensward south of Parrish Hall). The event was scheduled for late September. After the destruction of the Twin Towers in New York, that was cancelled. As the country struggled to cope, many feared the campaign would not succeed. No one knew, at that moment, what the economic, social or psychological cost of the disaster would be.

We paused to regroup and then determined to continue. Our institutions and our way of life had to prevail and even overcome this heinous challenge. Instead of the large event on campus, we held regional events in eight large cities, including London.

There was a chilling parenthesis at Swarthmore. At the time of the attack the college enrolled a handful of Saudi students. Every one of them was quickly flown home the next day, by their government. We never saw them again.

The other huge challenge to the Campaign was a December 2000 decision by the Board to eliminate football and men's wrestling from our athletic program. Al Bloom, in the most courageous decision of his presidency, initiated, led and shouldered the backlash for that. I agreed with him, from the first mention.

It was not an economic decision. The college subsequently reinvested all monies saved from dropping these sports into the remaining sports. Bloom had reached the conclusion that the college could not afford the "slots" it set aside every fall for football players. We were sacrificing slots that could have been filled by often much more qualified (academically) students in order to have a football team. And, importantly, the football program was and had been unsuccessful.

Bloom met little resistance from the faculty and not much from the student body. Moreover, he knew his board and, of course, talked with many of them before he broke the idea to the entire group. He did meet resistance, though muted, from his own direct reports, vice presidents and deans. One or two were ex-athletes. Others worried it might detract from the norm, from what college administrators love to describe as a "well-rounded" student population. I quickly supported him and did so, unreservedly, throughout the whole process. Even though I knew that I, of all the executives around the table, had the most to lose. We were in the early stage of a campaign for millions and there would be, we knew not how many, angry alumni/ae.

I confess I saw a chance to advance a long-held dissatisfaction with an overemphasis on athletics (especially football) in much of American higher education. If anything, this is even more apparent now, sixteen years later. Witness Penn State, Baylor, and a number of other scandals. But also, I had worked at two other colleges which had, at the time I was there, successful football programs: Carroll and Union. And I knew Swarthmore was not and would never be such a program. Neither most of the faculty nor most of the students cared a whit about it. It wasn't important to the surrounding community and most of our major donors would not miss it either.

Given what the college had accomplished academically, the small size of the student body which made freshmen "slots" one of our scarcest resources, and the way in which football warped and twisted the character and mission of so many colleges and universities, we'd do well to be rid of it.

At the end of the Campaign, in a lengthy evaluation, I wrote that "the athletic decision had a minimal effect on the overall Annual Fund (and on the Campaign)."

Swarthmore, 2006

Chapter

Years of Campaigning

As we built up the staff and enhanced our capabilities I now know, looking back, that I honed my own skills in raising money. I knew, early on, that I would have to spend a large amount of my own time in travel and one-on-one visitation. First, we were a staff-driven (vs. volunteer-driven) campaign. I had never been convinced that the time and energy required to recruit, train, motivate, and check up on a large number of volunteers was worth the effort. This is especially so in a small college where there is often no history of extensive volunteer activity. Secondly, the president came out of an academic (teaching) background rather than development and, except for an important group of board members who were capable of making very large gifts, did not take time for extensive personal solicitation. Thirdly, even though I hired two directors of development and a handful of major (capital) gifts officers, none of them traveled that extensively, except to favorite areas, and I knew I had to compensate, as much as possible, for their limited aggressiveness in solicitation.

I visited all of the board members, more than once, had a large number of assignees, and made a large number of first-time (exploratory) calls on prospects identified by our research staff.

I developed what I believed to be a successful pattern. I seldom stayed in anyone's home or office more than an hour. I wanted to be able to secure a follow-up appointment if necessary. I tried to avoid meals (too many distractions). I always made an "ask." Who knew if I'd ever get to see the visitee a second time? I devised a three-part formula. The first third of the hour was focused on my prospect: his or her family, work, interests. The second twenty minutes centered on the college: important developments, needs, prospects. The final third of the time was the ask – always for a specified amount and a specific purpose. For larger amounts ($25,000 or more) I usually had a written proposal prepared and presented it after making the request orally.

For the alumni who thought the college already had plenty of money and who insisted he or she was more interested in giving to other charitable causes (Planned Parenthood. The Salvation Army, Food Pantry, Cancer Society, literacy program, for examples), and would then ask, why shouldn't they direct their resources there instead of to the college, I had a well-rehearsed response. First, they were wrong to think we had enough. I reminded them of the expensive honors program, excellent labs and libraries, facilities and great faculty, and told them all of that was there for them only because others, before them, had given to make it possible. As to their interest in other charities, I explained that only if they helped Swarthmore to continue would it be able to produce more grads like them who wanted to help other people.

My favorite objective for which to solicit became endowed scholarships. I loved "selling" them. What is more attractive to a potential donor than setting up an endowed (permanent) fund, with his or name on it, producing income every year for the foreseeable future, to help a student with the cost of his or her education?

The largest construction project we worked on was the science building. It was dedicated in 2005. We also sought funds for a new dormitory, renovations, the restoration of Parrish Hall, and endowment to support various programs and faculty positions. Personally, I was especially pleased to have raised endowments to support both the Protestant and the Jewish chaplaincies.

I recruited a number of new board members. I worked closely with Larry Shane, of Swarthmore, Board chair. I also worked closely with John Goldman, Fred Kyle, Elizabeth Scheuer, Marge Scheuer, Pam Wetzels, Julie Hall, Jack Riggs, David Singleton, Gene Lang, and

Gil Kemp. Almost all of these men and women gave very large amounts of money to help make the campaign a success. Gil Kamp later became board chair. I considered all of them close friends and with several, we are still in touch.

The Development and Communications Committee of the Board met the day before each Board meeting, always on campus. The Campaign Committee met in New York City two or three times a year. I and others on our staff provided support and follow-up for these groups.

Among the most impressive people on our staff during those nine years were Mike Valores, Director of Planned Giving; Jeff Lott, Director of Publications; Lisa Lee, Director of Alumni Relations; Danielle Shepherd, Director of Parents Giving; Florence Ann Roberts, Director of Prospect Research; Ken Dinitz, Director of Corporate and Foundation Giving; Pat Laws, Director of Annual Giving; Ruth Krakow, Director of Donor Records; Diane Crompton, Director of Operations; and Connie Baxter, Administrative Coordinator to the Vice President.

Connie and I have remained close. She and her husband, John, have been to visit us twice. She and I became a well-coordinated team. She was so good I never had to tell her what to do. She raised money herself -- her telephone manner was that good.

Mention of these people (I could list many others) reminds me that in a well-run development office no gift is ever the sole doing of one person. From research to record keeping and all the steps in between, a contribution is the result of the work of many. Publications and other printed material, press relations, alumni activities - all of it is important, and each component part of a successful development program is essential.

Indeed, on more than one occasion, I said to the faculty, in reports I made at faculty meetings during most of the Campaign, that as we asked for money we were selling the work of the faculty, the educational experience they were providing to students. And, I told them, almost always, when we met an alumnus or alumna who felt especially positive about her or his student days, it was because of a close relationship enjoyed with a particular faculty member.

I traveled a lot, mostly within this country, in the northeast corridor, and on the west coast, but I did go to the south and the southwest a good deal. And, also, to England, France, Germany, Belgium.

The place I visited most was New York City. We had so many alums there. The Harvard Club, on West 44th Street, was very useful. I met so many people there. Sometimes Sidney would accompany me, on the train. She loved New York. We both enjoyed many aspects of it: the theatre, the restaurants, the museums, friends we had there.

Development work for a college is based on human relationships, as are most endeavors. In making friends and building friendships Sidney was invaluable. She easily relates to everyone and draws people to herself. Her empathy and sensitivity resonates with almost all. I am well aware that she has been an important part of the equation in whatever success we have managed in working for five colleges over the years

Chapter

Swarthmore's Community

I want to write more about the college, as it was during our years there. First, Al Bloom. A very talented, complicated and interesting man. In my estimation, the three most important leaders of the college have been two presidents, Swain and Aydelotte, and one of its board chairs, McCabe. Bloom ranks as the next most important president for the way he built on, and, in a sense, completed Aydelotte's defining work. He, Bloom, revived the Honors Program (35% were graduated with honors by 2002). He established new programs or concentrations in environmental studies, interpretation theory, Latin American studies, dance, linguistics, computer science, and Islamic Studies. He strengthened admissions requirements, but he also greatly expanded the admission of international students and study abroad.

Perhaps his greatest achievement was increasing, dramatically, the diversity of both the student body and the faculty. During some of the years I was there, the entering first year class comprised almost 50% persons of color. To walk across the campus was to be reminded of the United Nations. Both the founding Quakers and Aydelotte could be criticized for reluctance in welcoming racial minorities. The college did not admit blacks until the 1940s. Aydelotte was so committed to elitism in the recruitment of both students and faculty, he couldn't see beyond the de facto segregation this caused. Bloom corrected this and thus completed an otherwise impressive college community that truly became a national model. I was thrilled to be part of such a place.

Al Bloom and his wife Peggi were very kind, very supportive of Sidney and me. He was generous in his praise, forthcoming with budget provisions, and he gave me plenty of flexibility in managing my shop. When we disagreed we always argued about it privately and though he did not always follow my advice, I felt he listened. We were very different in many ways, but we recognized each other's talents and clearly acknowledged the roles each was playing to the college's advantage.

Bloom was a talented politician. I learned a lot from him and had I known some of what he taught me, in that area, I might well have avoided a number of earlier mistakes. He had been a member of the faculty and had a number of friends in that group. That was an enormous advantage. He depended on them to keep him informed of any dissent or dissatisfaction. At the first whiff of controversy he would meet with people, in his office, and get right to the heart of the matter. He and Peggi entertained faculty, in the president's house, frequently. Similarly, he kept a close eye on student mood and movement. As issues inevitably arose, he was quick to call student leaders or complainers into his office or to meet with groups of them. He was the best mediator, conciliator, and compromise facilitator, I've ever known. He was the most effective college president I know of at faculty relations. Just as in Aydelotte's day, he coddled the faculty. He made them believe they ran the place.

During most of the campaign, Al was unconvinced that we would meet the goal. I felt part of my job was to reassure him, as well as some of the board members, that the money was there, that we would find it, - and obtain it, on time, and we did.

Sometimes I shared with him, the board, and the faculty, a common-sense observation: You can raise almost any amount of money; the question is how long it may take to do so. If we had not met the goal by the stated time, we would simply extend the end date. But, one needs a target date. Deadlines are very important in fund raising.

Beyond the president, the person on his immediate staff for whom I had the most respect and to whom I felt closest, in style and values set, was Sue Welsh, the vice president for finance. I appreciated her integrity, her work ethic, her maturity. I felt the college's money was well accounted for and I always believed what she told me. We were not especially close, personally. We were both too busy. But I appreciated her very much.

Three board members became especially close friends. Gene Lang, as the alumnus and board member who gave the most money to the Campaign, and who was most involved in the college as well, talked directly with the president about almost everything that happened. Al Bloom was masterful in responding to and communicating with Gene. And Gene was, I felt, always very supportive, very encouraging to me and to our part of the college. Even his sharp questions and sometimes critical comments were meant to help. During the Campaign, he established an endowed scholarship and named it for Sidney and me. It was Gene who came up with the name of the campaign, "The Meaning of Swarthmore."

Larry Shane was raised a Quaker, grew up in Swarthmore, was graduated from the college and was the son of one of my predecessors as head of development. His parents had lived in the house where we were. He understood and appreciated what needed to be done. He not only did a superb job of chairing the board (he prepared better than any chair I'd known), he also provided splendid leadership for a key piece of the Campaign's success, the project to raise money from many alums to restore Parrish Hall. Sidney and I became fans and friends of Larry and Marty Shane and remain so today.

Gil Kemp is a board member I took credit for recruiting and helping to involve deeply in development activity. He understood philanthropy; he said he'd learned it from Gene Lang. He was extremely successful at founding his own company and selling it for a huge profit. He was and is very generous. He loved to set up scholarships or fund renovations and name them for other people. His pledge of $10 million, toward the end of the Campaign, after he'd already given a good deal, helped put it over the top. At a memorable board meeting when Al Bloom insisted that Sidney join the meeting, Gil and his wife, Barbara, announced that $1 million of what they'd pledged would endow the vice president's house and garden and both would be named for Sidney and me. At a ceremony for which Claire and Chuck Jones, and Andrew West journeyed to Philadelphia, the Dan and Sidney West House and Garden were dedicated. At the board meeting when this was announced I was speechless. It fell to Sidney to say thank-you in an appropriate way. Gil has remained a close friend, visiting us in Atlanta, and entertaining us, more than once, at his chateau in Cerisay, France, as well as at his homes in Scarsdale and Orlando.

Chapter

A Successful Campaign

The campaign ended in December, 2006. It had taken 7 ½ years. It obtained the largest amount ever raised by Swarthmore, a quarter of a billion dollars. The board members, current and previous, 85 in all, had given $111 million of that or 45% of the total. That's important. The board has to lead in development. If they don't why should anyone else? They know more about the college than anyone. As mentioned already, I made my own pledge, I solicited the president, the board chair, and then every other member of the board. After those pledges were on the table we were ready to ask everyone else. No one has any right to ask anybody for money until she or he has given first, as generously as possible. You'd be surprised at the number of colleges and other non-profits, even churches, where this is not understood.

Eighty-seven per cent of the alumni/ae had given at least some amount at least once during the campaign period. Among current and retired faculty, 192 had given a total of over $1 million. A total of 256 current faculty and staff gave a total of $361,440. It had cost 18 cents to raise each dollar (if the numerator of the fraction included alumni relations, publications, and public relations) or 11 cents if figuring in the cost of development activity only.

We obtained over $17 million in foundation grants. The Annual Fund (unrestricted annual operating monies) had increased from $3 million to $5 million a year. Over 4,800 personal visits were conducted. About 1,000 alumni told us they had included the college in their estate plans. The number of gifts in seven figures was 37.

A mini-campaign with 40 volunteers raised $4 million in 12 months to restore Parrish Hall, and captured a $1 million matching grant from the Kresge Foundation.

The Campaign generated 261 new endowed funds, the great majority of which were endowed scholarships. The minimum amount to do this was $100,000.

I had organized the time table into five phases: Launch (October 2001 – December 2002); Expansion (January 2003 – June 2005); Parrish Challenge (January – December, 2005); Consolidation (July 2005 – June 2006); and Inclusion (July 2006 – December 2006).

Important gains were also made in the participation of alumni/ae in on-campus and regional programming, as well as in media coverage, effective communication to our constituencies, and in enhancing the college's reputation and visibility.

Hundreds of alums made multi-year pledges for the first time. We dispelled the notion that Swarthmore alumni/ae were mostly modestly compensated or committed only to community service and social action charities. We learned that though 40% of our graduates worked for non-profits, many of them had done well financially.

I maintain that there is a huge amount of money in this country and far more of it than has been heretofore obtained for charitable purposes is available for the asking. We are, far and away, the most philanthropic country in the world. Many people in development work decry the competition among an increasing number of charities for the private dollar. I maintain that "a rising tide lifts all boats." The way to learn to give money away is to give money away, the more ways and the more often people are asked to give, the more likely they will do so.

I felt a great sense of accomplishment and completion. In 2007, we celebrated on campus and in several regional events, the end of the campaign. In some ways it was the capstone of my career.

In a strange way, my career in college work had been done in reverse. Most people will think of a presidency as the apex of college administration. Both of mine, however, were in lesser-known places and at struggling institutions. Then I moved to two vice presidencies, both of which were at far more visible places that had established financial bases and secure reputations, as well as stable enrollments. My experience, in the northeast, the wide-ranging contacts, the exposure to an older and more influential part of the country - all were far greater than I'd known before.

In two important ways, the direction I'd taken helped me dramatically. First, it enhanced my physical health. In 1990, while at Carroll, I was diagnosed with atrial fibrillation (irregular heartbeat).

Subsequently I acquired a pacemaker and I've been taking medication for this ever since. Twice I've had a procedure called oblation therapy to restore sinus rhythm. The cause(s) of atrial fibrillation are still not known for certain, but it's safe to say that stress is probably among them. While a vice presidency for development is hard work and there is plenty of pressure to produce, it does not compare to that of a presidency. Leaving the college presidency probably prolonged my life.

In addition, I was compensated far more generously, as a vice president at both colleges, than at either place I was president. And, even though the amount I've been paid has never especially motivated me, it was important for my family and my retirement.

So, it's strange, sometimes, how things work out, especially with the benefit of hindsight.

After years of working as a jack of all trades (surely an apt description of a college president's role) I'd found a niche in higher education in which I felt expert. My knowledge of the U.S. higher education system was extensive. I'd been a student in six institutions, a staff member at five others and a board member at still another. Thus, I had an inside experience with 12 colleges and universities, public and private, large and small, in as many locations in the country. While that may not be a record for a single individual, it was certainly unusual. I'd spent 34 years working for five colleges and I'd been active in development work that entire time.

In May, 2007, I was 66 years old. I wanted to work until I was 67, but beyond that? I was weary of travel so I began to think of retiring, after another year.

Chapter

Personal Life in Swarthmore

We had many visitors: our children and grandchildren, my siblings and members of their families, friends from other cities, and many college guests including board members, parents, prospective students, alumni, and prospective donors. Certain board members, notably Gene Lang, Pam Wetzels, and the Kemps, stayed with us each time the board met and became like family.

Sidney's major task was to run a bed and breakfast place. She had help once a week from Dorothy Dallam, a talented retiree of the college who'd been a housekeeping supervisor. And there was often another housekeeper, from the college staff, once a week. And, she had a caterer who helped with large events, but she did most of the work herself, without pay, as usual. Many spouses of college officials no longer do this realizing it really isn't fair for the institution to get two for the price of one, but we lived rent- and utilities-free in a lovely place, with maintenance staff always ready to repair and refurbish, and that was another type of compensation.

West House, Swarthmore College

During our years there, Sidney's mother, Louise Castles Childs, came to live with us, and we loved having her. She died in 2003, in her bedroom there. Sidney, Claire (who was visiting, with Shelby, at the time) and I were with her when she died, in the evening.

Sidney and I both enjoyed working in our garden, visiting museums and public gardens in the area, taking out-of-town visitors to the many tourist sites (Valley Forge, Winterthur, Longwood Gardens, Independence Hall, the Philadelphia Museum, The Franklin Institute, Reading Terminal Market and others). We loved the Philadelphia Orchestra, the Opera and the many theatres. We drove to Center City on an almost weekly basis to sample still another new (to us) restaurant. We often went with the Blooms, and with our down-the-hill neighbors, Naomi and Allen Schneider, who became some of our closest friends. Another close friend was Micheline Rice-Maximin, and her husband Edward, until his sudden death, who lived across the street. Allen was a professor of psychology; Micheline was a professor of French.

When I wasn't traveling, Sidney and I, and while she was with us, Louise, and any guests, would gather in the living room when I got in from work, around six, for end-of-the-day visit and sharing with each other. In the cool months, we always had a fire.

Sidney and I both enjoyed walks through the neighborhood or on the campus, adjacent to our back garden. There was snow and cold in winter but the spring, summer, and fall were very pleasant. It was a good time for us. Busy, but fulfilling. Hard work, but in behalf of a college we both believed in deeply.

I worshipped most Sundays at Bryn Mawr Presbyterian Church, on the Main Line, but 8 or 10 times a year, I preached at Presbyterian churches when a substitute or guest preacher was needed. I kept up with my reading (planes and airports are good for that). We took trips to England, Italy, Switzerland, Canada, Greece, France, Spain, Peru, Ecuador, and Germany, and tours of Eastern Europe, and the Baltic States. Sidney, on her own, did a tour of Viet Nam in 2005. Some of this travel was work related. Some was vacation touring.

We often enjoyed concerts, plays, lectures, performances on campus. We lived on campus; it was easy. We were surrounded by students (two former residences on our street had been converted to dorms), faculty and staff, but we made some non-college friends as well.

It was a happy and busy and interesting time for us.

As we prepared for retirement we realized how much we enjoyed the northeast and especially Philadelphia. We decided it was our favorite place to live. We'd lived in eight different cities since our marriage. Our stay in Philadelphia was second only to our stay in Batesville, in length. We thought we'd enjoy staying in the Philadelphia area. We'd miss being there. But, it was never a serious option. It was expensive, we owned a house in Decatur, Georgia, and, most importantly, Andrew and Claire and her family, were in Atlanta. There was no discussion; it was a given.

Sidney made three trips to oversee renovation of the house we owned. We'd bought it as an investment, rented it to Claire and Andrew and a series of their friends and roommates, then, just before moving, we'd leased it to three sets of strangers, in one-year leases. The latter, unlike our children, had not taken care of the place.

Sidney had the entire interior redone, to get it ready for our move, projected for January, 2008. I settled on the end of December as my last day.

As I prepared to leave a place I'd grown to love, I reflected more on Swarthmore, what it had meant to me and what I had given to it. I was not uncritical in my admiration. I worried, for example, that as a relatively wealthy college (the endowment grew to over $1.2 billion, in part, because of the Campaign), some weren't as careful as they should have been about spending money. I regretted that the student body was predominantly from the northeast and California, and not nearly enough geographically representative of the rest of the country. Half the students were full-pay; they required no financial aid (there were no "merit" scholarships). This meant that many students came from families who could afford fees totaling in the tens of thousands (now well over $70,000) each year. We were generous with financial aid (before I left we discontinued college issued loans), but we still had too few economically disadvantaged students. The culture of the place was stringently secularistic (though that has changed a bit since then). Even though I was comfortable with the decidedly progressive political climate on campus, I worried that it seemed insulated from the real world. I didn't think there was enough planning being done for the long-term future of the college. Someone said, "becoming number one is easier than remaining number one." And, there was this curious isolation from Philadelphia, not to mention distance, even, between the campus and the surrounding borough.

On the other hand, as I mentioned earlier, Swarthmore proved to me that it was possible to have a college where academic excellence was more than aspiration. It was the most intellectually stimulating campus I'd ever been on or known about. It was unashamedly a college, with no aspiration to be a "university." It was oriented, entirely, to the education of undergraduate students. It was a caring community, often energized about injustice or cruelty anywhere. It was internationalist, worldly, egalitarian, and committed to a more just world and a better society for all. It was an unusual place and I felt strongly that every student, every professor, every staff member, including me, was lucky to be there.

Now, as I look back, there is another important aspect to Swarthmore, as part of my life. It was a long way from Galveston, Texas. I left there at age 9. I left Texas, initially at age 19. I returned to Texas three times before finally moving away for good in 1972, at age 33. As our stay in Swarthmore ended, I was in a place very far, in several ways, from Texas. My home state has always been conservative, politically and socially. I am neither. Nor have I been, from a young age.

It is as though my life, my dreams, my ideas of reality, had moved, inexorably, from Galveston all the way to Swarthmore, with many varied stops in between, and Swarthmore marked the place, in my head, in society, in culture and politics and education, where I had always wanted to be.

Chapter 34

Move to Atlanta

A very large moving van took all of our possessions, including our old Buick (that dated to Wisconsin days) and lots of plants and books to Decatur, Georgia (a close-in suburb of Atlanta). Decatur is an older city than Atlanta, straddles a train track, and is home to Agnes Scott College (Claire's alma mater) and Columbia Presbyterian Theological Seminary. Our house, off Kirk Road, was halfway between these two campuses. I often walked to each. We were only a few miles from Emory University (Andrew's alma mater).

Our house had two floors, an attached, two-car garage, den, kitchen, living and dining rooms, and, upstairs, three bedrooms and two baths. It was plenty of house for two people, but there were three problems. We had far too much furniture; I required a study and Sidney was used to having one as well; and the garden behind was tiny. We moved in, and lived there, for over two years, to avoid paying capital gains tax when we sold it.

Sidney loved it. It was so much easier to manage and care for than the large houses we'd been in. It was in a cul de sac and we enjoyed the young families and many children. We made close friends with several neighbors. We enjoyed Decatur with its charming neighborhoods and many restaurants. I often used the libraries at the college or the seminary. But, most of my books, and a lot of our possessions were in storage and I had no place to grow vegetables or roses.

271

Not long after moving there, I was doing some research in the library at Emory one day when I got a call on my cell from Elizabeth Kiss, president of Agnes Scott. She wanted me to consider serving as interim vice president for development while they searched for a permanent one. I was surprised. I thought I'd retired. But, I cared about the college. I had long before decided there is still an important place for single-sex colleges, especially women's colleges. I knew what one of them had done for Claire. I know what a women's college experience has done for many others. I was happy to try to help.

I'd served on the Board of Trustees there for 12 years. I already knew Elizabeth Kiss and others on the staff and faculty. I knew many former and current board members.

It was energizing, and even fun, to jump back into "the work." Except for a man in the publications office, I was the only male in a staff of 30 or so in Advancement. Except for one other male I was the only man on the President's Staff. It was exciting. I loved working with so many talented and dedicated women.

I worked 10 ½ months. I tried to visit as many board members and alumnae as possible. I traveled to several places in Georgia, South Carolina, North Carolina, Virginia, California, New York, and Washington, D.C. I enjoyed working with Elizabeth Kiss, a very gifted and very hard-working president. It was interesting to get to know and work with another set of trustees. I initiated discussion about a capital campaign and urged it be done as soon as possible. I solicited several additions to the endowment, some of which were later realized. I worked to increase the annual fund, recruit new staff, train and mentor other staff members already in place, and build morale and momentum in development.

I teamed up with Rosemary Zumwalt, the Provost, to restart the search for a permanent vice president and, by August, we had one, ready to start. He was Rob Parker from North Carolina. He proved to be very successful. The campaign he launched and organized was completed, after he left to return to the University of North Carolina, Chapel Hill, in 2015, and it exceeded its goal.

Working at Agnes Scott further solidified, in my head, a number of convictions I have about successful college fund raising. For example, the most productive and the most efficient way to raise money is to have a staff person visit a prospective donor in their home or office, and ask for it.

So much time and energy is spent on other approaches: benefits (as in auctions or "awards dinners"), meetings, letters, phonathons, brochures, elaborate volunteer networks. Of course, all of these methods can be and have been successful, but none compare with one-on-one solicitation. I've decided that much of the enormous amount of time, money, and energy that is invested in events, for example, is avoidance behavior.

Also, every visit should include a request for a gift. On only very few occasions (a condolence call, or an effort to address a grievance, for instance) should a visit occur without an "ask." If the visited person is an established donor, it often should be a "triple ask." That means a request for an annual fund gift, an ask for a capital, multi-year pledge, and a question about including the college in estate planning. It is impossible, by the way, to do the last of these in other than a private conversation.

Always ask for a specific amount. Donors often give less than what they're asked for, but they almost never give more. It's unfair to make an open request. How does one read your mind? And, almost no one gives very large amounts unless they are personally solicited.

At every college where I worked, it was an effort to get some staff out the door and in front of a prospect. Why? Maybe because some people are afraid of failure, of being rejected. Having someone say, "no." So what? I often told staff, if you go to see someone and ask them for a gift, the worst thing that can happen is they will say no. Then, thank them for their time, leave the door open for another visit, and go on to see the next person! Meanwhile, there is no such thing as a wasted visit. Who knows when you may have planted an idea that will come to fruition later. I've seen it happen many times.

It's better to ask for a specific purpose as well as a specific amount. People have to be able to react, to know what you have in mind. If they aren't interested you can always ask for something else or for a lesser amount. You have to put down a marker, a starting place. And then you have to be quiet and allow the donor to respond. And, listen carefully. I often had to caution people with whom I worked to do this. The tendency is, if there is a pause in the conversation, people start filling in. You can't do that.

So, it was fun to test further such theories and share them with others. I felt very good about the chance to share accumulated theory and experience with one more college and to know I'd helped, even a little, with a school I care about deeply.

Chapter 35

One More Move

Sidney made our house in Decatur a very pleasant place to live. We had the tiny garden in back landscaped and, in May, 2009, we held a party to celebrate my 70th birthday, using the back deck and the garden.

I used one of the bedrooms as a study with shelves attached to two walls. But, the money we were paying for a storage place drove us both crazy. I missed the largest portion of my library. And, I missed a vegetable garden. As the second year there passed by, we looked for another house.

We moved in July, 2010. Our Decatur house went on the market in March and sold in June. We were very fortunate; the real estate market in Atlanta had tanked by then. The house we found, in Druid Hills, an area between downtown Atlanta and Decatur, next to Emory University, had been built in 1923. It is two

Druid Hills, 2010

floors, brick painted white, close to the Atlanta city limit, in an unincorporated part of DeKalb County, and only blocks from Emory's front gate on North Decatur Road.

It has a large living room, a dining room, kitchen, half bath, and an enclosed porch (Sidney's study) on the ground floor. There are three bedrooms and two baths above. We liked the house. We liked the gardens even more. The lot is 100 feet wide and 300 feet deep. It comprises ¾ of an acre. The "bones" of the garden were already well established. In addition to the front (a lawn and borders), there is a formal rose garden, a water garden with pond and small waterfall, a long, gently sloping greensward with borders, a lower garden, and, in back, behind the garage, a kitchen garden.

There is a large, two-car garage with a carriage house overhead that was originally intended by the previous owner, who built it, and who was a photographer, as her studio. For me, it made a splendid study.

We spent months, and lots of money, while living in the place, completely renovating, redecorating, restoring the house. Then, rearranging and improving the gardens, and, finally, redecorating the study.

The rose garden is much improved. It now has about three dozen plants, mostly hybrid teas. Elsewhere Sidney has done much in transplanting, watering, fertilizing, pruning. We've hired professionals to help with this and continue to rely on occasional help for the heavy lifting. But I manage the mowing, the roses and the kitchen garden. Sidney specializes in the front and most all else in back. She also repaints the decks and steps and outdoor furniture each spring.

We have inherited five trees (Water Oaks, a Red Oak, and a Southern Pine) which are well over 100 years old. They make the garden. We have lots of Boxwood, Azalea, Dogwood, Camellia, Japanese Maple, and more. We have bought very little plant stuff from nurseries. We already have more than enough to care for.

For me, an important decision, most days, is whether to work in the study or the garden. Sidney seems to enjoy working outside as much or more than anything else she does. I take much pleasure in the Roses. As Shakespeare said, "Of all flowers me thinks rose is best." We tell each other, frequently, it is a small paradise. We are very fortunate. I never dreamed, before 2010, we would finally land in such a delightful place. It seems just right. The house is lovely, but not palatial. The gardens are beautiful, but not lavish. We are very nicely situated here.

My study has a deck on two sides, overlooking the gardens. It has windows on three sides looking out to the trees. It is light-filled. Bookshelves, floor to ceiling, are on three walls. I have a desk, a sitting area, and a writing table. In addition to this memoir, I have written five articles, on theology, all now published in an English journal called "Faith and Freedom" (Manchester College, Oxford University). I write the Family Letter each week and the annual Advent Letter. I still write, in longhand, letters and notes and postcards. I walk to Emory to use their libraries. I'm reading and writing as much as I can and as much as I'd hoped to do during all those years of college work with little time to do either.

We entertain visitors several times a year. We enjoy Atlanta's many cultural opportunities. We love seeing our children and grandchildren frequently. Andrew usually stops by for dinner once a week. We enjoy a good many friends we have made here. We are blessed, so far, with good health, as we advance into our late seventies. We have a great deal for which to be thankful and we are.

Since coming to Atlanta, there have been only two clouds in our lives. Not long after we got here Claire was discovered to have cancer. It required surgery. We were very worried. She was brave. She had great care, an excellent young female surgeon, and was surrounded by the love of her family and friends. She recovered, and there has been no recurrence. We were relieved and remain thankful.

Andrew, as a Gunnery Sergeant in the Marine Corps Reserve, was mobilized in 2015, for a year, and was deployed to Afghanistan for six months. He was at a base in Helmand Province, Camp Leatherneck. Sidney and I drove to Camp Lejeune, in North Carolina, to see him off, and we were there when he returned. Those were anxious months, full of prayer and fervent hope for his safe return. In both instances, I was reminded of what I heard a man say, once, "If your kids are all right; you're all right."

We thought we would miss Philadelphia and we have, but we have been surprised at how much we enjoy Atlanta. Partly this is due to our experience in moving several times to new places and learning, thus, to make new friends, explore the new city, and afford ourselves of the opportunities at hand. So, the High Museum of Art, the Botanical Garden, the Symphony, Opera, other museums, many restaurants, are all enjoyable. It is clear we have become urban people. We've done small towns and small cities. We like the urban scene. The street in front of our house is very busy. Atlanta traffic is often "Impossible." Taxes and property values are high. The cost of living is, too. But, this is where we want to be. It is so much more interesting, varied, diverse, and complex.

We worship at First Presbyterian Church, on Peachtree, next to the High Museum. It's the oldest Presbyterian congregation in Atlanta. We are there because it's Andrew's church. Claire and the children are 20 miles north in Roswell, and part of a Presbyterian congregation there. We are members of the High Art Museum, and the History Center, and the Botanical Garden. We are season ticket holders at the Symphony and the Opera. We are often on Emory's campus, for concerts, lectures, seminars. Our lives are busier than I expected, surprisingly active, friends-filled, social. I could not be happier with what and where we are.

Chapter 36

Once More Into the Fray

In September, 2015, Don Weatherman, president of Lyon College in Batesville, called to say they had lost their vice president for development. He asked if I'd serve as interim while they searched. I hesitated. Sidney said, "You need to go over there and try to help."

For 4 ½ months I commuted between Atlanta and Batesville. I flew from Atlanta to Little Rock on Sunday afternoons, then drove to Batesville, where I worked for four days, leaving Friday mornings to return here. I loved being back on that gorgeous campus, and working again there in beautiful Arkansas. The commute, however, drove me crazy. I realized, all over again, how much I hate airplanes and airports. They are crowded, uncomfortable, unpleasant. Flying is undependable, subject to weather and so much else. Planes are often late. Flying is too expensive. It isn't any fun anymore, if it ever was. Other than that, I'm a good traveler!

I was thrilled to see the college's campus looking so elegant. The new buildings since we were there and the careful maintenance of grounds and facilities make it, truly, among the handsomest small colleges in the country. There were many physical improvements, but also much dedicated talent among faculty and staff. I met many impressive students. Sadly, the place still struggles with under-enrollment, under-endowment, and a sparsely populated host community. There had been three development vice presidents in six years.

I worked to train and mentor staff, hire a couple of new staff members, help with the search for a vice president, advise the president, and raise as much money as possible. I was astonished at how many names and people I remembered, after 27 years! I worked long hours, at near flank speed, starting early and often ending with dinner meetings. It was exhilarating in many ways. I was thrilled to learn I still had the energy and stamina for such work. I was happy to see so many people I'd known years before and enjoyed again. It was fun to see the changes in Batesville and elsewhere in Arkansas. (Northeast Arkansas is the new center of activity.) I loved working with the young people on the staff.

The president, Don Weatherman, announced his retirement while I was there, scheduled for summer, 2017. Sadly, he suffered a stroke in February, 2017, which effectively ended his work even sooner. But, in the years he worked as president, he accomplished much. I have already mentioned campus improvements. They include new residence halls and a new college union, replacing the one built during my tenure, which caught fire and burned down during his tenure. In addition, he has increased the enrollment and greatly strengthened the athletic program. The college remains an important part of higher education in Arkansas, among the best private colleges in the state. It is still a treasure in that yet undeveloped, relatively poor section of the country. It is still graduating students whose lives have been transformed by it.

It is very important to Sidney and me that Lyon succeeds and prospers. We have a great deal invested there. We still care about it deeply.

Chapter

Into the Future

Retirement is better than I imagined. I heard a man say, once, that when he retired every day seemed like Saturday. Our lives have become more structured than that, but I do acknowledge that the stress level is much diminished. For so many years I worked under great pressure. Much of it was self-imposed. My idea of work was to operate at a perpetual "all ahead full." But, the pressure also came from knowing I was responsible for the education of, and, in many cases, the livelihood of numerous others. I do not miss the stress and I know my health is better without it.

Nowadays our lives have settled into a routine and I've learned that the older one becomes the more important routine is. My favorite part of the day is the early morning. I've always been freshest, more alert, more creative, at that time. I must have tea (that started years ago, on the first trip to England) and then I have to read, in order, the New York Times and the Atlanta Journal Constitution.

I've read newspapers in many places and, where available in English, in other countries. None surpasses The Times. It is not perfect; nor is it completely objective. I can criticize it for being New York-centric, but it is far ahead of its closest competitor. Karl Barth once said that a Christian has to read the Bible and the newspaper every day. I agree, and I would be happy to do without television, radio, and on-line stuff so long as I had The Times thrown into my driveway each morning. The "AJC" as we call it in Atlanta, is surprisingly good as well, far better than the papers of many other

U.S. cities even larger than Atlanta (now six million). And, one must read it to stay aware of the latest scandal, the usual corruption, and the ethically challenged behavior of so-called leaders, public and private. What would we do without such muckraking newspapers? No other part of "the media" in this country exposes misdeed more effectively.

I try to walk each day, after breakfast, about 2 miles. Then, work in the study. Once or twice a week I work in the garden: mowing, pruning, planting, weeding. Sidney works outdoors every day she's not committed to be elsewhere. It's her favorite activity, and she's very good at it. I can't imagine not having a garden. I started this as a boy and I resumed as soon as I got out of graduate school and started my career. One of the reasons it is such a passion is that I know when I'm thus engaged nothing else comes into my mind. And, that is exactly what one needs for a hobby.

The afternoons are almost always occupied with work in my study. I've had some very nice studies, especially while at Arkansas College (in the Brown Chapel) and at Carroll (on the third floor of the president's house), and at Union (second floor, rear), but this one is best of all. I read, I write, I think, I surf the net, I take care of our finances, I file stuff, I try to organize my life. I discovered, soon after retirement, how much I had depended on talented assistants (Spencer, Wilkes, McCallie, Quinn and Baxter). Suddenly I had to try to do so much that they had done for me, and had done more quickly and better than I could have. Typing, editing, proofing, making appointments, arranging travel, filing, paying bills, and on and on. Now, I am a one-person shop. And the computer is the enemy!

In the evening, Sidney and I try to visit, to catch up on what the other has done and to whom we have talked, or about what we have learned or thought. And then, the PBS NewsHour, and then dinner. And then reading, or movies on cable.

This pattern is altered, of course, when we meet, for lunch or dinner, with others, together or separately, and on weekends, and when we go to performances, movies, museums, etc. From our initial arrival in Atlanta when we knew just a handful of people we have met and grown close to a much larger number. We love eating out with local friends or visitors. Trying out new restaurants is a passion. I especially like French food. Entertaining friends from out of town is a favorite sport.

Once a year, we manage some sort of large event to which we invite everyone we know in Atlanta. The occasions have included: important birthdays, our fiftieth anniversary, in 2013, and, in the last two years, the full blooming of the rose garden.

My reading has been widely varied. This is due, partly, to my friends John Scott and Bob Kibler, who got me invited to their book club, all male, comprising mostly retired Emory science and medical faculty. So, I'm reading stuff I'd never choose on my own. But, that's good for me. I continue to love biography, history, theology, and church history. I'm fascinated with politics (but not because I've ever wanted to do that or would be any good at it). I know it affects us all so much, and determines the direction of our lives and that of others elsewhere in the world. I remember that Mark Hanna said, "There are two things that are important in politics. One is money and I can't remember what the second one is."

In my writing in theology, I'm particularly interested in trying to understand how the Christian faith can be lived in today's context and remain relevant. I'm also deeply concerned about the future.

I'm fascinated with history, but not fixated on it. It serves my need to understand why what has happened occurred and then, what is going to happen next. As Cicero said, "Not to know what happened before one was born is always to be a child." I have never been nostalgic for some supposed bygone age. I don't believe there was some golden period in the past that was better than now. I find the present fascinating, exciting, full of exhilarating change, and, also, endlessly perplexing, confusing, often frightening. Importantly, as a Christian, I am filled with hope and fall back, always, on basic trust that God's purpose will prevail. The experience of my life has taught me, to use Mendelssohn's paraphrase of Psalm 121:4, "God, watching over Israel, slumbers not, nor sleeps."

My basic difference with conservatives, of any stripe, is that they too often look to the past rather than the future, oppose instead of propose, protect individual self-interest instead of looking to the general good of all. I serve a God who is still creating in a world that is still evolving. To be alive is to change. To be completely alive is to change often. My understanding of God is ultimate energy, direction, purpose, movement toward peace, love, reconciliation, community (with no one left out). I follow a Christ who represents the future God is creating and who, therefore, is far ahead of me in compassion, kindness, justice, and acceptance of all.

I learn from Jesus that the most important aspect of our lives are the relationships we develop, with loved ones, family, friends, work associates, community, the world. It is in reaching out, extending ourselves, forming bonds with others, that we find purpose and fulfillment, as I reflect on the most tragic events of my lifetime the list I would compile as among the worst would include: World War II and the Holocaust and Nagasaki/Hiroshima, the atrocities of Stalin and Mao, Viet Nam, the assassinations of both Kennedys and Martin Luther King, Jr., Nixon and Watergate, the election of Donald Trump.

Were I to compile a list of the most hopeful events during my life that would include: the founding of the U.N., Roosevelt's Social Security, Johnson's Medicare, the collapse of the Soviet Union, the end of apartheid in South Africa, King's civil rights movement, the election of Barack Obama.

The swings of history's pendulum between such devastation and such human triumph are breath-taking. I struggle to understand much of this. For example, I still, after years of reading everything I can find about it, cannot fathom Nazism. Germany was, arguably, the most civilized, scientifically advanced, cultured, Christian nation on earth. How did that happen? Economics alone does not explain it.

On the other hand, how, under Mandela, South Africa escaped bloody revolution, or, for that matter, how a black man got elected president of the United States, are equally puzzling to me. In the latter example, we are still arguing about and litigating issues that should have been settled by our Civil War!

There are forces, evil and good, in contention with each other, that extend beyond (certainly beyond my) comprehension.

My goals for the future are both numerous and modest. I hope for Sidney and me to be blessed with health. I pray for and give thanks for this daily. I want to get into research on the genealogy of my family. I want to continue an ambitious reading program. (I recently completed reading through Shakespeare.) I want to get this memoir published in some fashion. I have more articles in mind. I think I should write another book, about higher education. I hope Sidney and I can continue to travel (beyond the last trip, in 2017, to Germany, with Andrew, taking Shelby, our granddaughter, along). I hope to continue my weekly "family letter," and the annual "Advent letter." I treasure times with Sidney and our immediate family of six. I look forward to more Thanksgiving reunions with my siblings and their families. I'm grateful for every friendship, old and new.

As I evaluate the major activities and achievements of my life, I'm aware that I have had twin preoccupations: religion and education. I've wondered, occasionally, whether I would have been more effective and my career more interesting had I been one or the other: full-time church worker, i.e. pastor or church administrator, or full-time teacher or professor and scholar. But, I haven't worried much about what "might have been." I doubt whether either of those alternatives could have been more challenging or more interesting than what I did in combining them.

Religion continues to fascinate me because its subject comprises the most important questions: who are we, where did we come from, where are we going, and why? Education still intrigues me because I continue to learn how much I don't know, and because of the difference what I have learned has made for my life and my family's, and, hopefully, for those around me. As I read in Wisdom of Solomon (6:17), "The true beginning of wisdom is the desire to learn."

I know that among the greatest peak experiences of my life have been the commencement (including high school graduation, there have been five) ceremonies where I received a degree. Among the happiest days of my career have been the commencement ceremonies of the six colleges I served when I saw students march whose lives I knew I had helped enhance and enrich. Among my most treasured moments have been the occasions in which a former student or congregant or listener or work associate whom I had taught or spoken to, or preached to, or worked with, seized an opportunity to thank me for "changing my life." I need no further reward.

Education is not everything. There are and have been educated miscreants. But, in the main, education is a force for good. The earlier it begins the better. The longer I've worked in education the more importance I've placed on what happens to teach people in the very earliest stages, i.e. pre-school or even neo-natal. It is a privilege to be part of the finest higher education system in the world (largely because of the mix of public and private ownership) and it is a rare opportunity to reflect, as a religionist, on the deeper questions as well. As for what else, there is so much we yet don't know, starting with a largely unexplored universe and a still little understood human brain.

So, from Galveston to Atlanta and many places in between, the trip out of Galveston in 1949, across the causeway to the mainland was the beginning of a remarkable adventure which hasn't ended yet.

What intrigues me is the way in which each new place, each new experience, each new relationship, has expanded and enriched my life.

What are the comparative advantages of living in one place all one's life (the experience of many, perhaps most), or, of moving, many times and traveling a lot. In our case, the exposure to other areas, cultures, attitudes, has been thrilling. I realize that those who are more stationary often have a strong sense of belonging and acceptance, a great feeling of security. I have come to value, on the other hand, openness, progressiveness, flexibility. Thus, I fear that remaining in one place can often lead to reaction, conservatism, resistance to change, intolerance, fear of the different.

I know I have been fortunate. I've been given opportunities which most do not receive. I've been helped by many people. Yet, each new episode could not have expanded my understanding and lifted my sights without my own willingness to learn and improve. As Alfred Tennyson wrote, "I am a part of all that I have met." An attitude of openness, of teachable-ness, is also part of the learning I seek.

I've learned that life is complicated because people are complicated. Issues are therefore complex. Simple answers seldom help and often make worse the problems we confront today.

I remember Thomas Wolfe's third novel, "The Web and the Rock" (1937) which (he wrote (in an author's note) "was one man's discovery of life and the world." It was, he said, a journey that took him from "the little world around him" to "being in the city" and "a part of the whole adventure of … discovery."

Robert Fuller has written in his book on "Religious Revolutionaries" (2004), that "the key to spiritual living is to open ourselves to the directing activity of God." For me, in these retirement years, the main avenue to learning is reading books. The main avenue to understanding what I have read is writing. Someone said, "I write, therefore I think."

So, there are more causeways to cross, and a bigger world awaits.